Entrepreneurs in Pharmacy

Entrepreneurs in Pharmacy

AND OTHER LEADERS

GEORGE S. ZORICH

outskirts
press

Outskirts Press, Inc.
http://www.outskirtspress.com

ISBN: 978-1-4327-9583-2

Library of Congress Control Number: 2017915159

Cover Photo © 2018 thinkstockphotos.com. All rights reserved - used with permission.
Author Photo courtesy of John F. Cooper

Outskirts Press and the "OP" logo are trademarks belonging to Outskirts Press, Inc.

PRINTED IN THE UNITED STATES OF AMERICA

To Marianne:
my wife and best friend — with all my love!

To E.M.Z.,
my mother, who knew the value of education.

INTRODUCTION

When I was in pharmacy school at the University of Wisconsin in the 1970s, there were limited options upon graduation—you either went into a residency/graduate school or worked retail or hospital pharmacy. Our professors rarely provided any other guidance or examples of what we could do with our degrees other than traditional pharmacy jobs. As an example, my pharmacy jurisprudence professor took a survey in our final year and asked us what we planned to do upon graduation. We all eagerly filled it out, but it only listed three options: retail, hospital, or graduate programs. I wrote in a fourth line: "Sales—Eli Lilly."

I was enamored with Eli Lilly and Company, the pharmaceutical giant, and I was encouraged because they hired pharmacists exclusively. Everyone was required to start in sales, and I thought that sounded like fun, so I interviewed with Lilly in each of my final two years of school, and I never interviewed with another potential employer.

Imagine my embarrassment when the survey results were read in front of the class and most of my colleagues were going into retail, some into hospital, and a select few into residencies or graduate programs. One person was singled out as going into sales, and that was me. The professor chastised this individual for "wasting a pharmacy degree by going into sales." Ouch!

In 1978, I was convinced a pharmacy degree was a valuable springboard for anyone who was interested in healthcare; I thought you could do anything with it. I was happy to start in sales, but knew I would not end there. My mantra was to work hard and persevere, and eventually opportunities would develop for me. I also knew I would become more experienced and wiser with each new responsibility, position, and company.

I didn't know that one day I would work with private equity companies as a president and CEO and successfully build and sell those companies—I simply was willing to work hard and leverage my experiences. I enjoyed a thirty-five-year career in the pharmaceutical field.

The last fifteen years of my career were spent managing and leading companies with the goal of building them up and selling them. Developing successful business strategies, hiring world-class people, and then leading the team to execute that strategy ended up being my strength, but I couldn't have predicted this in 1978 as I was sitting in my pharmacy jurisprudence class filling out a survey.

As you read this book, take notice of the vastly different stories of the pharmacy entrepreneurs. The ten profiles dig deep into the entrepreneurs' minds. There are many commonalities in the entrepreneurs profiled: They all went to great schools of pharmacy and obtained a first-class education; all are smart but practical; all built a foundation of knowledge and experiences in their early years by working in some "traditional" pharmacy type of job; and at some point an idea or an opportunity presented itself and they took the leap. As entrepreneur Marla Ahlgrimm said, she was "vision ready" when the opportunity presented itself.

They were passionate about their ideas and what they were doing; they were decisive; and they all were hungry, worked hard, and had to make sacrifices to accomplish their goals.

It's also interesting to note that two of the ten entrepreneurs profiled were the last ones to get into their pharmacy class. Without someone changing majors or going to medical school, these great entrepreneurs would have been lost to pharmacy. It makes me think that we need to reconsider our admissions policies. Truth be told, I was on a waiting list and only got into pharmacy school because someone was accepted to medical school.

I've observed a few things while serving on several pharmacy boards, including those of the American Society of Health-System Pharmacists (ASHP) Foundation and the University of Wisconsin School of Pharmacy Board of Visitors: Pharmacists by nature are conservative and not prone to tremendous risk-taking. Entrepreneurs are willing to take risks when warranted and show significant self-confidence in their decisions and ideas.

Although schools of business, which are filled with future capitalists, or engineering schools, which are filled with Lego experts, builders, and tinkerers, may have a higher percentage of graduates who become entrepreneurs, there's no reason why pharmacy can't have more entrepreneurs in the future. At the very least, let's at least try to find ways to encourage more entrepreneurship in our pharmacy schools, especially with new Accreditation Council for Pharmacy Education (ACPE) guidelines that require entrepreneurship be part of the curriculum.

Pharmacists are the experts in drugs, and drugs are an expensive and vital part of the total healthcare picture. Business ideas are out there waiting to be discovered—and solutions to roadblocks and major issues in health care are waiting to be addressed. Curt Mueller, founder and CEO of Mueller Sports Medicine, noticed that high-school athletic departments were purchasing balms and liniments from sporting goods stores, and he couldn't see the logic of that. He founded a sports medicine business based on that simple idea and made it into a world leader. There is no one better to solve these healthcare problems than our current and future pharmacists.

I wrote this book is to reinforce what many pharmacy entrepreneurs told me, including Gordon Vanscoy, chairman and CEO at PANTHERx, who said, "If I can do this, why can't any pharmacist?"

One of the goals of this book is to provide solid examples and "stories" about how pharmacists have built their businesses. As you read the interviews, take note of the risks and challenges for each person and how each was addressed.

I read a statistic recently that stated 61 percent of Millennials want to be entrepreneurs. This large number makes me think that 61 percent of this surveyed group thinks that it is easy to be an entrepreneur and start a business. Building a business requires tremendous work, commitment, and sacrifice. I hope that after reading this book of interviews and profiles of pharmacy leaders that there's an appreciation for the thought process, hard work, and personal sacrifices required to turn an idea into reality, but also a clear picture of some of the challenges any new business owner and entrepreneur faces when climbing that mountain.

The second part of this book has profiles of what I call "Leaders in Pharmacy." These quick reads provide examples of the vast number of careers that a pharmacist can consider—careers that we call non-traditional because they are not in a drug store, a hospital, or a residency program. The leaders section includes pharmacists who are working in the following:

- The Drug Enforcement Agency (DEA)
- The U.S. Food and Drug Administration (FDA)
- The National Institutes of Health (NIH)
- Big Pharma
- Biotech

There's a pharmacist who's in Congress, others who are CEOs of hospitals, the CEO of a major chain drug store, healthcare recruiters, wholesaler executives, distributor presidents, GPO executives, State Board of Pharmacy presidents, pharmacy foundation CEOs, pharmacy association CEOs, drug shortage experts, 340B experts, pharmacy law experts, deans of pharmacy schools, experts in pharmacy compounding companies and practices, insurance company CEOs, and pharmacy benefit manager (PBM) executives.

You get the picture. Each profile is written by the individual leader and has tips for pharmacists at the end. These personalized stories provide you with an idea about how these leaders pursued their vastly different and exciting careers.

My point is this—the pharmacy degree should be thought of as a limitless degree, and my suggestion is simple. Start your career in a traditional role—whether it's in retail, hospital, the pharma industry, or graduate school. Always be on the lookout for ideas about how to better the healthcare system in the first three to five years of your career. For most of you, taking the leap into entrepreneurship, or even doing something completely different, may not be in the cards, but for some of you, it may be the beginning of a journey to unlimited challenges and excitement (and many headaches, too) as you create something new and/or better.

The career paths of the entrepreneurs of tomorrow may be similar to the profiles discussed in this book, but, quite frankly, they don't have to follow this roadmap, either. The entrepreneurs of tomorrow may be working part-time and being entrepreneurial part-time. As entrepreneur and podcaster Erin Albert told me, the new paradigm might just be made up of "intrapreneurs" or "multipationals." You'll learn about those terms in the book. Remember, any healthcare system problem or issue we face today can eventually be solved, and I'm confident pharmacists are perfectly equipped to do just that.

Enjoy the book.

George S. Zorich

University of Wisconsin School of Pharmacy, Class of 1978

Contents

LEADERS

ENTREPRENEURS

CHAPTER ONE

Marla Ahlgrimm

Founder of Madison Pharmacy Associates Inc.
University of Wisconsin School of Pharmacy

In the early 1970s, Marla Ahlgrimm, a talented musician capable of excelling in any of the schools at the University of Wisconsin, chose pharmacy over business or music. Four years after graduation, at age twenty-six, she co-founded the first pharmacy in America to focus on women's health and individualized prescription therapy. She was one of the first health providers in the United States to identify the symptoms of premenstrual syndrome (PMS) and to develop specific treatment options for these symptoms. Madison Pharmacy Associates was the first pharmacy to exclusively provide compounded low-dose, natural hormone therapy to manage PMS. Having reached more than 300,000 women and trained more than 7,000 physicians worldwide, Ahlgrimm's vision paved a new road for thousands of pharmacists.

She was at the forefront of outside-the-box thinking about this common health concern at a time when the medical profession claimed PMS was a psychiatric issue. Her problem-solving skills and business acumen led her to found Madison Pharmacy Associates, specializing in customized prescription therapy. Ahlgrimm developed and introduced natural progesterone dosage options and protocols to patients and practitioners in the United States.

Ahlgrimm's story should inspire any person who has an idea for a new business, but especially those who face naysayers and considerable adversity. The ever-changing healthcare market will need some of this creative thinking to create new solutions for the healthcare problems of tomorrow. Here is Ahlgrimm's story in her own words.

ENTREPRENEURIAL ROOTS

I grew up in an entrepreneurial family. My father was also a University of Wisconsin graduate with a degree in mining engineering. When he decided to open his own company, we moved from St. Louis to a very small town in Wisconsin. Of course, my brothers and I didn't really like the idea of moving. I was eight years old, and they were six and four years old. That was the first experience we had with starting a business. If you have ever lived in a small town, you know that most people have very deep family connections and a lot of relatives! We didn't know anybody.

When my dad started his engineering company, his office was in our house, so when the phone rang and it was a customer we, at an early age, were taught how to address the person, take the orders, and capture the phone numbers that were required for my dad to respond to customers' requests in the event that his administrative assistant did not pick up the phone. Dad introduced us to the customers who came to his office because, as was the case with many of them, we had already talked on the phone. We were exposed to the inner workings of business from an early age.

As we got older, my brothers started working with my dad, and that drove me crazy because I also wanted to work with my dad in the family business. During the summer between my freshman and sophomore years of college I was needling my dad about working with him in the quarries along with my brothers. My dad was a mining engineer who specialized in explosives for use in quarrying stone for road projects. In the summer, the quarries were stifling hot, often more than 115 degrees—quite frankly, not the place most parents would want their 18-year-old daughter to be working her summer job.

I clearly remember how I discussed a summer job opportunity with my dad in his office. He opened his desk drawer and handed me a brochure from DuPont. "It's a new construction product," he said, "something that you might want to learn about." It was a brochure about an innovative fabric called Typar®, sort of like Tyvek® wrap for new houses—but for road construction. I had the opportunity to introduce this product to the state of Wisconsin.

In the Midwest—but definitely in Wisconsin—we have many pot-holes because the gravel used below the layers of asphalt or concrete can mix with dirt and water and then sink, resulting in a pothole. Typar® was invented to be a water-permeable layer that separates the gravel foundation beneath the asphalt or concrete from the dirt layer. Water could move through the fabric, but the Typar® would not allow the gravel and dirt to mix, and this prevented the forma-tion of potholes. I remember thinking it was a really interesting and useful product.

Finally, this was the opportunity I was waiting for to work with my dad and figure this new Typar® business out. He handed me a list of all of his customers and told me a little bit about each of them. I then received the keys to the company car, a credit card, a sales presentation, and the opportunity to start making sales calls. I couldn't get out of the door fast enough to start this business.

My dad allowed me to name the company—I called it Ahlgrimm Sales—and started calling on customers. It was an interesting group because they were all city engineers. I was only eighteen and met with a lot of skeptical looks when I walked through the doorway to talk about this new construction product.

I would meet the city engineers at their workplaces or at the highway construction sites all around the site at 5:00 or 6:00 a.m. I stayed in hotels and ate at Country Kitchen—for a teenager, I was on cloud nine. Most of the city engineers told me Typar® wouldn't work, but one agreed to do a road construction test. I set up a demo project where Typar® was used in Racine County, and it proved that it was beneficial because it reduced potholes in that stretch of road.

It was a challenging and exciting time, and I was able to work—albeit indirectly—with my dad by asking him about the business, product pricing and discounts, marketing, and why this product was beneficial to each construction site. Because he knew all of the city engineers and construction company personnel, I also gained insight into an array of personalities and how to communicate best in my presentations to connect with various audiences.

I thought I was on my own during this time, and only later did I find out my Dad was looking out for me. I didn't know this until several years before my dad passed away, which was in 2010. It turned out he was there watching, at a distance, at all my stops throughout Wisconsin to make sure that I found the location, got there on time, and was safe. I was a somewhat naive young woman making her way in a man's world.

Today, my brother still runs the company I started, and it's very successful. This early experience was life-changing in that it allowed me to learn a lot about business principles without falling too far or crashing too hard. Only in retrospect do I see how valuable that was in forming my entrepreneurial attitude and confidence about forging ahead on my own.

So, by the time I was ready to start a business, I was confident. I knew that I had the support of my family, no matter what the outcome was. I would be a failure only if I didn't try.

PLANTING PHARMACY ROOTS

I used to walk home after school with our high-school guidance counselor because he lived next door to us in our small town. He knew I was interested in just about everything but was uncertain about my career path. One day he said, "Marla, have you ever thought about pharmacy?" I replied no because I came from a family of engineers, and my mom was a home economics teacher with a chemistry minor, so pharmacy as a career choice wasn't on my radar.

He encouraged me to talk to our local pharmacist, and I when I did, I thought I hit the jackpot. Here was an opportunity to work in a science field knowing that I was potentially making a difference in someone's life.

You don't necessarily start a business because you want to make a gazillion dollars; you do it because you are passionate about making a difference in someone's life, or improving a process, or solving a problem. So, that's what I ended up doing. I enrolled in the school of pharmacy at the University of Wisconsin, but I kept my double major in the school of music until my junior year when I had to decide whether I was going to select pharmacy or music performance as my major.

As a student, I was interested in doing something entrepreneurial and starting my own business. I always knew that I was not going to be working in the basement of a hospital pharmacy or for a chain pharmacy, either. When we were pharmacy students, we all struggled with those choices. We all wanted to take care of patients, but the state of pharmacy practice in those days was a bit limited. I knew I wanted to be practicing in the area of pharmacy and patient care.

I finally graduated from pharmacy school and finished my internship, and I had started planning from the time that I got my internship to eventually start my own business. However, I didn't really know what or where it was going to be.

I started my career at the Prescription Pharmacy at 1 South Park in Madison, which was a clinic pharmacy. The staff consisted of four pharmacists, several pharmacy interns, a nurse fitter for Jobst stockings and colostomy/ileostomy products and we had a hearing aid specialist. We carried the Allercreme and Almay lines of cosmetics, especially for patients who had scarring or allergies to cosmetic ingredients. We also had one of the largest compounding inventories in Madison. It was a good place for me to start because I was in a clinic and it helped me to build a lot of the confidence working with physicians that I would need later when I started my business.

A Woman's World

In 1978, I read an article in the local newspaper about a woman who suffered from severe, cyclic symptoms that included depression, mood swings, and irritability. She had gone to Europe for treatment because she found that no physicians in the United States could help her. There, they had a name for her symptoms — Premenstrual Syndrome — and treatment options in the form of natural progesterone therapy. Her symptoms sounded so much like those suffered by my preceptor's wife that he contacted the woman in the article to learn more.

Another woman suffered the same symptoms and wrote an article in the Milwaukee paper, which the preceptor's wife happened to bring in to work, and she described the same symptoms that the first woman had. So, there were two people who had these symptoms that seemed to disappear for half the month and then return again. Intrigued, we started working on how to alleviate the symptoms for both women. In Europe, the symptoms were treated with natural progesterone, but there wasn't a source for that hormone in America.

European Connection

Katharina Dalton, MD, is the European physician who coined the term Premenstrual Syndrome, and she wrote a book about it titled *Once A Month: Understanding and Treating PMS.* Her book served as the source of information we needed to understand premenstrual syndrome and its management.

Everett Roley, MD, who practiced in Madison, was the doctor of my preceptor's wife. He prescribed progesterone for her, and she said it was as if a cloud lifted. Her symptoms were instantly relieved. Dr. Roley was the first physician in the United States to prescribe progesterone for managing the symptoms of premenstrual syndrome.

At this point, we had to confirm to ourselves that progesterone was safe for patients to use. We spent many hours at the University of Wisconsin Medical Library studying progesterone, how its molecular structure compared to medroxyprogesterone, allowing for differing effects and side effects. It sounds simple today, but you have to remember that progesterone and estrogen receptors had not been identified yet. Practitioners assumed that all progestins and estrogens had the same effects and side effects. There was a lot of misinformation written about these hormones, which made it very difficult for us in our study of steroid hormones.

It was common for a physician to stop by the pharmacy and ask what we were working on. We'd tell them about PMS and progesterone therapy, and each would say, "Hmmm, I've got a patient who sounds just like that! I haven't been able to help her, so let me send her to see you." Two patients became five patients, and then we grew to fifty patients during the next two years. Our practice was growing by word of mouth alone.

Eventually, we flew to Europe to meet with Dr. Dalton to learn how to manage PMS. She prescribed progesterone USP injection or progesterone suppositories because those dosage forms were available in Europe.

Although progesterone suppositories were typically compounded for luteal phase defect, we did not compound progesterone suppositories for our PMS patient population. The very first progesterone dosage form we developed and compounded in the United States was a rectal suspension. We also had to develop something to measure dosage amounts, a rectal applicator, and to understand how to individualize dosing. We quickly learned that dosage amounts varied per woman and varied based on the day of her menstrual cycle. We also began to notice how other medication effects varied in our patients throughout their menstrual cycles. It was the beginning of our recognition that all patients are unique, and one size didn't fit all. It was the first stage of personalized medicine.

The use of a rectal suspension was less irritating and allowed each patient to titrate the dose to better manage her symptoms. Dosing could range from 25 mg to 400 mg per application, depending on the patient and her symptoms, and it could change throughout her menstrual cycle. One of the challenges was to provide a formulation to which patients could be taught to adjust easily and accurately.

Progesterone is metabolized via the first pass effect, so oral options weren't available yet. That's why vaginal and rectal routes of administration were most effective. We began asking questions about the effects of progesterone particle size on absorption and relief of symptoms.

We struggled with micronized progesterone because the particle size was so small, and it resulted in formulas that were very thick. Milled particle size, on the other hand, was too large and resulted in formulations that gave inconsistent patient results.

We contacted the Upjohn Company and persuaded one of their scientists to help us. He eventually acknowledged that the idea made sense. Using equipment at Upjohn, he was able to manufacture progesterone in the particle size ranges that were most appropriate for us. Upjohn eventually used this work to enhance manufacturing for many of their finished tablet dosage forms.

ALLEVIATING SYMPTOMS AND SUFFERING

Patients lined up in the pharmacy to learn about PMS and their prescription. We were teaching menstrual cycle physiology and dietary changes and were listening to symptom histories right in front of other patients. It wasn't an ideal setting for them.

Our first patients had very severe symptoms, and some were hospitalized every month. Many had lost their jobs or couldn't work due to symptom intensity. Others feared losing their children due to divorce related to their symptoms, which were considered to be a mental health concern at that time. However, at the end of each consult, the patient would say, "Thank you; you've changed my life!"

From 1978 to 1982, I was the happiest I could ever be at the pharmacy. I was working with patients, providing education, customizing therapy, and working in a setting where doctors relied on my medical therapy knowledge for each patient they referred.

Early in 1982, I came to work one morning, looking forward to the day, and found the owner of the pharmacy standing at the end of the long dispensing counter. It was obvious he was irritated about something. In a loud, booming voice he said, "Marla, why are you wasting our time anyway? All women are neurotic and should be on Valium."

So, that was a very important day because I was what I call "vision ready." I had been preparing for something like this my whole life. I was a pharmacist, I was doing something I loved, it was beneficial, and I was doing something to help others. I had been saving my money, I had my house, and I was all ready to go to the bank — I just didn't know what form the business would take. When the owner of the pharmacy said, "Why are you wasting our time?" and that, "All women are neurotic and should be on Valium," this is what pushed me out the door to open the very first pharmacy to specialize in women's health and hormonal disorders in the United States.

FOUNDING THE FIRM

I founded Madison Pharmacy Associates in April 1982. It was not easy back then because this was a revolutionary idea — and resisted by most of the medical community. But the pharmacy owner's words from that fateful day still ring in my ears, and they have every day since I left.

The only call I made to discuss my new business was to Pam Ploetz. She was one of our clinical instructors during pharmacy school, and I respected and trusted her. She was a clinical pharmacist at the University of Wisconsin Hospital and Clinics and was a national thought leader for issues related to the expanding roles of pharmacists in the United States. Her opinion mattered to me. I asked her what she thought about the idea of a specialty women's health practice focused on PMS and other hormonal issues. She replied, "Marla, this is revolutionary; this is one of the most wonderful and needed ideas I have ever heard. Yes, you should try it; you should do this." I remember hanging up the phone and being confident about my next steps. We have stayed in touch over the years. I always tell this story to emphasize the importance of having a mentor when you're an entrepreneur. Pam Ploetz has truly been my North Star throughout my business career.

The important thing to remember as an entrepreneur is you're looking at each problem as a whole world of possibilities. You are not looking at the world and agreeing that things must always get done the same way. Saying "because we always did it this way" is the antithesis of an entrepreneur. An entrepreneur is always looking for solutions to problems and how to do something better. We used to say, if a doctor tells you it has always been done this way, or a pharmacist says they teach that in pharmacy school, we need to step back and reevaluate the answer. A number of the things we were taught which we thought were universal truths were not.

When we were starting out, there was no pharmacy practice to copy, no place to buy sophisticated compounding equipment. No computer software had been written for individualized compounded prescription therapy with care plans, and the idea of specializing in the care of women was unheard of in 1982. Not to mention that to start a pharmacy, I had to find a space to rent. I thought it wouldn't be too hard, but no one would rent to me because I was a 26-year-old young woman pharmacist going into an area of business that had never been done before.

Finally, I found a businessman in Madison who believed in me: Jim Imhoff, owner of First Realty. I called him to rent my first pharmacy space, which was on Monroe Street. It was a perfect 700-square-foot space that had previously been a pharmacy. He explained the rental contract to me line by line and reminded me that by signing the contract, I was agreeing to rent for three years—whether the business was successful or not. I could not sign fast enough! I did not think finding pharmacy space was going to be one of the hardest parts of starting my business.

The next unsuspected hurdle appeared when I applied for a pharmacy license. The Board of Pharmacy rejected my application the first time because there was no precedent to approve or regulate a specialized pharmacy in the state of Wisconsin. There were only two types of practices in 1982: hospital pharmacy or retail pharmacy, the latter of which included everyone, from children to geriatrics. There was no specialty pharmacy for women, and they were reluctant to listen to my idea about starting a women's health pharmacy. At that point, my business partner had also left the pharmacy where we had been working, so there were two of us saying we really would like to launch this business. I don't know how we got the license, but at the end of it all, I felt the board thought we weren't going to get into any trouble specializing in women's health, it was a crazy business idea, and we'd be out of business in a couple of years, so why not? Today, there are many specialty pharmacies throughout the United States.

Once we had the business running, another stunning surprise was how resistant many women and female physicians were to the idea of hormonal imbalance. PMS at that time was looked at by many in the women's movement as just another excuse to discriminate against women. A woman couldn't run for president or be an airline pilot, for example. When we brought Dr. Dalton to Madison to give a lecture, people from the women's community in Madison protested. As we began to grow, protesters even got involved with some of the doctors we worked with throughout the country. They picketed in front of their offices and tried to block women who had appointments from entering. I was shocked. I thought Madison would be an accepting place, especially for women's health, and it wasn't.

As a result of our work, we were seeing women getting better, going back to school and finishing their degrees, getting new jobs, and moving on with their lives. Plus the quality of their lives was improving.

EVOLUTION REVOLUTION

Despite the initial hurdles, gradually patients began to be referred to us from doctors throughout the country. The state medical board challenged us because, of course, we were teaching doctors and their patients. We spent the majority of each day educating women and their health care providers about hormonal imbalance, how to identify it, what could be done about it using specific diet, exercise, and lifestyle changes, which was new information at the time. Then, we recommended drug therapy if these changes weren't enough. We were getting most women off the typically prescribed medications, including Valium and Elavil. Relying on dispensing medication as a revenue stream in our pharmacy was not a good thing because we were finding that many patients had prescriptions for medications that they really didn't need or that they were taking too much of.

After four years, we had about 500 patients throughout the country, and everything in our pharmacy world was perfect. We had faced challenges from the medical society, the women's community, and from every doctor who said PMS was all in a woman's head and that our business idea was crazy. The bank never loaned us any money; we started with our own money. We bargained and bought our first compounding equipment from antique stores, purchased used counters and shelves from a local pharmacy, and our first used torsion balance came from Rennebohms. Our pharmacy looked beautiful and completely professional, with no outfront merchandise to distract the patients once they came in.

I don't know how they found out about us, but *New York* magazine flew a reporter out to visit us and do an interview about this new women's health concern called premenstrual syndrome. I thought this was a breakthrough. We'd be able to tell more women about what premenstrual syndrome is, how it can be managed with diet and exercise, and, if that wasn't enough, it could be managed with natural hormone therapy. It turned out that the reporter wrote the most negative article possible. She thought we had identified another way to discriminate against women and was not sympathetic at all. I was deeply disappointed. However, that was when I learned that any media, whether positive or negative, increases awareness. Within the next year, we grew from 500 patients to 5,000 patients in our tiny pharmacy with two telephone lines.

SCALING FOR SUCCESS

Faced with explosive growth, we felt like there weren't enough hours in the day because the business was growing so fast. I had to stay on top of cash flow, keep up with the patient consultations and doctor education, compound each prescription, start hiring more help, and deal with business and bookkeeping at night after the pharmacy had closed.

Each day, I would go to the mailbox and find more mail squeezed into it. We didn't have time to open the mail, much less take the checks out. Our accountant was a friend of my business partner, and he put a simple accounting system together for us because we hadn't learned any accounting techniques in pharmacy school. Everything was done by hand because computers were just beginning to be used — but only in very large organizations. We were more pharmacists than business experts, but I knew we had better figure the business and cash flow part out pretty quickly.

We had to learn about telephone systems to buy a bigger system, quickly hire more pharmacists and technicians, negotiate with shipping companies, locate compounding supplies, and create solutions that weren't easily obtained. I called my dad and asked him if he could help us find a bookkeeper. I wasn't sure how to do an interview for a bookkeeper.

We ordered a pharmacy computer system from QS1; it was huge, and we were the first retail pharmacy in Madison to be computerized. Eventually, we had seven people in our small pharmacy. I could hear every conversation from everybody else's phones at the same time, and it was chaotic.

I approached the building owner about obtaining more space, and he suggested we move across the hall to the 1,500-square-foot office space that was available. Now, we were remodeling a space, building shelves and counters, setting up phones, getting new furniture and trying to hire.

Throughout all of this growth, there was no roadmap. We were learning, trying to take care of our patients, traveling to teach physicians throughout the country, developing different hormone formulations, writing a women's health newsletter, and becoming experts in an area that had not been considered a significant health issue by anybody previously.

We desperately needed health information to send to callers, so I began writing brochures, physician information, and, eventually, a newsletter. One of our patients was our graphic designer who helped with logos, colors, and layouts. Over time, we were able to hire a medical writer and enlist the help of a small advertising agency to organize our outreach. We were desperate for knowledgeable doctor referrals, so we developed a two-day training program in Madison for physicians.

In 1999, I wrote two books with colleagues: one was *Self Help for Premenstrual Syndrome* and the other was *The HRT Solution.*

REGULATORY SCRUTINY

We were facing questions from every angle, especially from a regulatory perspective. The first issue had to do with the perceived overstepping of our role as pharmacists. Were we acting too much like doctors by consulting with patients and teaching physicians? Were we making medical claims and dispensing unapproved drugs? Or, were we simply providing customized prescriptions for a specific patient, working with his or her physician, and also educating the patient? Understanding labeling, approved claims, and proofing marketing materials for compliance was complicated, and, from the regulatory perspective, very threatening to our business.

We knew that we needed to stay within the lines, but we didn't really know what that meant, so we hired an FDA attorney. We let the law firm evaluate what we did, said, and wrote for compliance so we could focus on the professional side of our business.

After spending quite a bit of time and money evaluating materials and products we were developing for commercial resale use requiring FDA approval, we got a letter from them saying they were not responsible for anything they had advised us to do! Obviously, this was a shock. They were not going to stand behind us even though they were the ones who recommended the pathway.

The next time our Navy jurisprudence professor marched in to see us, I asked for a recommendation. He referred us to a wonderful FDA attorney who worked with us for the next twenty-five years!

Each state regulates its pharmacies and pharmacists. As long as the prescription triad— physician, pharmacist, and patient—is in place, the state is involved in regulation. Once a medication is manufactured or distributed for resale, the FDA gets involved and regulates manufacturing, marketing claims, drug efficacy claims, approved uses, and drug safety. The FDA even regulates type font size, label layout, and container size for products that are commercially distributed.

A pharmacist can compound a dermatologic product on prescription and dispense it to a patient. Once a pharmacist starts telling others they can compound a specific dermatologic formula for rosacea, for example, you cross over into FDA regulation. We had doctors prescribing hormonal products for their patients, but we could not do mass marketing or manufacturing in bulk without FDA approval.

The FDA has attempted a number of times to regulate the practice of pharmacy. In the early 1990s, we had more than 40,000 consumers write to the FDA in protest of their efforts. It took a grassroots effort to keep what we were doing from being eliminated. Of course, the FDA was being hounded by major pharmaceutical companies, so they were putting pressure on the FDA, too. Plus, we were in the forefront, so we were the first company leading this charge. We always had a big target on us, but it was a threat to all pharmacists who were moving past the traditional practice of dispensing, counting, and pouring.

Not to mention that competing pharmaceutical companies saw us as a threat. I could read their complaints to the FDA with our pharmacy listed. We were their target, and we had to be stopped because we were a liability to their business. The way I looked at it, the Premarin market and the Provera market were huge at the time, so why bother with a little retail pharmacy? But our little operation cut into their sales, so they looked at us as a big threat. I was constantly aware of that. When I lectured for practitioners about hormone therapy, I might speak about the differences between progesterone versus medroxyprogesterone or estradiol versus conjugated estrogens. There would be MD/JD lawyers in the audience who were hired by the pharmaceutical companies to stand up and challenge what I was saying in front of the other doctors. They tried to intimidate me, but I always had my armor on.

The next wave of regulation involved OSHA and their regulation to provide safe pharmacy work environments. We were ahead of the pharmacy field in that area. We eventually moved into a state-of-the-art 17,000-square-foot building complete with sophisticated HEPA filtration, isolation rooms, robotic dispensing, compounding protocols, and air and surface monitoring techniques that I developed.

As far as safety for employees and patients, pharmacy as a profession has come a long way since we were in pharmacy school. We never thought about nor were we taught that we had to worry about ventilation systems in any pharmacy that was drawing in micronized powders and blowing them back onto the employees and customers in the store.

POWER OF POSITIVITY

Throughout all the challenges, if I began to doubt myself, I remembered the encouragement that Pam Ploetz gave me when I was contemplating this business. I surrounded myself with inspiring, and positive people, too--people who made a difference to others in the world. My mom and dad were unconditionally behind me, even though they never did figure out what I did in my business. I also live in Madison, where we have many entrepreneurs and small businesses. They had won some, occasionally lost some, but always picked themselves back up and kept going. You have to surround yourself with people who energize you and aren't riding your coattails to take from you.

QUALITY PATIENT CARE

Despite the many business hurdles, we always kept patient care front and center in our business. A doctor would refer a patient to us, and because we had usually trained the doctor, we knew that he or she would be sending us a patient who really needed our help.

Initially, we would spend about an hour over the phone or in person with the patient going over her symptoms, teaching her how to chart her symptoms, teaching self-care options that included diet and exercise changes, and we recommended books to read. We developed our own menstrual cycle symptom chart that was used all over the country. Then, they would start a specific nutritional supplement, which I developed.

What we found is that once a patient started appropriate dietary and lifestyle changes, which included exercise three or four times a week for thirty minutes, and a nutritional supplement that emphasized B vitamins and magnesium, we could start weaning patients off of other prescribed medications. If she needed a hormone prescription, we found the dosing required was lower and the symptoms more completely managed.

We were one of the first companies to incorporate changes in diet, lifestyle, and nutritional supplementation as the foundation of health before drug therapy. This unleashed a fury from practitioners who accused us of practicing voodoo medicine.

We showed the significant influence that self-care can have on health. Initially, we were working with patients who were hospitalized nearly every month because of the intensity of their symptoms. The idea of weaning women off the usual drugs of choice, including Elavil, Valium, Xanax, and Prozac, was revolutionary.

We established a number of unique symptom patterns that women experience due to hormonal fluctuations, beginning with ovulation when progesterone is produced. Symptoms usually intensify daily until menstruation begins. On her chart, you could see the diagram of a menstrual cycle, and mid-cycle is indicated with a simple line. Then you would see an increasing line from ovulation to menstruation, and then you would see the lines fall off. Every time we talked with that patient, we were reminded about what her pattern was, which was significant to her, and was significant to us, as far as dosing was concerned. We listed the top six most intense symptoms that we had taught her to chart.

Every consultation began with a review of patient improvement since the last visit, what the key symptoms were, and what the symptom intensity was. All of this determined what would come next. Would it be lifestyle and nutritional supplementation, which is how we usually started? Then, in two to three months we added drug therapy, which was hormone replacement or supplementation. Sometimes symptoms were so severe that we'd start prescription hormone therapy with diet and exercise and then lower the dose over several months.

Our whole goal was to eliminate blood sugar swings, which women with PMS are very sensitive to. We taught women to eat six small meals a day, emphasizing complex carbohydrates and proteins, and eliminating things that they craved, like sweets or simple carbohydrates.

As for the exercise component, we recommended a brisk 30-minute walk three or four times a week. As a woman, she often was the last person to be taken care of because family members always came first. In this case, for severe premenstrual symptoms, the family had to help.

Once a patient leaves our office or pharmacy, she has a whole life out there that brings its own challenges with medication compliance. That was our attempt to get the family involved in supporting her care, and, overall, it was a good attempt and it helped in many cases.

We were devoting a lot of hours per patient to deliver care, but we didn't think about it that way at all. We hadn't really learned about pricing and margins in pharmacy school. It was left to be taught during our rotations, during internship, or to be learned independently. Prescription insurance reimbursement for compounded prescriptions was always a challenge because the time taken to research a formula and consult with a patient was not reimbursable. The ingredient cost was always the lowest. For this reason, many pharmacies didn't take insurance for compounded medications. We were fortunate that we had numerous doctors who signed on to work with us early on. They were frustrated that they could not help their patients, and we were the solution. Because of the early referrals and dedicated doctors, we always had a steady stream of revenue coming in. This enabled us to build each "care plan," provide the health education information for patients, and to fund our operational expenses.

We learned that perseverance is key. I can't keep track of the number of times someone said: it can't be done, you won't get financing, you're practicing voodoo medicine, you can't license that business model, you are too young, you are a woman, this is a joke, and you are going to be out of business in months. All of this was unrelenting, and it went on for thirty-five years.

Self-belief, self-assurance, and self-confidence are critical. Getting pushback from major pharma, the FDA, the state medical board, and the state pharmacy examining board can be very intimidating. I spent a lot of time just trying to put that into perspective: Am I really that off base? Is this really a bad idea? What you conclude is that you are doing something different, and you are changing the way it has always been done before. Of course, others may not see your vision. It can be very lonely, and because of that, self-doubt can be a hazard.

Another is to question the status quo. I used to teach that in our pharmacy. If a doctor said, "It has always been done that way," I would automatically become more inquisitive. An example is, "Marla, it has always been done this way; we give oral contraceptives for women and it protects against bone loss." Now, we were taught that in pharmacy school, but once we were given the ability at my pharmacy to test the rate of bone loss in urine, we found it wasn't true. Thirty- and forty-year-old women taking oral contraceptives were losing massive amounts of bone, so it changed another paradigm. The lesson was, if it has always been done that way, you better check it.

The lessons are that if you are going to change the way things have always been done, you have to be confident and brave. You have to be a visionary because there is no roadmap, you have to be resilient, and you have to be able to withstand the forces that are going to come at you from all directions because of the change you are creating.

I was always "vision ready" and tried to be internally and externally collaborative. It doesn't hurt to be an extreme optimist, either! It's important to maintain vision readiness so when an opportunity presents itself, you have thought about it enough to recognize when it is staring you in the face. For me and my business, this was the saliva testing and the NTx rate of bone loss testing. If I hadn't really thought about ways to prove to the doctors that the amount of medication really did make a difference and that medication was necessary and should be individualized, I may have delayed the success of my business. Plus, the appropriate dose for each woman was probably lower than doctors had been prescribing, and we were individualizing each dose for each woman — in essence, trying to instruct the medical community on how best to manage PMS, perimenopause, and menopause.

The doctors, rightly so, did not know how to practice that way because prior to that they would prescribe ibuprofen 400 mg and 800 mg, and that was it. Vision readiness is important and is part of being an entrepreneur.

Another success factor is that I ran a collaborative practice. We worked with clinicians and researchers around the world; we worked with anybody who would share information with us. Being collaborative was something that helped us immensely. People would say, "Well, in our area of practice, we do it this way," and after discussions with us, they would say, "Oh my gosh, that would be perfect for our practice; I have never seen that." The ability to be collaborative not only from outside resources but from your inside resources, especially within the staff, is so important. Just because you hire someone as a pharmacy technician doesn't mean he or she can't grow into becoming an analytical chemist for you. My staff helped create world-changing technology.

I look back at our time at the University of Wisconsin School of Pharmacy and constantly reflect on all the wonderful things it gave us: our ability to think critically, to be exposed to all different ways of thinking, and all different types of people.

Collaboration made our work easier. I never found it difficult for a nurse to respect the knowledge that I had, much less a doctor or a researcher. They all treated me in a very collaborative way. In my business model, we ended up writing the protocols, providing physician, nurse, and patient education, and really being an extension of that doctor's practice.

Thus, we automatically became more collaborative, and, in doing so, we were able to progress a lot faster with a more rewarding business practice than would have been possible by just waiting for the prescriptions to come in and dispensing them. When we first started in practice, we were supposed to say to the patient, "If you have any questions about your medicine, talk to your doctor." We did not do this in our business model. Pharmacy missed out early on in changing a major paradigm, which, of course, now they are doing, which is wonderful. We didn't know we were being trained as medication experts, which was a good thing, but, on the other hand, it did not let us grow to our full potential as a career.

We always wanted to be a member of the healthcare team, but we were kept siloed. Even in pharmacy school, we sat in the same classroom and the same seats every day, and the professors came in to us. Now it's different, but how great would it have been to spend some time working on meaningful rotations, interacting more with other healthcare disciplines, and allowing everyone to see the skill set of the pharmacist. It's encouraging to see that we have become a true healthcare profession versus a group of highly sophisticated technicians. The challenge will be: Can the pharmacists of tomorrow truly become the center of "all things drug therapy related?"

There are some exciting areas in which pharmacists of tomorrow can get involved in health care, but this doesn't mean it's necessary to keep adding pharmacy schools. It is clear that the corner pharmacy as it has always been is evolving. That's exciting!

But what is a pharmacist going to do when 3D printers are ubiquitous and patients can order their own medications, have them printed, and sent to them? What will the role be for robotic dispensing and counseling? Right now, there is no interface with all the wearables that people are using to monitor and collect health data. Who is evaluating it and getting it to the right health professionals? A pharmacist may be the most important health professional to monitor and adjust dosing based on these data. Individual genetic testing is becoming so cost effective, a pharmacist needs to be the one to evaluate appropriate drug therapy using that information. Pharmacies as wellness centers could be a great resource for rural areas or highly populated areas in the United States. I am not sure what our role will be, but I know in the future it is going to change dramatically, and we need to change with it versus keeping these old models going.

Healthcare costs and runaway drug pricing are definitely a *current* problem. But it may be managed by eliminating pharmacy benefit manager tiers, modifying how an insurance company bills by streamlining drug pricing options, opening options for foreign drug acquisition, and changing the cost of dispensing using 3D printing, artificial intelligence (AI), and robotics. In addition, if the impact of corporate lobbyists and their influence on the FDA and Congress was lessened, you may see even more savings to taxpayers and the healthcare system.

I can envision a patient sitting at home and an alarm goes off on a smartphone after the last tablet is taken from a prescription vial, and it reorders the medication. Once you tap yes on your smartphone, it provides several competitive options where you can get it printed, filled, and delivered. Maybe it is included in your online grocery order. Either way, you eliminated the pharmacy altogether. Now you have AI or wearable technology that is monitoring compliance for you. It notices how many times you have opened your prescription vial or if you put it back in the refrigerator where it needs to be stored. It's monitoring your blood pressure with a wearable app and it auto-sends a printout to your family practitioner alerting him or her about a trend that requires a dosing intervention. These are examples, but we are in for some big changes, and it is going to eliminate the need for many of the technical tasks that all healthcare providers do—including pharmacists.

Many people do not want to drive to pick up a prescription or wait in line. Why wouldn't I open up my computer and talk to a knowledgeable expert via telemedicine? If I could get my questions answered and not leave my home or my workplace—that seems appealing. If I were disabled, I wouldn't have to use my energy to get to the doctor or the pharmacy. If I wore a patch that was testing my levels of insulin, wouldn't it be nice to get an auto reminder for a dose adjustment—or a notification that I need to improve my diet or get back to my exercise program. There will be opportunities for pharmacy professionals, but there will also be a need for fewer of us in the brick-and-mortar settings.

There are so many pharmacists working at the two major chains today, whether it is CVS or Walgreens, and they have a lot at risk to their long-term job security. At the major chain level, they also may be able to start incorporating more and more of these services that are new occupations with which we are not familiar today, and they all have to do with data management. AI is bound to create new opportunities for pharmacists but it will also eliminate many of the dispensing functions. If I were a pharmacist today, I wouldn't be worried that it is going to change tomorrow, but I would be concerned that in five years, what I am doing may look completely different.

Exit Strategy

I have enjoyed my time as an entrepreneur, but I always wanted to sell my pharmacy in my mid-50s and possibly do something else, which is exactly what I did. I had numerous offers to merge or be incorporated into other businesses. The problem with that was our business model was a detailed, hands-on operation using customized care plans and compounded prescriptions, nurses, a nurse practitioner, analytical chemists, pharmacists, custom computer algorithms, along with a large support staff. It was very patient-oriented, and a lot of people didn't understand that. I ended up selling

to a person who loves the specialized and custom compounding pharmacy business. He basically left the model intact with plans to grow it over time. It all turned out well.

When considering whether to become an entrepreneur, you have to look yourself in the mirror and do a self-assessment. Your business is your values in action! I would approach it more from that perspective. Are you disciplined, are you honest, do you have integrity, are you generous, are you self-serving, and are you willing to make a difference in the lives of your staff and your patients? Or, is the difference you want to make only self-serving? I would look at all of those first and say, "Do I have the values that it takes to become an entrepreneur, and will those values allow me to grow with my business?" Sometimes, you don't even know what the opportunity is going to be until it hits you between the eyes, and you have to be ready to do it. Remember what I said about being "vision ready"?

I knew I was going to do something like this, but I didn't know when or what form it would take until the day the pharmacist at my pharmacy said to me, "All women are neurotic and should be on Valium. Why are you wasting our time?" That would be a good ending to my story because it brings it full circle.

CHAPTER TWO

Bruce Paddock

Founder, President, and CEO of Paddock Laboratories Inc.
University of Minnesota School of Pharmacy

Bruce Paddock had to grow up faster than he wanted when his father—and hero—passed away when he was twelve years old. His
determination in the face of adversity is inspirational to all.

It's difficult not to be in awe of the work ethic Bruce developed in
his youth; he worked many jobs growing up. Why is it that so many
entrepreneurs from his generation had paper routes? Did it force
them to be not only an employee but also an independent business-
person at the age of twelve or thirteen? It was essential for them
to manage time, priorities, and cash flow—and learn how to make
collections weekly—in person.

After pharmacy school, Paddock gained a variety of work experiences, including getting a job at the CR Canfield Company. After
working there for three years, it was clear the company was not
doing well and was on the road to bankruptcy. Bruce found a way
to get financing, including using all of his personal savings, which
totaled $20,000. He acquired the company and then during the

next thirty years built it into the pharmaceutical leader, Paddock Laboratories, which he sold to Perrigo for $540 million in 2012.

I first met him when I was at the pharmaceutical giant Eli Lilly and Company as a product manager. I was at an American Society of Health-System Pharmacists (ASHP) midyear clinical meeting in the mid-1980s in New Orleans, and we had about twenty staff attending, all gathered around a gigantic exhibit envisioning dinner that night in the French Quarter. While walking around the exhibit floor, I noticed a single person at a 10-foot exhibit, the smallest exhibit size available. It was Bruce Paddock working and hustling like there was no tomorrow—selling what I think was an activated charcoal product of some kind for a company called Paddock Laboratories. It was his company and his life's passion, too.

That encounter exemplifies Paddock in those early days—CEO, chief salesperson, with unlimited energy and nonstop work. He did everything he needed to do to build up Paddock Laboratories and make it a success.

I got to know him much better as the years went by and would see him at ASHP meetings or the Generic Pharmaceutical Association (GPhA) meetings—now called the Association for Affordable Medicines (AAM). We would usually run into each other at the gym or a reception. He was always fun, down to earth, and never a phony. He was the kind of person that if he promised you something, you could bet that he would deliver.

Paddock's story is a great read about building a business and its inherent challenges, but it is also about overcoming obstacles in life. Bruce did it all and never changed who he is at his core—maybe that is his biggest accomplishment. Here is his story.

MIDWESTERN ROOTS

I was born in Duluth, Minn., in the late 1940s, and my life in Duluth through the 1950s and 1960s formed the foundation of my life. The lessons I learned from parents, teachers, and coaches informed my successes and failures.

My parents were firm believers in the children helping to keep house, and we all had duties and responsibilities to the family. There was no playing with friends until our daily chores were completed. We rented a small apartment until I was ten years old, and then we moved into a modest home about one block from our rental unit.

My father had a small furniture-refinishing business that he operated out of our basement and garage. I worked alongside him, helping at first with cleaning up and organizing his tools. Later, he would employ me to complete basic refinishing of furniture, from sanding and finish removal to sweeping the floors. He taught me the benefits of hard work and finishing a project to perfection. My father was my mentor, friend, and hero. Unfortunately, he died at age forty-eight, when I was only twelve years old. It was the most devastating experience I had in my young life. From that time on, I worked various jobs, mostly menial, entry-level roles.

I had paper routes from ages twelve to seventeen, eventually landing the largest paper route in Duluth, delivering papers to the wealthy upper east side of the city. Many of my customers were professional people, including doctors, attorneys, and prominent business owners in the city. It was this experience that gave me the drive to become successful in my adult years. I had the opportunity to enter customer homes on collection day, usually Friday of each week, to see how these successful and wealthy people lived their lives.

For the most part, they all had new and expensive cars in their driveways and garages, and their children all had bicycles and toys that I could only dream of. It didn't take me much time to realize that most of these successful people all had one thing in common, which was higher education. It was this experience that made me realize at a very young age that I needed to go to college and develop my skills to increase my standard of living as an adult.

Manual Labor

As a teenager, I pumped gas at a service station after school and on the weekends. The owner was a friend of my father's, and I think he felt sorry for me after my father died—but he also knew my mother was making minimum wage sewing drapes at the local drapery store in downtown Duluth.

Another friend of my father's was Ivan Grossman, owner and president of the local North American Van Lines. I was a big, strong kid by the time I was fourteen. I moved furniture for North American for five years, through high school and college. Eventually, I secured my chauffeur's license to drive trucks for local deliveries. I made the most money working as a furniture mover because we were unionized and my hourly salary was double or triple what I made at my other minimum-wage jobs. This was not my chosen profession, and I quickly realized that I could not move furniture for the rest of my life.

I had numerous jobs during this time period, including working as a busboy, dishwasher, "salad girl," and eventually a waiter at the Highland Supper Club once I turned twenty-one. These experiences reinforced the fact that education was my only way out. Most of my co-workers were adults with families, but they had little chance of advancement.

My other jobs included mowing lawns, laying sod, gardening at the local Northland Country Club, and Christmas gift-wrapping during the holiday season. There wasn't much that I didn't do during my formative years in Duluth. If there was a job to be had, I was the first to apply. It was through these various jobs that I learned the lessons of hard work and reaped the financial rewards that gave me the independence I craved.

FROM A BOY TO A MAN

After my father died, I accepted the responsibility of maintaining the household because my mother worked full-time to put food on the table. I learned how to re-roof our modest home, paint, caulk windows, perform plumbing and electrical repairs, and I stoked our coal-fired furnace, not an easy thing to do during the cold Duluth winters. My bible became the *Reader's Digest* encyclopedia of home repairs.

During my junior and senior years in high school, I took as many shop classes as I could, and most were required classes for boys during that time. They included woodworking, sheet metal work, plastics, printing, auto mechanics, and learning how to be an electrician. I was convinced that one of these vocations was my chosen profession because I excelled in all of these classes. Many of my projects were entered in city industrial arts contests, and I was proud to have won several ribbons and awards. Little did I know that I would need these skills later in life when I started my pharmaceutical business.

I also discovered that I had math and science skills to supplement my mechanical skills. My counselors encouraged me to take physics, chemistry, biology, and advanced math courses. I didn't have a great interest in them because my natural skills were mechanical. The math and science courses required studying, and I had little time for that because I was working most of the time after school and on the weekends.

Believe it or not, I somehow found time to participate in athletics. I lettered in football, basketball, track, and softball in junior high and football and track in high school. I don't want to take too much credit for these athletic milestones, because back then if you tried out for the team, you were on it. We didn't have to commit to one or two sports to be successful like young men and women do today.

A COUNTRY AT WAR

Back in the 1960s and early 1970s, the United States was fully engaged in the unpopular Vietnam War. There was a mandatory military draft, and all males once they turned eighteen had to register with the draft board, as I did the day I reached that age. I had just graduated from high school and wasn't sure if I wanted to go to college or a trade school. I found out that if I went to college, I would be granted a four-year military exemption, or 2S deferment, until I graduated.

My close friend, Scott Baldwin, enlisted in the Army due to poor grades in his first year of college. He was killed in action within months of arriving in Vietnam and came home in a box. Attending his funeral at age eighteen was a stark reminder of how fast life can end. My path was now very clear, as I determined the military draft was not an option for me. I had too many things I needed to accomplish; I had to go to college.

I enrolled at the University of Minnesota-Duluth (UMD) because a public, subsidized education was my only option. I explored the idea of attending West Point because I was an Eagle Scout and I had good, but not great, grades in high school, but my mother and I did not have the means for me to attend, nor did I have any political connections.

During my first year in college, I became a double art and business major, and I took an occasional math and science course because I started developing more interest in those subjects. In the 1960s, there was a shortage of pharmacists, and I found out that pharmacy was a five-year curriculum and one-year internship. The military draft board would give me a five-year military deferment if I completed the required courses and graduated. Pharmacy looked to be an attractive profession, but I was not the best student in college—mostly a B and C student with a 2.7 grade point average (GPA) before entering pharmacy school.

Luckily for me, entry to pharmacy school was pretty simple in the late 1960s. You needed a 2.0 GPA with an emphasis on math and science courses and a minimum of two years of college. As I said, there was a severe shortage of pharmacists at the time because of the war, and the school needed to increase its graduating class numbers to fill that void.

I declared pharmacy as my major and applied to the school. I had to meet the dean of student affairs to get in. There was no pre-test and no references required--just an interview with Dr. Frank DiGange, and I was in.

The interview went poorly, and he commented that I didn't have the required courses for entry, didn't have a strong GPA, and he felt that I was not pharmacy material. I begged for his reconsideration and committed to going to summer session before fall entry to complete my organic chemistry, calculus, and biology coursework, promising to earn a B average. He believed me and gave me the OK—if I honored my commitment. That summer was the longest and least fun of my life. No work, no play, and all school, but I made it—I was admitted to the school of pharmacy.

INTIMIDATION AND ANGST

I was immediately intimidated when I entered pharmacy school. My first class included about 300 students from all over the state. I was convinced that I was the least-prepared of all the students. Many had made pharmacy their chosen career path at a very young age. Others had fathers and family members who were pharmacists. Some had four-year degrees and were seeking higher education, and many were military veterans who were going to school on the GI bill—and they all seemed more confident than I was.

The dean of student affairs, who was also my stern admissions professor, was my first professor in analytical pharmaceutical chemistry, my poorest subject. Dr. DiGange's nickname was "Black Frank" because he was known to intimidate students and had flunked more people than any other professor. When he entered the classroom, he immediately told us to look to our left and then to our right because by the time we reached our senior year, two out of three of us would be gone. There were only seventy-eight senior compounding benches in the laboratory. He was right; we graduated seventy-eight students.

He was the toughest professor I ever had. I worked hard for my B grade and was proud of my accomplishment. After my graduation, Dr. DiGange and I became friends and served on many committees together. It wasn't until years after graduation that I appreciated his commitment to pharmacy education and his love for the profession—and his students. I will always remember him as an influential mentor in my pharmacy career.

PHARMA LIFE

While in school, I committed to the life of a pharmacy student. I studied hard my first year, didn't work, and lived off savings from my jobs in high school. I sold my car and didn't have a TV. I lived in a one-bedroom, lower-level apartment in a modest South Minneapolis home. My roommate, David Larson, had a small Volkswagen that we drove to school each day. We studied together every night, mindful of the challenge that Dr. DiGange laid before us, keeping in mind the anticipated attrition from 300 students to 78.

My roommate's father owned Falk's Pharmacy in Duluth, and he was expected to join the family business. He felt the pressure from his family, and I felt the pressure from and fear of the Vietnam War. I also did not want to go back to moving furniture and waiting tables; I was determined to be successful. I wanted to move to the east side of Duluth—the good side of town.

After my first year, I slowly gained more confidence as I realized that with hard work I would make it, but I had a money problem: I was running out. I needed a strategy for reducing my expenses, increasing my income, and still maintaining my level of study. I had to complete my coursework in five years before the military draft board caught up with me.

I decided to join the Phi Delta Chi fraternity. They had a house with cheap room and board at $80 per month, and they had a great cook, Clementine Kosie, who was our surrogate mother. They also had years of test files from all the professors at the pharmacy school, and the house was a good source of camaraderie and commiseration. I loved living in the fraternity house and met many friends that I still have today.

By the end of my second year of pharmacy school and my first year at Phi Delta Chi, I became the pledge master to the new students and a member of the college board. I was starting to feel a real connection to my chosen profession of pharmacy rather than thinking of it as an academic excuse to avoid the draft.

CONFIDENCE BOOSTER

My roommate in the frat house was Gary Rein, a fellow student from Duluth, who became a member of Rho Chi, the pharmacy honor society. He helped me as a student because we became best friends and studied together. He got the As and I got the Bs. He simply was smarter than I was. By the time I made it to my senior year, I was elected president of Phi Delta Chi and was working in retail at Cranes Pharmacy in South Minneapolis and at the University of Minnesota Hospital Pharmacy. What great work opportunities for a student to experience both community and hospital pharmacy. At that time, we didn't have rotations, there was no managed care, and industrial pharmacy was generally unknown to us.

By the senior spring quarter, I had fulfilled most of my required coursework, and I decided to take two elective courses that had great appeal to me: parenteral products and pharmaceutical manufacturing. Both were taken as pass/no pass credit. I had great passion for both and enjoyed these classes more than any other in my college career. Again, I had no idea how important these classes were to me at the time because I was convinced I was going into community pharmacy and would own a retail store — that was my goal.

After having at least four positions offered to me, my first position was as a staff pharmacist for Nabors Drug in St. Paul, Minnesota. I was told five years earlier that there was a shortage of pharmacists, and that was true. I simply went with the highest-paying job I was offered.

I worked for about eighteen months at Nabors Drug, and it became a mundane position. I needed greater stimulation; therefore, I applied and entered Northwestern Chiropractic College in Minneapolis. I left Nabors Drug, entered school full-time, and started working part-time for Snyder's Drug, a small regional chain in Minnesota.

During this time, I got married, finished chiropractic school in two years, and passed national basic science exams, but I never completed my internship for chiropractic. At that time in the mid-1970s, chiropractic was not covered by many insurance companies, managed care didn't exist, most chiropractors' revenue was from private payers, and economic success was limited.

At the end of my very short chiropractic career, I applied for the chief pharmacist position at the CR Canfield Company in South Minneapolis. Canfield was a local pharmaceutical manufacturing company that Carl Canfield, MD, originally owned.

He sold his company in 1970 to several Minneapolis-based athletes in the twilight of their careers: Bob Allison and Harmon Killebrew from the Minnesota Twins, as well as some other well-known athletes and celebrities. Allison hired me because I had some manufacturing experience that I picked up in my elective coursework in parenteral products and pharmaceutical manufacturing during my senior year in pharmacy school.

Little did I know at the time when I took these two elective courses that they provide the entry into industrial pharmacy which would shape the balance of my pharmacy and business career. After three years of a new and exciting position with the CR Canfield Company, I had found my niche, and it was both stimulating and challenging.

I was using many of the technical skills that I learned in pharmacy school: analytical, calculations, formulations, compounding, and applying methods and formulations from the USP and NF, plus my compounding courses. It was right in my wheelhouse of ability and interest.

In late 1977, after three years of employment there, I discovered the Canfield Company was having serious financial problems and was not paying its bank loans, which were in default.

In January 1978, the bank foreclosed on the assets of the Canfield Company and scheduled to put the company up for public auction shortly thereafter. I was approached by several business owners of local pharmacies, wholesale drug businesses, and private investors to stay on and run the small compounding business. I had other plans; I was working with a local bank, Summit State Bank in Richfield, Minnesota, to secure financing for asset purchase. I was able to secure a $30,000 Small Business Administration (SBA) loan and planned to put my personal savings of about $20,000 into the business, too.

Two weeks after the foreclosure, the bank conducted a public auction sale, and I was the successful bidder and acquired the assets of the Canfield Company for $20,000. I then purchased the company delivery van for $1,500 at a special sheriff's auction and purchased the existing master formulas and trade names by paying off the attorney's fees for the previous owners. Within a two-week period, I acquired all of the assets I needed to stay in business for the bargain price of $30,000, leaving me with about $20,000 in working capital to reorganize the bankrupt business and continue operations.

I opened the business under the name of Paddock Laboratories Inc. My humble little company occupied about 5,000 square feet in the basement of a South Minneapolis commercial building, and my staff started with an office manager, two lab technicians, and me.

Our first-year sales were modest at $183,000, and I was just able to meet payroll and operational expenses. During the first three years, I rarely took a salary and supplemented my income by working part-time at night and on weekends as a pharmacist. By 1980, I was able to take a $30,000 annual salary, and I retired from my community pharmacy positions. We had grown to ten employees with sales of about $400,000.

In the beginning, it was the Bruce Paddock show; I did everything, including sales, administration, shipping/receiving, manufacturing, packaging, quality control, regulatory, and even managed to clean the toilets and sweep the floors. I didn't know where I wanted to go with the company, and the business was driven by Canfield continuing business and customers who came to me with product ideas and formulations. All of the business was local and within the state of Minnesota, with very limited regional sales in the surrounding states of Iowa, Wisconsin, and North and South Dakota. Most of the products were ideas and formulations that various hospital and retail pharmacies approached us about, including Glutose, which was a concentrated sugar for insulin reactions that originated from the local Diabetes Education Center to fulfill patient needs for treatment of hypoglycemic insulin reactions.

Another product was Emulsoil, a self-emulsifying, flavored castor oil used for bowel evacuation before colonoscopy. The idea came from Mount Sinai Hospital and was driven by the radiologist who used castor oil. Other products were Actidose with Sorbitol and Actidose Aqua. Actidose was a liquid charcoal used in poison emergencies after gastric lavage, which was supplied to St. Paul Ramsey and Hennepin County poison centers. There were repacked chemicals used in compounding, including hydrocortisone, neomycin sulfate, triamcinolone acetate, progesterone, and testosterone. Finally, there were about twelve different compounding vehicles.

I decided to streamline the product line and pick various products that would have a national appeal; otherwise I would continue to be another regional compounding company with little opportunity for growth. We decided to create a compounding company that supplied various compounding vehicles and chemicals to the industry. At the time, the Minneapolis FDA inspected us on a regular basis, and we received many Form 483 deficiencies. The FDA required us to follow current good manufacturing practices (cGMP), which included chemical identification upon receiving, certificate of analysis from various chemical manufacturers, blueprint and resin specifications of all packaging materials, stability studies on finished products, and detailed analytical finished product standards.

By 1982, we had passed the $1 million mark in gross sales, and we had about twenty employees. We had outgrown our 5,000-square-foot manufacturing space and needed to make a commitment to build, move, and/or lease again. I spent several months talking to several banks in Minneapolis to secure at least a $500,000 business loan. Finally, I convinced First Bank System, the predecessor to U.S. Bank, to loan us the required $500,000 for construction and working capital required for the move and expansion of the business.

I had created a three-year business plan that had us tripling our sales in five years. At the time, I had no idea how I was going to execute such an aggressive sales plan, but I needed an optimistic plan to show the profit and cash flow to service our debt. First Bank believed me and approved the loan with security of everything I owned, including all inventory/equipment/accounts receivable and a personal guarantee with all of my personal assets pledged. Failure at this point would mean the loss of everything.

I rationalized the decision to myself by thinking that if I lost everything, I was still in my early 30s and could always go back to working as a pharmacist. It was always my fallback position, but the reality was that I would not accept failure and was determined to accomplish my goals.

I don't remember the exact terms of the transaction, but this was in the early 1980s, and inflation and prime interest rates had exceeded double digits. I believe our interest rate was somewhere around 14 to 15 percent. It's hard to believe, but my current interest rate before our sale in 2011 was around 3 percent. It was a lesson learned; when you really need money, it is cost-prohibitive, and when you don't, all the money in the world is available to you. We broke ground in November 1982 and moved into our 15,000-square-foot manufacturing facility in summer 1983. We had tripled our square footage and were swimming in space.

HATCHING A MILESTONE

The year 1984 marked another milestone for the generic pharmaceutical industry because Congress passed the Hatch-Waxman Act, which allowed a regulatory pathway for generic pharmaceuticals. We now only had to demonstrate bio-equivalency of the referenced listed products. We did not have to prove safety and efficacy with new drug applications. It provided new energy to the generic pharmaceutical industry, but it would be several years before we made a commitment to generic pharmaceuticals. By the late 1990s and 2000s, bioequivalent generics would contribute to our most dramatic growth and result in about three-quarters of Paddock Lab sales.

In 1987, Jerry Nelson from Upsher-Smith Laboratories contacted me, stating he'd like to become a partner in Paddock Laboratories. He left Upsher-Smith in 1984 as a full partner and had a three-year covenant to not compete with the company after being bought out by his partner, Ken Evenstadt. Nelson was the manufacturing/operations person at Upsher and had developed a line of suppositories, and he wanted to enter the pharmaceutical industry again.

I talked him into starting his own company, Nelson Pharmaceuticals, and I rented him space inside the Paddock Laboratory building. I put up $120,000 and he contributed $180,000 to start the company. We purchased a Pharma Due Suppository machine and an automated packaging line from Italy that year. By 1990, he decided he wanted to retire due to business failures and legal battles with his ex-partner at Upsher Smith. I bought him out of his equity in Nelson Pharmaceuticals for $180,000.

Paddock was suddenly in the suppository business. Sales were less than $100,000 when I took over the business because Nelson had a hard time generating sales in a niche market. From the acquisition of the suppository business in 1990 until the sale of Paddock Laboratories in 2011, we grew that segment of the business twentyfold to about $20 million and became the largest manufacturer of generic suppositories in the United States, with more than 250 million suppositories produced annually.

By 1990, the company had expanded to about fifty employees and $10 million in sales. After three expansions, we now had about 30,000 square feet of space, doubling our building size. We were ready for another major expansion because we ran out of space in our current location. However, major financing was always a problem. The company was growing, and most, if not all, excess profits had to be reinvested in accounts receivable, inventory, and new equipment.

We needed about $4 million to build a new building, increase working capital, and increase product development for further growth. The city leaders of New Hope, Minn., were starting to take notice of our growing business because they were at our site on a regular basis to provide permits for building expansion. We were becoming a major employer, and the city planning commission and city council were taking notice as we outgrew our facility and needed new space.

The city manager said there was a 10-acre building site one block away from city hall, and the city would be interested in sponsoring an industrial revenue bond to help keep us within the city limits. After consulting with local business law firm Fagre and Benson, we applied for a $4 million industrial revenue bond, which the city of

New Hope sponsored and approved. We stayed and continued to grow; we broke ground in 1992 and completed our move into our new 70,000-square-foot building in 1993.

By then, the company had grown to about 100 employees, and we added a director of human resources (HR) who relieved department managers of day-to-day HR functions so they could focus on their department operations.

I wrote our first business plan, including the mission statement, company values, and one-year strategic plan that included measurable goals, objectives, and an action plan to accomplish those goals. All department goals were tied to a bonus plan for each member of the management team.

Later, in the mid- to late 1990s, my executive staff wrote the business plan, and they recognized participation by all. This was the same year that I started having management meetings every Friday morning to get updates and reports from all department heads. These meetings allowed each department head to know and understand what other departments were doing. Later that year, we started to have monthly company meetings. The business was getting so big that my daily communication was limited, and I felt I needed to connect with all employees on at least a monthly basis.

Monthly meetings consisted of the introduction of new employees, recognition of employee accomplishments, including an award of excellence that was given out each month to one employee who had performed to a high level of accomplishment. It might be a cash award, a trophy, tickets to local sporting events, or a dinner for two at a local restaurant. Another one was a team-building award. This was usually department-driven and given to a group of employees. Finally, we had a President's Award, which was given annually to an employee who had contributed the most during the last year. The award was limited to non-exempt employees, and management was not eligible.

The balance of the monthly meeting was to review inventory, gross sales, top-selling products, and general business updates from all departments. Later, we would have a guest speaker, which was usually a department head who discussed his or her role in the overall success of the business. It was important to me that every employee understood the complete business, not just his or her department.

In addition, we always had sports teams that we sponsored. I felt strongly that if employees could play together, they could work together. In the end, we had four softball teams, a basketball team, a billiards team, and a volleyball team. I participated in all team events, but I retired at age fifty from most teams. I continued to participate on the billiards team.

BUILT FOR SUCCESS

Paddock laboratories, from the very beginning, provided me with the challenges, stimulation, and excitement that I would have never experienced in any other career in pharmacy. I miss all the many wonderful and talented people with whom I had the pleasure of being associated for more than thirty-four years. This not only included employees, but also vendors and suppliers, customers, and our many partners in the industry.

Many of these lasting relationships have developed into lifelong friendships. Paddock Laboratories provided a forum for people who were hard working, dedicated, educated, and committed to their work, family, and community. I was privileged to have worked with these great employees, and it was these employees and my relationship with them that has shaped my life and career and made me a better person.

We crafted a mission statement in 2000 that really said it all about the company, the employees, and what we stood for:

"The people of Paddock Laboratories are dedicated to providing affordable, specialty pharmaceutical products to meet the ever-changing needs of our customers through commitment to innovation, excellence, integrity, and teamwork.

Exit Strategy

By 2000, I was just past age fifty and started to think about an exit strategy. My options included:

1. My 20-year-old son, who was in college at the time, could take over the business.

2. I could sell the business to highest bidder: We had several offers over the years to be acquired by private equity and other pharmaceutical companies.

3. I could pass on the CEO/president position to current executive management or to an outside hire, and I could continue as chairman and a board member.

4. We could acquire other pharmaceutical businesses to supplement our growth, which would mean continuation of management.

I planned my vision in five-year increments. At the end of each five-year period, I would consider all exit options, but it wasn't until I reached age sixty that I acted on any option.

At that time in 2008, I hired a president named Mike Graves from Par Pharmaceuticals to run the day-to-day operations. The company had grown to about $100 million, and we had more than 250 employees. I needed to focus on overall strategy, product development, and the future of the company. We had more than thirty generic products in development, and sales were stagnant due to the difficulty of getting FDA approval for our thirty development projects. We also brought on a senior R&D person and several others in product development, operations, quality assurance, regulatory, and business development.

We now had a senior management team that would give us the leadership to drive the business forward and to position ourselves for either merger or acquisition during the next five years. Our new focus was product development, because generic pharmaceuticals was now our forte and product life cycles had diminished as the competitive landscape in generics became more difficult.

By 2011, we had doubled our sales and had more than fifty products in development either in early stages, clinical study, or pending Abbreviated New Drug Application (ANDA) approval at the Office of Generic Drugs.

I made the difficult decision to sell the business that I had spent thirty-four years creating.

After lengthy interviews with more than nine advisory bankers focused on mergers and acquisitions, we decided to go with Jefferies, a New York mergers and acquisitions firm, and used Greene Holcomb & Fisher, a local mid-market advisory firm in Minneapolis.

At the end of the process, which was long and arduous, we had one standing buyer in Perrigo, an Allergan, Michigan, over-the-counter (OTC) generic firm that was a leader in the private label OTC market and wanted to expand its generic prescription market after acquiring Clay Park Pharmaceuticals in New York City a couple years earlier.

The final sale price was $540 million, including all business assets and buildings in two locations. In the end, we had grown our humble generic business from $183,000 annual sales to $220 million. We had more than 400 employees when we exited, and our financials were impressive with thirty percent earnings before interest, tax, depreciation, and amortization (EBITDA).

THE BEGINNING OF THE END

We were proud of our accomplishments, and, at age sixty-five, I was ready for retirement. I was convinced that upon the final sale, I would be handing the keys over to the new owners and they would continue to build on the success that we created over thirty-four years. I was wrong.

Within the first year, Perrigo terminated all the vice presidents, dismantled our business development and sales and marketing teams, and discontinued most of our product development projects. They had turned the company into a manufacturing site supported by quality and regulatory.

It took me thirty-four years to build the business and a little more than four years to dissolve it. The last four years were arduous and painful.

Our purchase agreement was executed in January 2011, and it took more than six months for closing to take place, in August 2011. Delays included working with Perrigo's attorneys, accounting and operational reviews. Regulatory and quality were a focus for the due diligence of the entire operation.

Even after six months of scrutiny, not all components of the purchase agreement were completed. Open items included asset allocation, inventory value, equipment value, accounts receivable, real estate value, IRS review of Sub Chapter S status, and review of all supply agreements and contracts, including all fifty state Medicaid agreements.

Our biggest challenge was negotiating with the state of Texas's attorney general's office on all Medicaid claims dating back to 1996. Texas has been challenging Medicaid claims in the pharmaceutical industry since 2005, and because Perrigo was under investigation, Paddock Labs was brought into it after the purchase. We didn't settle with Texas until 2015.

The constant investigation of the pharmaceutical industry by the many regulatory agencies from local, state, and federal agencies was burdensome. Many of these regulatory agencies have the same redundant regulations from local to state and federal. My observation is that the degree and depth of inspection by all regulatory agencies has become increasingly more burdensome as time has gone on, without any degree of benefit to the pharmaceutical industry and the public it serves.

As a pharmacist and leader in the pharmaceutical manufacturing industry, I can assure the public that the safety and effectiveness of drug products today is no better than it was thirty-five years ago when I entered the industry.

Eye on Future Entrepreneurs

You'll face many challenges, but my best advice to pharmacy students is to keep your options open as you progress in your career. Your focus and interest may be community pharmacy, but opportunities can and will develop in other areas of pharmacy as you progress. Graduates have so many more options today than I had forty years ago, including in community, hospital, managed care, pharmaceutical industry, wholesale drug, and distribution. The options are endless in each general category.

Whatever you do in your vocation, perform it with passion, desire, and competitiveness. Take pride in your work, no matter how technical or menial. Hard work and focus will reward you with success.

I consider myself very lucky to have had a rewarding career in pharmacy. I never could have imagined the success I eventually achieved when I was a pharmacy student and young pharmacist. I simply kept working hard and looking for opportunities. I have no regrets and enjoyed every day of growing my business.

CHAPTER THREE

Dan Buffington

Founder, President, and CEO of
Clinical Pharmacology Services (CPS)
Mercer University School of Pharmacy

Dan Buffington has developed a business model that can be ideal for a pharmacy practitioner who desires to use his or her education to the fullest, one that I can only hope more pharmacists turn to in the future.

After completion of his pharmacy degree at Mercer University, Buffington did a residency at Emory University and got his first job at H. Lee Moffitt Cancer Center in Tampa, Florida. He asked a critical question of himself: Could a pharmacist follow a similar career path as a physician? Why couldn't he be a specialist in pharmacology just as medical doctors specialized in neurology or cardiology?

The founding of Clinical Pharmacology Services was the culmination of answering this question and trying out this concept. After all, shouldn't the pharmacist be looked at as the absolute expert on everything related to drug therapy?

Buffington has made this his passion, his business, and his livelihood. The pharmacy profession, pharmacy schools, and faculty can benefit from studying this business model. Here, he recounts how and why he founded his company.

FLORIDA ROOTS

Growing up in Tampa, St. Petersburg, and Orlando, Florida, I had an interesting first job. I can't tell you how I got started in it, but I started making marionettes. Everywhere I took them, they would sell out, including at airports, malls, and all sorts of places. It was an arts-and-crafts kind of thing and also a cottage industry.

I came from a family of craftspeople, which included wood cabinet-makers and a seamstress, and I learned how to create by being in their presence. When I made a few marionettes and they sold like hotcakes, it was an interesting first business experience.

My mom was an elementary school teacher, and my dad owned a gas station for several years and then went into the health insurance and life insurance business. I observed him as he went through the experience of being a broker and entrepreneur.

HEALTHCARE HABITS

I was interested in medicine from an early age, and I always showed interest in friends and family members who had medical appointments or ailments for which they needed to be treated. I knew I was going to be in the healthcare field. I was predominantly looking at medicine as a career, and I remember as a kid being drawn to optometry and reaching out to get information about medical and optometry schools. To this day, I still remember correspondence from the schools, which included kind words of encouragement.

When it was time for college, I chose Mercer University. I was looking at football programs at a couple different schools, and there was an issue with getting my transcripts sent to one of the teams. As a result, I decided to go to the University of South Florida (USF) for the first year, with the goal of moving on to another university after one year.

I got to USF and really liked their natural science program and was pointed toward the premed program. Several friends — both fraternity friends and family friends — mentioned a new program called PharmD, and they thought my interest in biochemistry and pharmacology warranted looking at it.

I met the recruiting director for Mercer University while I was considering the University of Florida, Mercer, and Auburn University. I was impressed with the interview process and the level of professional engagement at Mercer. I was accepted there and decided to pursue PharmD and still take the MCAT while there and apply to medical school. I thought it would be a nice blend even if I finished the PharmD program.

I got to Mercer and quickly realized that their PharmD program definitely was what I was looking for in terms of a career path.

While I was a student at Mercer, I had the opportunity to do some clinical rotations at Emory University in Atlanta. Emory has always had a strong residency program and was in the process of starting a clinical pharmacology fellowship. The person who was in charge was Victor Lampasona, PharmD. He was a preceptor while I was in school, and then I applied and did residency there. I also applied to their clinical pharmacology fellowship and did that at Emory as well.

Dr. Lampasona was with Emory for years, and after I left, he helped to build their clinical research infrastructure across the university. He has worked with several companies as a medical science liaison (MSL). MSLs can help recruit and build teams and build the infrastructure for groups in transition. It's an important role, and one that is probably underutilized in the industry today for many reasons.

After my fellowship, I took my first position at H. Lee Moffitt Cancer Center in Tampa, which is on the USF campus. At that point, USF did not have a college of pharmacy—they have only had one for about seven years. My interest was in what Moffitt offered, which was a very strong clinical support role: I worked with the gynecology, oncology, and infectious disease service. Because of my clinical research background, I was doing clinical trials, as well as acting as an investigator. In a very short period of time, I was recruited to be a full-time faculty with USF Medicine, specifically within the division of internal medicine.

This led to a very interesting project of helping USF to develop a division of clinical pharmacology within internal medicine to be able to help write clinical research trials, recruit these trials, and teach faculty, residents, fellows, and other faculty about clinical research trial design and management. It included developing a consult service for clinical pharmacological service.

It was during this time that I began to ask the question: What is the difference between a physician graduating from medical school and going into practice and a pharmacist graduating pharmacy school and taking a job? I was looking for differences in terminology, semantics, and climate that were progressively leading pharmacists down a path of employment for some other entity instead of opening their own practices.

These entities where most pharmacists were seeking employment encompassed a progressive consolidation with either larger health systems or larger chain pharmacy management entities. I asked myself the question: Could a pharmacist follow a similar career path as a physician — but as a clinical practitioner separate from a traditional pharmacist employer entity? I had to research the different types or infrastructures of medical practices, including primary care versus medical specialty practice office, and solo practitioners versus group practices, etc.

What I realized is that pharmacists are generalists, meaning we have to know all therapeutic categories and all therapeutic entities for medications. We behave more like specialists when we're integrated into the medical practice setting.

That becomes a little perplexing when people say, "Wait a minute; I see a great opportunity for pharmacists in primary care practices." My answer to that is the primary care practice didn't bring you in to be the primary care practitioner; they brought you in to be a specialist in pharmacology and clinical pharmacology in that practice setting.

If you look across many of the large national and international trials that have looked at promoting or evaluating interdisciplinary care models, you see something interesting. Pharmacists bring closer coordination of care between primary care and various specialties or allied health specialties. This reinforced my concept that pharmacists as clinical pharmacology practitioners operate more like specialists, and that is true because patients are referred to you.

If you look at oncologists, cardiologists, and gastroenterologists, patients are sent to them because they rise to the level of need on a particular specialty condition in which that specialist is engaged. They're either referred to or are collaborating with the primary caregiver. That is the ideal physical construct or infrastructure that works best for us as well. You can put a pharmacist in a primary care setting, but your value is that you are a specialist in that environment.

BLAZING A NEW TRAIL

I asked these questions not just for me but for other pharmacists. I am still doing what I did then, just in a more diverse way — and more of it. Overlapping that time period, I started to utilize the medical specialty practice model and was doing consultations for hospitals and medical practices across the Tampa Bay area. Even if the work I was doing was at a hospital, it may have been consultative support for the department of pharmacy in specialty services, pharmacokinetics, total parenteral nutrition (TPN), drug information support, or it could have been for medical practitioners at those hospitals.

I looked at medicine and how medical services were reimbursed. My theory at that point was: How do you look for the best practices within the medical service models to apply those as a clinical pharmacologist and specialist? I felt that if I adopted the best practices in medicine for everything, whether it was documentation, referrals, or reimbursement, that it would be for all parties to understand or comprehend. Then I was on to demonstrating the value of the services that I provided.

I wasn't reimbursed by insurance companies in the beginning, but there are a lot of medical services that even today aren't reimbursed by insurance companies. There is an entire realm of what is referred to as elective medicine, so I took that approach that it was a specialty and off of the standard scope of benefits, and I moved forward with that.

BREAKING OUT OF THE MOLD

One of the things our profession has suffered from the most is failing to recognize that it doesn't have to be part of the standard scope of benefits. There are many medical practices that function outside of standard insurance and are viable practices. Just because large corporations have wanted things to be tidy and exactly the way they wanted them, we fail to understand the realities of how things truly run in medical practices today.

I was modeling this practice and then converted to USF full-time faculty and began developing this as a non-USF practice model. I eventually went to the dean of the college of medicine at USF and presented the concept. I was managing a full book of clinical research business at the university, and we had many protocols where the research was there, but the university couldn't perform it. Maybe a particular specialty department didn't have enough faculty, or they were short on clinical research nursing support, or they had a competing protocol, among other reasons.

I made an agreement with the university that I would continue to recruit and do research with the university as a faculty appointment. In addition, I would build a private practice model with another practice locally — a non-university faculty practice. It has been a great recipe for many years for my business.

There is a high level of interest in how we are structured, how it's been sustainable, and what the growth opportunities are. I have had two people here recently who are interested in building upon what we have already done. Can it be done on a larger scale? Can we apply these principles to different types of pharmacy practice areas and types of services?

Despite the interest in this model, there are a couple reasons why I think this type of practice hasn't exploded in popularity yet. We have a service at a concierge level where, for example, yesterday we accompanied a high-intensity patient to her primary care practice to do that same function as a service for the patient. The goal was to look at refining her drug therapy. We don't do that often, but it is a high level of care—one where you're accompanying one of your patients to his or her medical office appointment for the purpose of a comprehensive med refinement with the primary care physician.

We have certain patients who have sought us out for concierge service, but it does not comprise the majority of our business. Most patients perceive our standard visit as a concierge type of role because we are an unbiased party that is trying to help them. The virtues of medication therapy management (MTM) include helping patients refine their therapy, reduce their spending, and get multiple practitioners on the same page when it comes to their treatment.

The backbone of our practice is medication management, patient counseling, and comprehensive review for medication management. There could also be a hospital-based consultation. Not that we have privileges and are running in and out of many hospitals, but the practitioner who is managing the case could be a primary care physician who is managing a patient in a hospital or emergency department and may still call for consultation.

You are playing an active role in support of the other practitioners and their patients. It is not simply a sit-down meeting with the patient in your office. There is diversity in the work, and we have some telehealth patients for whom we manage medications from a distance.

Clinical research has been part of the business since the early phase, and it is still there. In a light year, there are two or three primary clinical trials; they're typically phase II and phase III studies. The most active clinical research years have included fifteen to twenty research protocols.

I look at our scope of services and think that, like an investment portfolio, you want to be able to dial up or down the blend of services you are providing. You want your business to be viable and sustainable, so there are some years that clinical research opportunities are prevalent and play a more active role in the practice's activities.

Another part of the business is drug information support, and we divide that into two categories: clinical and forensic. With clinical, you are getting calls from a hospital to help develop prescribing pharmacy policies or medication-management policies. An example might include opiates or anesthesia medications. It could also be from another medical practice where they want to ensure that they are prescribing appropriate medications and are using the most up-to-date and cutting-edge therapies. It could be from a health plan looking for assistance with their benefit design or prior authorization service model.

The other side of drug information that has evolved over the years is on the forensic side. Medication questions constantly arise in the legal system. It could be law enforcement, public defenders, or medical examiners who have questions about a case where there is a pharmacology or toxicology component. It has also led to serving as an expert witness on cases, and that's an active part of what we do in the practice as well.

I look at those as being no different than clinical consults, but in this case your client is the court system, an attorney, or a law enforcement agency. The cases could be criminal cases, civil cases, or product liability and patent disputes.

The other piece of our business model is healthcare consulting, including with pharmacy and medical entities, health plans, and healthcare IT. We help to develop analytic tools, electronic health record modules that focus on prescribing, patient management, and medication-management issues.

Our early activities were a blend of patient consultation; inpatient clinical consultation; consulting for larger healthcare facilities, including hospitals and nursing homes; clinical service development; and clinical research. Over the years, we added drug information support in both the clinical and forensic roles—and then added health policy and health IT consulting. As we became more experienced and our reputation grew, we started providing services to government agencies. I have been serving as a medication safety expert with Medicare and the healthcare reform team for more than four years now. Those doors only opened based on my level of industry activity and engagement.

BREAKING DOWN BARRIERS

There are two key reasons why this type of business hasn't taken off, and money isn't the first issue. You could do this even if no insurance company would ever pay you. What will help is resolving the barriers to being included in the standard scope of benefits. What will help move the dial? The work I am doing with the Centers for Medicare and Medicaid Services (CMS) and on the Affordable Care Act (ACA), as well as on other national projects that focus on demonstrating the value in the return on investment (ROI) of what pharmacists bring to the patient care setting.

When we are included in the standard scope of benefits, pharmacists won't be compelled to say that we can only bill for product and, therefore, have to figure out a way to add enough margin to pay for the service we provide. That is the kiss of death for pharmacy because business pressures have driven the margin down. It used to be the margin that funded pharmacists in all the other things that we do in supportive care and don't bill for.

The margin is vaporizing, and so is the need to demonstrate ROI because a lot of medical payment models are shifting toward quality and value. You have to be able to show the reason that your component of the overall infrastructure of care is imperative not just clinically but also physically. We are at the point where we just have to keep moving that dial for pharmacists.

So, the first part is resolving the reimbursement issue and becoming part of the standard scope of benefit. The other issue is a bit more challenging. My challenge, and I think it's the other significant issue, is the fact that the people who would start businesses like this are other pharmacists. There is no higher-trained pharmacology expert in the entire healthcare field than a pharmacist, and with that we are the logical provider of these services to create the greatest value and impact. However, our curriculum and our experiential training has devolved to produce what the big box retail pharmacy market wants as employees, not as entrepreneurs.

When we can resolve the reimbursement issue, it will affect people who are in pharmacy practice settings who are decision-makers. But even when we resolve that issue, we still have a deficit of twenty to fifty years of an efficient curriculum. The pharmacy curriculum has made some amazing strides. We have evolved the clinical knowledgebase and the experiential training for direct patient care activities, but it has been at the expense of teaching how to develop the business acumen it takes to know how to build, manage, and sustain a medical service.

TURNING THE TIDE

When I give presentations on this topic, it leads to audience questions like: "How do you get our faculty doing this to where they are adding revenue to the bottom line, billing, and offsetting the cost of their existence?" and, "How do we show our students through experiential practice that this really does happen, and you can build a practice and provide services separate and apart from product?" (which we have done for years). Then, there is the question: "How do you build a practice model?"

It is one thing to say, "Go do a service and see a patient." The questions that remain are: Where is that money going to go, how much are you going to charge, do you need a contract with the facility, and what is the issue in terms of contracting with payers? All of these things in a medical practice are managed through the practice and its team; you have the practitioner, office manager, billing department, and others. In every medical school, they have their own practice models and academic practice models.

If I say to you that I have created nothing new, but I have borrowed the best of the best practice medicine and have applied it to pharmacy as a dynamic experiment, and it works and continues to work, that is my answer and a blueprint for success. Let's go do it.

The pharmacy deans are excited and say, "Wait a minute; let's tweak our practice setting and faculty to the point that they behave more functionally like a medical practitioner." Then they look back at their curriculum and say, "Where are the gaps and the holes in content?" In today's market of evolving payment models and evolving interdisciplinary, interprofessional practice structures, how do we infuse that and inject it back into the curriculum so we are rapidly and effectively training a functional future pharmacist?

The answer is that I can show you exactly how it is done in medicine, where they bring it in. We can be creative with an overlay. The Accreditation Council for Pharmacy Education (ACPE) that gauges school curriculum for accreditation is now open to even more creative models, so we could do overlays of classroom work with other types of work even before experiential training. It is not rocket science. It is helping them find the void and get recommendations about business and leadership skill development with live models in the process.

Does this type of education work better in an institutional setting or in a patient care setting outside of a hospital? I say it works in both. I could show you why; it just depends on where and how you want to structure yourself—the same questions a physician would ask. You could have emergency medicine, radiology, critical care, and anesthesia—all of these medical practices that live in a hospital but have an outpatient practice overlay. They touch and have a footprint in the inpatient facility setting all the time.

You could do this in a large interdisciplinary setting, too. We have a medical practice around the corner from us in Tampa that has more than 250 physicians integrated across multiple buildings. We have another orthopedic practice around the corner that includes more than 125 physicians. There are physicians who just do fingertips in that practice, surgeons who just do achilles, there are people who — you name it--if it's orthopedic, they do it. I can show you that in any of those structures; it depends on what you want to build. I could just as easily work with any physicians of one group versus the other.

PHARMA OF THE FUTURE

To achieve change, we first have to build pharmacy and academic practice models to reflect active and clinical practice entities. Pharmacists have to operate like other healthcare professionals — they can't continue to give the service away.

As I mentioned, the second part is to identify opportunities and evolve the curriculum to prepare future pharmacists with the business skills to develop, manage, and drive business in future healthcare markets.

The American Pharmacists Association (APhA) and the American Society of Health System Pharmacists (ASHP) are aggressively identifying where pharmacists are not at the table. This could be in the area of electronic health records, reimbursements, or the value statement of healthcare and attempting to represent the profession to articulate those points. Some of that is legislative; some of it is engagement with other disciplines and their associations. That work is in progress, and it's probably the most promising that I have seen in my career.

I'll give you an example of how advanced medical practice is present in this area. I have been able to serve on the American Medical Association's (AMA) Current Procedural Terminology (CPT) editorial panel. It's where billing codes are crafted, changed, and/or eliminated. It has been a tremendous experience to see the total interplay in medicine. Pharmacy has about twelve national organizations that vary in size, roles, and contributions; medicine has hundreds.

Medicine has done an amazing job of respecting the niche for our incremental roles of different organizations and coalescing that voice through the AMA. We have seen a maturing toward an AMA-like voice with APhA and some successes through collaboration in respecting each organization's contributions and roles. To me, that is a positive and healthy place to be. That's the highest level of collaboration in an organizational respect that I have seen throughout my career.

It will be easier for others to understand and accept us as pharmacists and as practitioners if we apply or emulate the medical model. My perspective is to adhere to and participate in what is changing and evolving for medicine. If I do that, then I am on the right road.

If we as a profession are reluctant to depart from what we did in the past, then it is going to be difficult to separate from a product-based revenue model, and it is going to be difficult to engage in new reimbursement lines in clinical services. Finally, it is going to be difficult for payers and other practitioners who may refer patients to us to accept this if their stereotype is still that prior legacy model.

I am not trying to be a primary care doctor; I am a medical specialist. My degree happens to be PharmD, but the medical specialty that is universally understood is clinical pharmacology or pharmacology, of which no one in the healthcare field has more training or clinical practice preparation than we do. Our problem is that when you get into an employment setting, many of those employers don't fully optimize or utilize the skill set that pharmacists have.

Many of us don't reposition ourselves to perform in this manner because we have a deficit in entrepreneurial preparation. I am confident the entire profession can do what I am doing, and nothing would please me more than to help lead that change.

ADVANCEMENT ADVICE

If you want to make a shift in the direction I mentioned, do some very deep soul searching about where your passion lies. Understand that from one terminal degree, the PharmD degree, your opportunities are limitless. For many people, that much freedom is overwhelming, but for others it is liberating.

Given that caveat, start off by deciding which direction you want to take, and look at the 10,000-foot view. Think through what you would like to endeavor in your career and how you would like to use your skills. This is like any other planning exercise: Write your thoughts down and come back and revisit them. Make it a document that you come back to and refine.

I can remember a class I took at Mercer with John Murphy, one of my professors, who one day said to put our books away, take out a pen and paper, "and think about what your perfect professional role is. Design it and describe what it is."

I just did this with a class that I taught this year. I told them to start with that and put it in a place where they could revisit it and keep coming back to refine it. The reason I bring it up is a couple of years into my practice, I came across one of my old college textbooks, opened it, and found that document in there.

The note basically spelled out exactly what I am doing now. It was important to have that sense of introspective goal-setting. Don't diminish it. Write it down and then keep refining your vision to the point that you are adding granularity. Identify what you need to get there and what could keep you from getting there; what are those hurdles?

I completed an MBA and overlapped the curriculum with my PharmD at Mercer, but I didn't get to finish it until a few years later. That experience was invaluable, but I would add that I didn't need it to achieve the same outcome. That said, maybe it added some degree of self-esteem, self-confidence, and resourcefulness to my personality.

If you grew up in a family business or in a family pharmacy, you will have gained all sorts of business training and education. If you pursue an MBA, try to do it as affordably as possible. Start with basic business principles, confirm that you have a passion to go that direction, and if you can, pursue a post-PharmD MBA in an executive program. I won't say it is imperative, but I will say it is informative.

Also, identify mentors who can give you advice along the way and help you with networking; you cannot put a price on that. Identify people who you feel are doing what you are interested in and have demonstrated success in their careers. Be transparent with them about your goals, and that relationship may turn out to be the equivalent of an MBA.

I look at John Murphy, Earl Ward, Marty Jobe, Richard Jackson, and others in the industry, and realize what I saw in them—which is what I have just shared with you. These are people who at the time were providing and instilling that into the curriculum and doing it in a live, functional fashion along with many other mentors, both clinical- and business-focused. However, I don't think the current curriculum has entrepreneurial, fiscally sound, clinical practitioners who are delivering services, billing, and coexisting in a medical practice-like manner.

One of the things that an MBA program teaches you, no matter which school you go to, is the importance of being able to analyze and deconstruct a process and a problem. When you can see where the flaws are and realize that you can't solve the problem alone, you are going to need to seek out someone with the skill or proficiency to help you achieve that goal. MBA programs teach you how to be resourceful and do that. Being resourceful is a capstone description of my career; I have many people to whom I owe a tremendous debt of gratitude and appreciation for how they have affected what I've been able to accomplish.

CHAPTER FOUR

John Gregory

**Co-Founder of General Injectable and Vaccines (GIV);
King Pharmaceuticals; Monarch Pharmaceuticals;
Founder of NFI Consumer Products
University of Maryland School of Pharmacy**

John Gregory always wanted to help people, so being a community pharmacist made sense to him. Throughout his career, he has turned his ideas into successful business ventures, always with his eye on helping his employees, patients, customers, and, of course, his shareholders. Everyone seems to gain in a John Gregory venture.

After pharmacy school, Gregory worked in a retail setting, but he had a desire to own a pharmacy in an underserved area. He consulted government databases and found several counties in the United States that didn't have a single pharmacist in them. He pursued establishing pharmacies in those counties, targeting one in southwest Virginia.

After working for several years, Gregory and an attorney friend, Randall Kirk, saw a possible solution to a business need. Rural physicians didn't need boxes of vaccines — they just needed one or two individual vaccines per week. Gregory and his partners established

General Injectable and Vaccines (GIV) to deliver vaccines and other injectables in small quantities to doctors' offices — first locally, then regionally, and then nationwide. They established an overnight delivery service, all the while maintaining the cold chain during shipment, one that became a leader in the vaccine-distribution industry.

After selling his shares in GIV, he and his brothers founded King Pharmaceuticals, one of the first specialty pharmaceutical companies in the United States. Although he acquired a manufacturing facility and some contract manufacturing business, his acquisitions and deal making were key in driving the company's growth. King's strength was taking existing good, undervalued products and making them into great products. He repeated this formula over the years, and in 2010, King Pharmaceuticals was sold to Pfizer for $4 billion. Gregory exited the company by 2002, but you get the idea: He built a company with tremendous market value.

In typical entrepreneurial fashion, Gregory decided to try his hand in the consumer market and acquired NFI Consumer Products. He has seen one of its key products, Blu-Emu, take off with the added marketing muscle he put behind it.

Gregory's story is interesting in that his main goal in life has always been pretty simple — helping others. He believes you need a strong business model and a strong focus on rewarding your employees, and the rest will take care of itself. What follows is his recipe for success.

———————

I grew up in Rockville, Md., a suburb of Washington, D.C. My father worked for the federal government as an accountant for the General Accountability Office. We had a middle-class lifestyle. I was part of the first graduating class from Rockville High School and played on the baseball and basketball teams.

Growing up, I played a lot of sports while trying to do well in school; I was probably a B student. My parents insisted that we study and do well—their goal was to make sure all of their kids had the opportunity to get a college education. At one time, my parents were paying for four kids to go to college at the same time, and I don't know how they did it. They borrowed a lot of money and were able to send all of their kids who were interested in going to college.

I grew up with four brothers and one sister, so there were six of us in all. I was a year younger than Jim, one year older than Joe, and two years older than Jeff. We grew up not only as brothers but as friends, and we did a lot together. Whether it was football, basketball, or baseball, when we played, it was the brothers Gregory against everybody else. We grew up in a competitive family environment, and that was one of the things that helped my brothers and me succeed in the business world.

My brother, Jeff, is a pharmacist and an attorney. Joe got a degree in business administration, Jim got a master's in public administration. Henry got a doctor of medicine degree, and I got a pharmacy degree. We were raised with a lot of discipline and attention to doing well. We grew up with traditional values that helped shape our thinking. This also helped us when we got into business and wanted advancement. Our upbringing spurred me on.

In high school, I was a pretty good baseball player and had some scouts looking at me. I wanted to play baseball in college and pursue a physical education teaching degree. My father didn't like that idea, and he said, "Well, I would like you to be a pharmacist." I had no idea what that was. At first, I thought he said "farmer," and I said, "You want me to be a farmer?" He said, "Not a farmer—a pharmacist, like the guy behind the counter over there at People's Drugstore."

At that time, the culture was such that you did what your parents wanted you to do—especially what your father wanted you to do—so I went to pharmacy school.

As I mentioned, I was a B student, and I was the last one to be accepted into the University of Maryland School of Pharmacy the year I enrolled. Someone dropped out the week before the start of school, they sent me a letter, and I got in. I have attended and spoken at the University of Maryland School of Pharmacy graduation ceremonies several times, and I've mentioned this fact. The university gave me an honorary doctorate of public service one year when I did the commencement speech for all the medical schools—pharmacy school and nursing school included.

FINDING A MENTOR

I worked with David Knapp, PharmD, who at that time was a professor of pharmacy administration. He later became the dean of the pharmacy school and was there for about thirty years. He gave me a job doing drug utilization review and had me gathering data. The thing about it that really affected me was the fact that I was a data collector and he was paying me about $6 an hour. This really helped because I used that as my spending money when I was in the school of pharmacy.

I have been published twice in my life, both times when I was in the school of pharmacy. Each time, Dr. Knapp added my name as a co-author, and the articles were published in the *Journal of the American Pharmacists Association* (JAPhA). Drug utilization review was a big deal at the time, and he was considered a thought leader. It was a big deal to me, too. I have often mentioned this point to the dean and the faculty: Just because someone is the last one to get into the school of pharmacy, it doesn't mean he or she won't have a significant effect on the pharmacy school someday.

As my career progressed, it was a privilege to be one of the largest donors they have had at the school. I was blessed with all the resources that I got from starting King Pharmaceuticals. The seeds of success were planted by Dr. Knapp when he included me as an author on those articles.

ACCOUNTING MAKES A DIFFERENCE

I was back at the school of pharmacy one year, and they assembled some business leaders and the students asked questions. A student asked me, "What was the most important class when you were in the school of pharmacy?" I will never forget that the first year I participated; I said accounting was the most valuable class. The accounting teacher stood up and everyone clapped for him. I don't think they teach accounting anymore in pharmacy school, and for me that is one of the shortcomings in the curriculum.

I was constantly telling the school to focus on accounting and business courses. Even if you don't own a pharmacy, it is important to understand a profit and loss statement, a balance sheet, and how to manage accounts receivable.

In your retail career, you may be a district or regional manager at Walgreen's, CVS, or Walmart. Your bosses will expect that you can put together a budget. If you can't read a balance sheet, understand cash flow, or communicate about accounts receivable, you are at a disadvantage.

The thing about the accounting course I took in pharmacy school was that it taught me some of those basic skills. These became very important to me, especially in the early days of running my first startup. When I needed a bank loan for GIV, they required a business plan, which required me to produce a budget, balance sheet, and cash flow statements.

When you are establishing a business, you don't have enough money to hire a fancy accounting firm or some type of business planner. You have to figure it out yourself—at least you had to back then. The fact that I had the background in accounting was crucial; otherwise, I wouldn't have known the difference between a debit and a credit.

WORLD OF WORK

The first job I had was as a retail pharmacist working for Michael Skiba, who was the owner of Connecticut and Knowles Pharmacy. It was on the corner of Connecticut Avenue and Knowles, an area in Kensington, Maryland., a suburb right outside of Washington, D.C. I had been talking to individual pharmacies to see if they had an opening close to my home, and this pharmacy was about ten minutes from where I lived in Rockville, Maryland.

I went to work for him the day I got out of pharmacy school. I will never forget it: I went to work one day, and the next day Skiba and his wife decided to go to the beach on vacation. He was going to be gone for two weeks—talk about being thrown into the fire. I was now a full-time pharmacist. As the boss of the store, and especially at that independent pharmacy, everything ran through the pharmacist. You made all employee decisions, closed the store, filled all the prescriptions, gave all the advice, and — on the second day — I was the pharmacist in charge. What a baptism by fire, but I made it until he got back. I worked there for about three years until I moved down to Bland County, Virginia. I had the fever of wanting to own my own retail pharmacy.

When I started to research where to start my business, I wanted to find a place where they really needed a pharmacy, because I felt that was my best opportunity for success. Before my wife and I got married, we would go around on dates to different restaurants in Washington, D.C., and I always looked for the best place to put a pharmacy. I wanted to put it where there was a need. I looked in some government publications to see where there were shortages of pharmacists, and there were several counties in the United States where they didn't have a pharmacist. One of the counties was Bland County, Virginia. I knew a little bit about Bland County because my grandmother lived on a farm in Lee County, Virginia., all the way in the corner of southwest Virginia. We used to go down there all the time on vacations when I was growing up.

I went down there to check it out, and, sure enough, there was not a single pharmacist in Bland County. I didn't have the capital or cash to start a pharmacy, but the government had a program where they would subsidize your salary and get you started if you worked in an underserved area. After a few years, you could buy the government out for cost and take over the store, so that's what I did. I was now the owner, and I ran Bland County Pharmacy for about seven or eight years.

As I mentioned, I was the only pharmacist in the whole county. It was a real pioneer pharmacy type of job. I loved it because I went out and helped give injections – and that's when pharmacists didn't give shots. I went out and took patients' blood pressure, made house calls, and helped the only dentist in the county pull teeth. There was one doctor, one pharmacist, and one dentist for 5,000 people in the entire county, so everybody depended on you to do a little bit of everything. You became a "jack of all trades" healthcare provider.

When I say I gave injections, I mean all types. We had several terminal cancer patients in Bland County, and I gave them their shot of Demerol at home. When you do those types of things, it is not just about providing a medical service; it is about building a relationship with the person. You no longer had to worry about competition when you had a relationship and when people looked at you as a friend.

We built a really nice pharmacy there, and we were making close to $100,000 a year in prescriptions and were providing a tremendous service to the area. I used the money we earned from the pharmacy to start GIV.

I remember thinking that there weren't very many companies providing injectables and vaccines to doctor's offices. Darby and Schein were the big providers of injectable products to physician offices. They had big catalogues, but they weren't providing many vaccines. Most of the vaccines had to be ordered directly from the manufacturer in quantities that many physicians' offices didn't need. They wouldn't sell individual shots – you had to either buy a box of twelve or twenty-four.

This was about thirty years ago, and I felt that vaccines were starting to come of age. If we could buy some in bulk and break them into individual vials, we could sell the vaccines to doctors' offices by providing them in "onesies and twosies" instead of a box of twelve or twenty-four.

At that time, the hepatitis B vaccine was a big deal, and it was pretty expensive. So, I started off selling small quantities in Virginia, and then it became so popular that I decided to go national. I discussed the idea with Randall Kirk, the only attorney in Bland County at that time, and he liked it. We got together and started this company called General Injectables and Vaccines (GIV).

We used a typical distribution model where you buy products in bulk, break them down, and sell them in individual quantities. By doing that, you are able to earn enough margin. Initially, the margins were 40 percent, and toward the end of my time at GIV, they got down to about 30 percent, but there was enough margin for us to create the business.

In the ten years I was there, we grew GIV from startup to about $100 million in revenue. Initially, our first GIV orders were typed on a typewriter. Within about six months, business computers started to become available. We hired some technology people who built us proprietary and custom software on our computers. Today, it's not a big deal to do something like that, but at the time we had some state-of-the-art call center software. When a person called in, his or her account popped up and it showed the most recent orders, but it also showed the specials that made the most sense for that physician specialty.

Giving Great Customer Service

We hired ladies from the community to handle the phone orders, and they were so pleasant. They loved working at GIV, and it came across over the phone. I don't know how many times I would have doctors' staff send letters saying, "We love your ladies; they have a beautiful Southern drawl, and we just love talking to them."

By the time I left GIV, we had about 50,000 doctor office accounts on the books that were ordering products from us. We were the first national supplier to physicians' offices to offer a toll-free number. With Darby or Schein, they were the market leaders, but you had to mail in your order. Or, if you called, you had to call their East Coast area code. It was those types of things that allowed us to stay ahead of the competition. Our sales were driven by our first-line employees—our customer service reps—and how pleasant they were.

Another point of differentiation was that instead of using Styrofoam chips to pack orders, we used popcorn, mainly because popcorn is biodegradable. This was way before the push for environmental marketing that is ubiquitous today. Doctors loved the fact that we packed with popcorn instead of Styrofoam. Little things like that made an impression on our clients.

We also collected personal data about those who worked in the doctor's office, including things like physicians' birthdates. We had a 90 percent participation rate in this program. We would send out a birthday card and a birthday cake by FedEx to the doctor the day before his or her birthday so it would arrive on the birthday. At one time, we had a whole operation where my stepfather did nothing but bake birthday cakes all day long, and we were shipping 200 to 300 birthday cakes a day. We would get a ton of calls to tell us how much the doctors appreciated this gesture and just how unique it was. It created a memory that they didn't forget, and the office staff remembered us and liked our company.

Not only did we make inroads with our clients, but we endeared ourselves to FedEx and the phone company. We were in an isolated location that was challenging to access, and it didn't have good service when it came to FedEx or phone lines. We got the phone company to string a direct line for us due to the call center's high volume. We became FedEx's No. 1 account in that whole southwest region, including Morgantown, Charlotte, and Knoxville. They had vehicle after vehicle at our dock, and we developed such a great relationship with them that we got good rates on next-day and second-day air, and they would do almost anything for GIV.

STARTUP No. 2

After the success of GIV, I co-founded King Pharmaceuticals. If I knew exactly how challenging it was going to be, I may not have started it. One of the things that all entrepreneurs need to realize is that you have to be flexible. You have to be able to adjust to what you are seeing and what you are up against. The idea was that we would backward integrate and make some of our own injectables because we were doing such a huge volume of generic injectables at GIV. About that time, Randall Kirk and I had a bit of a falling out, and he decided to stay with GIV. My brothers and I left to start King Pharmaceuticals.

We acquired a 500,000-square-foot manufacturing facility from RSR Inc., and the owners were former employers of SmithKline Beecham. This facility was the former North American headquarters of Beecham Pharmaceuticals. Many pharmacists dream of going into manufacturing, so this was like we died and went to heaven. Part of pharmacy school is about pharmaceutical compounding and manufacturing, so I was so excited.

However, there were some things I passed over in the process of founding this new company, including the reality of being a pharmaceutical manufacturer. We paid about $1 million and RSR Inc. gave us a $9 million note, so it cost us $10 million to buy the facility and their business. As part of the deal, we maintained the contract manufacturing business with SmithKline Beecham, which shortly thereafter became GlaxoSmithKline. It was doing between $10 and $15 million in revenue and making about $1 million.

We soon found out that pharmaceutical manufacturing is hard — very hard. There are a lot of regulations around it — far more than in the distribution business. Manufacturing requires a lot of smart people, and their salaries are high. You have to constantly be recruiting people with advanced degrees from around the country to work with you. I quickly realized that the pharmaceutical manufacturing contract business was going to be hard, so we had to supplement it with something else because the gross margins were low.

Step one was to acquire some name-brand products, and the first one we bought was Tussend Cough Syrup. I saw that Dow Chemical owned Tussend Cough Syrup, and they discontinued it. I called them up and I asked them if we could buy the brand name and trademark. They sold me the trademark for $50,000. We formulated it there at the factory and relaunched the Tussend product. We got it out the door and sold $1 million in the first year. Because it had a 90 percent margin, I liked what I saw.

We were making some products for GlaxoSmithKline, and I realized that they weren't selling a lot of Nucofed, a cough syrup that had 20 mg of codeine per dose versus the standard 10 mg per dose. It was a high-dose codeine cough syrup with 30 mg of pseudoephedrine and was a Schedule V product. It included the liquid and a capsule dosage form, and they were selling about $1 million annually. They sold it to us for $2 million. We had a product that was already doing $1 million, and we grew that a little bit. All of a sudden, I saw that there was a real business model in buying small products and trying to improve sales by promoting them to doctors.

We got in touch with GlaxoSmithKline, and they said they would sell us their cortisporin product line, which had gone generic. This included cortisporin ophthalmic suspension, cortisporin otic, and cortisporin ointment and cream. It was doing $15 million in revenue, and they were willing to sell the line for $21 million.

Part of this business model was understanding how to reinvigorate a brand. Would our priorities be in marketing or through line extensions? Was there a reason to perform a new clinical study? Was this a product that was challenging enough to formulate and manufacture? Could this be affected by drug shortage where the generic was not on the market for a period of time? There were several parameters we looked at to determine whether the target products were going to be good candidates for acquisition and for increasing our revenue. If you have a 90 percent margin and an increase in revenue, you can make up your acquisition cost pretty quickly.

We did everything right and then had a little regulatory luck. Steris Labs in Phoenix was the company that provided so many of our injectables at GIV, both aqueous and suspension products. They also made generic cortisporin products, both ophthalmic and otic. The FDA office in Phoenix was giving them a hard time about their facility, stating they didn't build it in compliance with the Current Good Manufacturing Process (cGMP). We knew about these issues brewing with Steris when we were at GIV.

We bought the cortisporin product line, and it was doing $15 million in revenue—$10 million of that was the cortisporin ophthalmic suspension. Within four months of our acquisition, the FDA made Steris take its generic cortisporin ophthalmic off the market, so our brand of cortisporin ophthalmic suspension went from a $10 million brand name to a $27 million brand name the first year we owned it. We paid $21 million for the product line, and the first year we owned it, we made $25 million in gross margin. In the next five years, that product line made $30 million in gross for us each year.

We funded the acquisition by convincing the local coal company to invest. Bristol, Tennessee was coal country, and United Company was king back then. There were several coal barons, and one of them was United Company's CEO, Jim McGlothlin. We convinced him to invest in King Pharmaceuticals for $15 million, and he would get a third of the company. He has written a couple of biographies, and in them he mentions that the best investment he ever made was in King Pharmaceuticals. His $15 million investment eventually netted him $300 million.

We used the money he invested with us to buy the cortisporin product and transfer the manufacturing to our plant. All of a sudden, we were doing $50 million a year with a net income of $15 million. We had established an acquisition business model called Specialty Pharma. We weren't the first specialty pharma company—Dura Pharmaceuticals probably was—but we were one of the first.

Dura was one of the first companies to acquire products from a pharmaceutical company, build up the business, and then go public. They showed us that there was value in this business model, and that helped us—especially when they went public and had a $1billion market capitalization. They proved that the model was desirable to Wall Street and bankers, so when we went public, it was easier for us.

After the success of cortisporin, we kept upping the ante. We made larger and larger acquisitions, whether it was products, companies, or mergers. Each of my brothers had a different role: Joe was the sales guy, and he ran Monarch Pharmaceuticals and promoted all of our products; Jeff was the regulatory and operations guy, and he ran Parkedale, the sterile facility in Rochester, Michigan. Jim ran the King operation, and he had a background in public administration. Henry was the medical officer for the whole facility. Jeff and I did the deals, and we probably did a couple of dozen deals in the ten years that I was at King Pharmaceuticals.

In another acquisition, Altace® proved to be a game-changer for us because it was doing about $90 million in sales, and they wanted $360 million for it. That would not be an abnormal multiple today, but it was back then. The usual multiple at that time would have been 1.5 to 2x sales. Those lower multiples were great for guys like me; you could get a payback in two to three years on these products because they had margins of 90 percent. Over time, those multiples quickly changed because people were willing to pay more as more companies got into the specialty pharma business model.

We went big on Altace®. One of the reasons was we thought we understood this market. Everyone was going to the angiotensin II inhibitors, and although this was an angiotensin inhibitor—the first generation—we saw two interesting things with Altace®. One, we still had a ton of patent life; there were about ten years left on the patent. Two, we knew about the HOPE Study, the goal of which was to show that the drug could decrease mortality in heart disease. If that did not get validated, we still had a good product with ten years of patent life. If it was shown to decrease heart disease mortality, we would have a blockbuster.

Within six months of acquiring the product, the front page of *USA Today* read, "Altace: the new wonder drug that decreases heart mortality." During the next couple of years, the product went from $90 million to $500 million. It enabled us to do other things, like a co-marketing agreement with a Big Pharma company like Wyeth. The co-marketing wasn't the biggest part; we now had a platform and relationship to do many more deals with Wyeth. Because we did that deal with Altace®, they sold us other products, including Bicillin and Wycillin, neither of which had generic competition. We were the sole source on Bicillin and Wycillin products, and that product line grew to $50 million annually at 95 percent margins. By the time I left in 2001, we were approaching $1 billion in revenue, about $300 million in income, and had a market capitalization of close to $10 billion.

Having a pharmacy background helped me with all of the product acquisitions. You use your pharmacy background to determine the possibility of doing line extensions on these products: Is it difficult to copy and make into a generic from a chemical point of view; what are the formulation challenges; and what is the possibility of doing another clinical trial that could give you an indication of some new type of disease prevention?

We looked at the HOPE study from every angle and felt that there was a good possibility for success. The study showed a decrease in mortality, but it also showed something else that didn't get as much play: Altace® showed stoppage of renal degradation due to diabetes whenever you started taking it. Now, it didn't cure any damage that had been done, but we got a secondary indication that it stopped any further degradation of your kidneys if you had diabetes. I thought that was as big as the decrease in mortality indication. We tried to play that up to get it listed as a No. 1 indication, but the FDA wouldn't let us do it.

We were surprised that Hoechst Marion Roussel (HMR) was willing to sell Altace® to us before they found out the results of the HOPE Study. They continued to show interest in selling, so we pushed them to sell it before the results were out.

About a year after we did that deal, the CEO of HMR was on a conference call with Wall Street analysts, and one pharma analyst tore him up because he sold Altace® to us. He asked, Why did he do that, and why didn't he know about the HOPE Study, because the HOPE Study had been going on for several years. It's not like they didn't know about it, and the CEO got an earful from that analyst.

Even if the HOPE study didn't work out in our favor, we had a good ten years to market it and try to improve it. We felt comfortable that we could get it up from $90 million to $150 million, no matter what. We didn't think we would be able to get it to $500 million like it got up to with the positive HOPE Study. We felt that at $150 million, it was going to be a very successful drug for us.

KING'S EXIT

King Pharmaceuticals sold for $4 billion to Pfizer in 2010, but I was out of the company by 2002. I had $1 billion in stock, and I wanted to give a lot to charities and do other things. The company itself was a really good one, and when King sold to Pfizer, it was doing $1 billion in annual revenue. Surprisingly, one of the biggest things Pfizer got from buying King was the Alpharma animal health business. When they combined that with their own Pfizer animal health division and then sold off the entire animal health business to Zoetis, they got back double what they spent on the King acquisition. Overall, Pfizer did very well on the King acquisition.

However, Pfizer wanted to get rid of the Bristol, Tennessee pharmaceutical plant. They were going to close it down, and that crushed our family because we had built the facility to something that was important in the community and provided a lot of jobs. I hated the idea that it was going to go away, so we structured a deal to buy the factory. Pfizer had about $100 million of capital investments in plant improvements. We offered to buy it back from Pfizer for $10 million. The interesting part of this story is that we originally paid $10 million for the factory when King acquired it twenty years earlier.

We bought the facility and moved our current pharmaceutical business into it. I had a small, 30,000-square-foot contract manufacturing facility in Baltimore called UPM, and we moved that back to Bristol into the new facility we just acquired from Pfizer. We continued to do contract manufacturing for Pfizer, transferred some contract manufacturing that we were doing in Baltimore to the new facility, and we were thinking of developing some generics and specialty pharma products.

Instead, I started looking at over-the-counter (OTC) brand products and thought it was a good model for the future. I believe we are going to see more products going OTC to reduce healthcare costs, and I wanted to be where the future market is headed. I have seen more interest in OTC brands than ever before. NFI is doing very well, and I'm excited about the potential.

Acquiring Blu-Emu

In my continual product research, I noticed that Blu-Emu topical oil got great reviews on Amazon and was getting an average of 4.5 stars. I read all the reviews from customers, and 80 percent of them loved it. Of course, some said it didn't do anything for them and it must be mayonnaise, but many gave testimonials about how they used to use narcotics for their pain, but now they use Blu-Emu. It wasn't like there were fifty reviews; it was more like 1,000 positive reviews, and it seemed to have a tremendous following. They had not really done much advertising, and I felt that if we put some advertising and marketing behind it, we could really get this product going.

To date, we have grown from $8 million in sales per year to $30 million per year, and not with price increases — they were pure volume increases. In our first year, sales went up to $15 million, in year two it was up to $20 million, and we anticipate more than $30 million in year three.

We've learned a whole lot about how to do an OTC brand and business model in the process, including how to work with consumer advertising and how to do line extensions. We've already done three line extensions on the Blue-Emu product line, and much of it was due to my pharmacy background and understanding that segment. We learned what we could and couldn't do. As a result, the OTC business model is something we feel really good about.

We recently acquired the e.p.t. Early Pregnancy Test Kit from Prestige, and we have plans to reinvigorate it and do line extensions as well. This is a product that has not been advertised for the last five years, and it was the original pregnancy test kit. I am excited about this new business model because it reminds me a little bit of the beginning of the specialty pharma business model at King.

That said, the No. 1 challenge is getting products on the store shelves. CVS, Walgreen's, and Walmart are the big three, you have to have a product that is doing enough business and is growing for them to want to carry it. If you can't get it on the store shelves, it is hard to sustain a consumer model. The e.p.t. has an advantage because the name is widely recognized and already has wide distribution.

Celebrity endorsements can help with name recognition, which can translate into a boost in sales. The previous owners of NFI had just signed Johnny Bench when we bought the product, and we ended up doing all the commercials with him, and they were shot by our marketing group. We have had a great relationship with Bench, and he loves the product. We also used the golfer Jack Nicklaus on the Altace commercials. We found out he used Altace and had benefited from it, so we used him for several years, and it was a successful ad. In our experience, celebrity endorsements worked.

BUILDING A BOUNTIFUL BUSINESS

When I was age thirty-three, and prior to starting GIV, I was an alcoholic and struggling with my life. My pastor helped me through many personal issues, and I became a Christian. I started reading a lot of books, but one caught my attention: *Money Matters* by Larry Burkett. It said that when most people have a strategy as an entrepreneur, or when they go into business they think of themselves first, then the bank debt, then their customers, and then their employees. It went on to say that as a Christian business owner, you should flip that order and take care of your employees first, then your customers, then your bank debt, and yourself last. If you do that, it will work very well for you. If it doesn't make you a fortune, at least it will be pleasing to God.

I tried my best to implement that strategy by doing the maximum we could for our employees. At GIV, my goal was to become the highest-paying company in Bland County. It didn't matter that many employees only had a 10th-grade education; we wanted to pay them the highest amount we could and have the best and most unique benefits.

We paid for employees' daycare in a special program we put together. We allowed them to use their relatives to babysit. They had to get certified, and that allowed them to watch up to six kids at a time. Many of the customer service representatives had their mothers get certified, and then GIV would pay them to watch their own grandchildren every day. All the employees loved our daycare program, and they were so appreciative. It made them happier at work, which came across whenever they were on the phone with doctors' offices.

Another benefit we offered at GIV was a chaplain, and we also offered it at King. The chaplain would visit every worker's extended family if a relative was in the hospital. He or she was there to consult with any employee who was going through adversity and stressful times. This is an area of the country where community and church are very important, and it was considered to be a special benefit.

When entrepreneurs start businesses, the immediate thought is not that you will have hundreds of employees; you are just trying to grow a business. But if you take care of your employees, you are going to have a better business. I found this to be true in all the different businesses that I have had the honor and privilege to own.

Maybe that is the key point—remember how important your employees are to your business and how important it is for the business to do well so that your employees can do well and prosper. After King went public, we gave stock options to everybody in the company—all 300 employees, including the maintenance workers. This was unheard of at the time. The only person who didn't get stock options was me; I didn't take any the whole time I was CEO of King.

One of my most cherished memories was when one of our maintenance employees paid a visit to my office. I always had an open-door policy, and Chris came in to tell me how much he appreciated getting the stock options. King stock had gone through the roof the first couple of years, and the stock options became worth a lot of money. He told me those stock options allowed him to buy a house. Those types of things really make you feel like you are doing something right. I encourage everybody to remember how important your employees are when you start your business, whether it's the CFO or the maintenance staff.

CHAPTER FIVE

Curt Mueller

Founder of Mueller Sports Medicine
University of Wisconsin School of Pharmacy

Curt Mueller combined his pharmacy degree, merchandising acumen, and his experience as a University of Wisconsin power forward with some true grit to establish Mueller Sports Medicine, a company focused on outfitting all athletes with the most advanced sports medicine products available. His business popularized the term "sports medicine," and it became the premier supplier in the area he serves.

In the 1950s, Mueller was a power forward for the University of Wisconsin basketball team. While earning his pharmacy degree, he took a communications class where he was asked to give a persuasive speech. He decided to present to the class about how to sell products inside a pharmacy, and while doing so, he realized he loved discussing merchandising and retailing. As you will read, this is a man who liked the front of the store—the retail side—as much as he liked the back of the store—the prescription side.

After graduation, he served in the Medical Services Corps in Texas, worked at a Walgreen's store in Chicago where he picked up some valuable merchandising and shelf-space expertise, and then he gravitated back to his hometown of Prairie du Sac, Wisconsin, where he worked with his pharmacist father.

Mueller started distributing athletic products to local high schools, including liniments, balms, and bandages. When one supplier increased his balm and liniment pricing, Mueller decided to compound his own product and realized his pharmacy school compounding classes had taught him some valuable skills. He was making compounded product at 10 percent of what his distributors were charging him, and then he expanded it to other products in the typical athletic supply catalogue—and a business was born.

His first twenty years in business were about growth, and Mueller Sports Medicine offered innovative products like Quench Gum for salivation; various branded antiseptic, analgesic, and antibiotic disinfectant sprays; and ointments, balms, and even skin tougheners. During the next twenty years, he expanded the business into wound care products; a complete line of patented sports braces; high-tech ACL triaxial hinged braces; pre-wraps, including team-colored wraps; and the popular Mueller No-Glare® eye black strips that are worn under the eyes of so many football players. Today, Mueller Sports Medicine is a worldwide company with sales in more than seventy-five countries and a product line that features continual innovation. One of the company's recent product introductions is called Mueller Green, an environmentally friendly line of braces and supports that are made of recycled plastic.

Whether you're a world-class athlete or a weekend warrior, we owe Curt Mueller and Mueller Sports Medicine for bringing these products to the front of the store and making them a retail item in drugstores and other retail outlets today.

I sat down with Mueller at his sprawling global headquarters in Prairie du Sac, Wisconsin, about twenty-five miles away from his alma mater, the University of Wisconsin, where he played basketball more than fifty years ago. We discussed how he built his thriving company, but, more importantly, I heard some of his colorful stories in the way that only he can tell them.

I started my working life in my dad's pharmacy. He would let me work the soda fountain and take care of the newspapers, but I had nothing to do with the pharmacy except just being there. I wanted to be a basketball coach, but my dad talked me into going to pharmacy school because he went to pharmacy school in Minnesota.

When I got out of school, I ended up going into the Medical Services Corps in Texas. When I came back, I found out I could make more money in Illinois rather than working for Rennebohm Drug Stores in Wisconsin, so I went to Walgreen's in Chicago. If I started with Rennebohm's, I would have made $4,800 in one year, but at Walgreen's I made double that because I could work overtime, and I was always willing to give them fifteen to twenty more hours per week because I was interested in making money.

Walgreen's gave me a chance to run the health and beauty aids retail area, and that's where I learned a lot about inventory control and retail sales. I may have been focused on toothpaste at this store, but those lessons would serve me well when I was figuring out the best shelf-space strategies for Mueller products years later.

Eventually, I moved back to Wisconsin because my dad wasn't feeling well. I told him, "I will work with you, but not for you," so he made me a partner, and I eventually paid him back. When I got

Curt Mueller

there, we were struggling with how we were going to have two families making a lousy $20,000 at his downtown drug store.

I needed a strategy to boost our revenue. First, I went to my former high-school classmates who were running their dads' farms, and I ended up selling them veterinarian-type products, including injectable antibiotics and iron supplements for cattle. I called on these farmers frequently, and every time I stepped out of my car, a German Shepherd would come up and growl at me. I wasn't exactly fond of that so, I ended up going to strategy No. 2, which was trying to do some new things at the front end of the store.

There was a place in Madison right on State Street called Lou's Tobacco Store, and they had Latakia, which is a strong tobacco, and I bought my tobacco from Lou. I ran some ads in the local paper that asked, "Have you seen Lou?" I had all my buddies smoking this heavy-duty tobacco with pipes, and that worked out well.

As a third strategy, I thought, "Why don't I go over and sell some products to the local high school?" The athletic director and football coach was buying a product from Badger Sporting Goods in Madison, and I told him I couldn't understand why he was buying medical supplies from a sporting goods store — I just didn't get it.

I contacted the company that was supplying Badger Sporting Goods and wrote them a letter asking if they would sell those products to my drug store. They sent me a letter saying they would sell them to the drug store at 35 percent, less 2 percent cash, which is 37 percent. I had one catalogue and one school price list, and I called on three schools and sold them liniments and other related products directly against Badger Sporting Goods. That was really the start of my business.

I said to myself, "This is pretty easy." I was lucky because the people in the sporting goods business never went out and promoted the products I was selling; the products were in their catalogues, but they were not marketed. They were interested in selling clothing, helmets, shoulder pads, shoes, and socks, etc., but not the medical products.

MARKETING MEDICAL PRODUCTS

Most of the people in the sporting goods business feared having to answer questions about medical products. The balm product they were offering didn't make any sense to me. I worked out of the basement of the drug store in my laboratory to make analgesic balm. I will never forget that after making some batches and looking at the cost, I realized that I could make it for 10 percent of what Badger was charging me. My father warned me that this type of product would take some marketing, but my response was, "That is what we do here; we are marketing people." I would get up at 4:00 a.m., drive north in my Volkswagen, and call on schools and make my deliveries.

The liniment we offered was a combination of menthol and salicylic acid in a vehicle. We ended up selling a lot of product and were doing pretty well. I was all by myself, and I would go out and sell some product, come back, manufacture it, and then ship it out. The invoices were handwritten because we didn't even have a typewriter.

Later, I was on a vacation in the Bahamas with my wife, and when we got back to Florida, we had a long drive back to Wisconsin. I started thinking about all of the schools that were out there and of all the potential, but I realized I couldn't get to all of them in person. When I got home, I looked up the National Sporting Goods

Association, and I offered their members some deep discounts on our products versus what the competition was charging.

I got out of the direct-selling business and sold only through sporting goods stores, which eventually turned into medical houses. To this day, most of the product in American high schools is sourced from medical houses like Schein — the really big distributors.

A Fateful Meeting

In 1969, I attended a very important meeting. I was part of our Lion's Club, and we were running a raffle. I usually got the drug reps to buy $5 raffle tickets when they stopped by the store. I never saw the rep from Marion Laboratories, so I sent a letter directly to the owner of the company, Ewing Kauffman. He owned the Kansas City Royals baseball team and had founded a very successful pharmaceutical company. In the letter, I asked him if he wanted to buy a raffle ticket. He sent me $10, told me he could afford $10, and said, "If you are ever in Kansas City, look me up."

It didn't take me long to go there. One of the big sporting goods store owners in Kansas City picked me up at the airport, took me over to the Holiday Inn, and as soon as I opened up the hotel room door, the phone was ringing. I picked it up and confirmed that I would be at the Royals game that night to watch the team play and meet Mr. Kauffman.

I went to the stadium, and there were limousines everywhere. I went to the top floor of the Kansas City Club and asked for Mr. Kauffman. A man told me to sit down and that Mr. Kauffman would be there shortly. He asked me if I wanted a drink, and I told him no thank you.

All of a sudden, he walked in. He wasn't very tall, but he burst into the room and said, "I am Kauffman; where is Mueller?" and I said, "Over here." He pulled out his corncob pipe and Half and Half tobacco, poured himself a stiff drink, and said, "Let's watch this game and then talk business."

Afterward, we sat in the corner to have some privacy, and I asked him about all of his businesses. He had race horses and owned a baseball club. What made him want to do all this? He said it came from within him — he had to be financially successful.

We ended up talking about his career, and then he said, "Well, what about you?" I told him I had a pharmacy, but I really liked the idea of growing the sports medicine business I started by selling to high schools. I told him I really didn't know what to do. He gave me the greatest advice: "You cannot ride two horses at one time." I said, "Well, you just made my decision." I shook his hand and left.

Once I got back, I asked my dad if he wanted to buy the pharmacy back from me. During that time, I was making more than $50,000 a year in 1968-1969 with the drug store and calling on schools. That wasn't too shabby. For context, this was at a time when teachers were making about $5,000 a year and pharmacists were making about $10,000 a year.

My dad didn't want to buy the pharmacy back, so I sold it to a drugstore in Sauk City, and then I scrambled to find money to expand my sports medicine business.

I ended up putting this building up for collateral, and I sublet part of the building to a guy who was interested in the dairy supply business. I gave him ten hours per month on my outgoing calls, all costs included. He could also warehouse his products there, have an office, and even use the toll-free wide-area telephone service (WATS) line. Of course, we had the usual banking relationships, loans, and lines of credit.

Branding the Future

Once I got the company up and running, one of our vice presidents called to tell me there were representatives from a certain company visiting, and I needed to see their products. I went to meet them, and there were three guys from Ashland, Wisconsin showing wrist, back, knee, ankle, and shoulder braces, and they had U.S. patents on a lot of them.

I immediately saw the Mueller name on these products; that was our future. It was a big swing for us. I personally took these products to the sporting industry to promote how they could sell directly to consumers and not keep those products in the back room or available only through physicians' offices. It was analogous to how we merchandised pre-wrap with consumer packaging, making it available out front for the retail customers. As a result, my company designed retail packaging for most sports medicine products. Everyone was selling to the University of Wisconsin football team, and there were 100 football players on the sidelines. I was trying to teach them how to sell to the 77,000 fans in the stands, where the marketing power was.

I was the first one to take these products to the retail level, which is why I was inducted into the Hall of Fame in the sporting goods industry. I showed them ways to make money. It wasn't "what can you do for me;" I showed them what I could do for them, and I got it going. I bought a GMC motorhome and went across the United

States several times with a display showing them how to sell these products at retail.

The private-label braces put Mueller on the map, and then I took them to the pharmacies. Right now, we are in Walgreen's, Walmart, CVS, and thousands of other pharmacies. Many of our products are made in the United States—our basics are made right here in Wisconsin, including our pre-tape underwrap, disinfectants, and instant cold packs, and the reusables are made right here, too. All this local manufacturing we do increases margins. We also make all of the No Glare® athletic strips that football, baseball, and softball players wear under their eyes. But, instead of our bracing products being made in Ashland, Wisconsin, they are made in Mexico, Taiwan, and China.

GOING INTERNATIONAL

Around that time, I came up with the saying, "Today, Prairie Du Sac; tomorrow, the world." You could run the best pharmacy in Prairie Du Sac, Wisconsin, but how much business would you do in Japan? The only way I could expand was to go out and sell a lot of product. In Japan, they love American products. We had a partner there called Mutoh, and they were our exclusive distributor in Japan for more than twenty years.

It all started opportunistically. Mutoh needed a U.S. tape manufacturer because Johnson & Johnson took their athletic tape business away. I was skeptical about selling to them because I thought it would be too short term and they would eventually source their own product and come over and compete with us in the U.S. market. We solved the problem because they needed help with the football helmet supplier Riddell, and we wanted the tape business. We worked out a deal and did business for decades.

THIRST FOR INNOVATION

In addition to selling our staple products, one of our more innovative products was Quench Gum. We started with a liquid spray, and it was one of those trigger mist kinds, and we sold a lot. I would call on a coach and paint this picture to him of having to go to the grocery store, buy some oranges, slice them up, give them to the athletes, and then dispose of them. I told him that whenever the ball players come over, shoot this in their mouths instead—it would get their attention. It was great for salivation, and eventually we put it into a gum.

Another innovation was an antiseptic spray that is used on wrestling mats to prevent staph infections. One of our top employees suggested the product: Ron was a wrestler at the University of Wisconsin-Madison, and he thought it would be really great if we had something that cleaned and disinfected the mats. He came up with the name Whizzer®, which is a special hold in wrestling. It has been approved by the Environmental Protection Agency (EPA) to kill viruses, including HIV and H1N1, also known as the swine flu.

My pharmacy background helped me dissect the competition, especially when they didn't have diddly squat for product—I caught them sleeping. I found ways to copy their catalogues and manufacture "me too" products, but it also helped me improve upon those products.

I felt like I had one foot nailed to the floor when I worked in the pharmacy, and I wanted to get the hell out and do bigger things.

Pharmacy was the start of it all, but it was a matter of coordinating the parts and moving on to new things. And, as they say, the rest is history.

THE VALUE OF PHARMACY

As you can see, pharmacy has allowed me to build the career and company of my dreams, and it can happen for others, too. You take this guy right down the street who graduated from the University of Wisconsin Pharmacy School and opened his pharmacy about fifteen years ago. A good friend of mine made a comment about how this pharmacist helped him during his battle with cancer. He simply said, "The pharmacist really gave a damn about me."

The most important thing in a career is to choose something that you love to do; it starts there. Learn everything you can early on, whether it's in retail, at a hospital, or working at a drug company. If an idea looks good, go ahead and start your own sales company and sell to other pharmacists.

The reason the sporting goods stores were getting the liniment business was because pharmacists did not call on athletic departments in schools. To get any business—or expand into any business—you have to know where to go. For me, it was knocking on the door to the athletic department of the local high school.

To own any business, you also have to have a positive environment and good, hardworking people who give a damn—that's important. Young pharmacists have a lot of opportunities, but to be entrepreneurs, they have to want to do something different than filling prescriptions for Mrs. Jones's kidney pills once a month.

CHAPTER SIX

Katie MacFarlane

Co-founder of SmartPharma Inc.
Purdue University School of Pharmacy

Brian Zorn

Co-founder of SmartPharma Inc.
University of Kansas School of Pharmacy

Katie MacFarlane and Brian Zorn met during a Rutgers fellowship and became friends, which eventually led to starting a business together. Along the way, they gained valuable experience working for Big Pharma in medical and marketing areas, where they were employed for years. Although they remained friends, they went their separate ways for several years. When circumstances allowed, they founded their marketing consulting company, SmartPharma, specializing in commercial and strategic consulting for biotech and pharmaceutical companies.

They have built a business model that combines skills in pharmacy practice, medical affairs, marketing, market research, and communication skills. This is an exciting business model to consider for young entrepreneurial pharmacists once they have built a résumé of experience in medical, marketing, and sales areas. Their stories illustrate how they eventually became co-founders.

Brian's Story

I grew up in Great Bend, Kansas, which had about 20,000 people but fed into a very large high school. It is right smack-dab in the middle of Kansas, so if you put your finger in the center of the Kansas map, you would be on Great Bend. I have an older brother and an older sister. It was a small, kind of isolated town, but it was the biggest city in a 50-mile radius. If you wanted to go to a bigger city, Wichita, Kansas, was two hours away.

Neither of my parents went to college. My dad worked for a farming implement company for thirty-five years, and my mother was a bookkeeper. They both graduated from high school, which was unusual, because most of their siblings did not. They had instilled in us the knowledge that we were going to college and there was no debate, so I followed my brother and sister through school. I helped my brother with his paper route when I was about five or six, and then I had my own paper route starting at age ten until about twelve. I also worked at Sonic as a carhop and at a retail store called TG&Y.

My parents stressed hard work and getting good grades. I was expected to work forty hours a week in the summer and, ideally, get a second job to earn even more. My brother and sister were both strong academically; one went into petroleum engineering and the other into accounting. My sister was valedictorian in high school, and my parents were so proud of her. Although I was a freshman at the time, I told them I was going to be a valedictorian, too. I ultimately was valedictorian, and it was simply because I couldn't let my sister beat me.

When it was time for college, there was no going out of state; that wasn't an option. I had the choice of going to the University of Kansas (KU) or Kansas State. I decided to go to KU, which is where my brother went; and because he was an engineer, I was going to be an engineer, too.

I applied to become a chemical engineer, and because I was high school valedictorian, I got a full ride scholarship to KU for that major. I pretty much had made up my mind that once I left Great Bend, I was not going back. I ended up coming back for a single summer. Great Bend was one of these very small towns, a farming and oil town, but the successful people were doctors, accountants, and insurance salespeople. There were no big businesses, only a few small factories like where my father worked.

My brother graduated from KU the year before I entered, and he went on to be a petroleum engineer for Conoco in Oklahoma City. I was in the process of getting all of my prerequisite science courses for chemical engineering. In my first semester, I did quite well early on. I went into finals with all As and came out with all Bs and one C.

My parents were upset, but they weren't nearly as upset as I was, and I vowed that those subpar grades would never happen again. Nevertheless, I realized I wasn't enjoying chemical engineering.

We had an introductory chemical engineering class, and we had to take a programming class in Fortran, which I did not understand at all. The second semester of my first year, I decided I didn't like the engineering part.

I was learning more and more about what chemical engineers do, and they were talking about working in a factory where you determine all these processes. It seemed awful, and I thought I would hate it. I decided I was not going to continue in engineering. Because I didn't know what I was going to do, and because I wasn't going to take engineering classes, I lost most of my scholarship.

I started looking around for another major and was considering pharmacy. My parents had suggested this at one time because we had a local pharmacist in town who they knew pretty well. I met with him in the spring of my first year. Most of my classes fit, so I was not going to lose any of my courses, and I decided pharmacy made sense. I found out what I needed to do for the pre-pharmacy courses, and after our first semester of our second year, I applied to pharmacy school.

Pharma Life

I entered pharmacy school and seemed to do the best in the hardest classes; if they didn't challenge me, I tended to get a B. I found dispensing lab and those types of classes to be boring. Medicinal chemistry and pharmaceutics intrigued me, and I really enjoyed them.

I had to work part-time as a pharmacy technician throughout school, and then I ended up working in a lab that analyzed asbestos. After my third year, I got an opportunity to do an internship with a pharmaceutical lab that was started by a pharmaceutical chemist who was a leader in modern pharmaceutics. He had started a lab and built it up over several years, and then Merck acquired it. Merck then started a summer internship program, and I applied for it and got an internship working for Merck in Lawrence, Kansas.

During that time, I started delving into pharmaceutical chemistry. I worked with PhDs, and that's the career path I was thinking about, but then faculty started talking about starting a PharmD program, too. The University of Kansas didn't have a PharmD program at that time; it was a bachelor of science degree. KU decided they would start an eight-person-class PharmD program, so I decided that was what I wanted to do. I applied to the PharmD program, interviewed, and got in.

KATIE'S STORY

I would say I had a very middle-American upbringing. I grew up in a suburb of Cleveland in a middle-class house with my mom, dad, and two brothers. My mom was a social worker and my dad was an engineer. Probably like most kids in the Midwest at that time, I had various jobs growing up. I had a morning paper route for *The Plain Dealer* when I was ten. I figured out pretty quickly that I could use my gender to my advantage. I would wait to collect on subscriptions until the weekends because the husbands were home and they would give me bigger tips. *The Plain Dealer* was $1.40 a week, and the women generally would give you $2 and want 50 cents back; the men would give you $2 and let you keep all of it.

As a part of my middle-class upbringing, it was just assumed that I would go to college. I always liked the idea of working in health care and helping people. As kids, my brothers had been hospital-ized for serious illnesses, so my family idolized physicians.

Freshman year of college, I was thinking about going to medical school, and I started out as a chemistry major. I was in freshman classes with all the chemistry and chemistry engineering people, and I was getting killed. I knew I didn't want to get a PhD in chem-istry. I scored high for pharmacy on the Myers-Briggs test, so I went and checked it out. However, I knew from the get-go I didn't want to be a pharmacist in a drug store, which had no appeal to me at all.

I met with Nick Popovich, a professor at the pharmacy school at Purdue, and he said to me, "Oh, my gosh, there are so many other things you could do with a pharmacy degree." He talked about working in a hospital, industry, or in sales. He had talked about sales, and there was a part of me that thought, "Maybe I could be a sales rep." I knew he was right about a pharmacy degree, so that's when I decided to go to pharmacy school.

I knew what I wanted to do, and I was slowly making my college choice. My dad was an engineer and had worked with several guys who went to Purdue and had lots of good things to say about their time there. I took a road trip with my neighbor, visited the campus, and, honestly, I got there and it felt like college. I looked around and thought, "This is what college looks like," so I decided on Purdue.

I knew I didn't want to pursue a chemistry major, and I kept go-ing to the office of student services and changing my major. I was picking classes randomly based on what my friends were in; I had no idea what I was doing. Finally, one of the counselors gave me some advice and said, "Let's talk about the kinds of things you like to do." She had me take several of those interest surveys like the Myers-Briggs, but there was another survey that focused just on careers, and this test had pharmacy rated very highly for me. Of course, it also had forest ranger rated highly.

JOURNEY TO SELF-SUFFICIENCY

I wanted and needed to do something that allowed me to be self-sufficient. My parents paid for college, and my dad's deal was that he would pay for four years, but it ended there. I distinctly remember the day my parents dropped me off at college. It was a seven-hour drive from Cleveland. We unpacked in my dorm room, and they went back to the hotel.

I wanted to stay in the dorm that night, so we met for breakfast the next morning before they left town. We were sitting at breakfast and all of a sudden, my dad got really serious, which he didn't often do. He said, "Look, I will pay for four years, and that means four years from now. If you take time off in the middle, that counts. If it is going to take you extra time, you better figure out a scholarship or something to pay for it. You'd better study very hard, and let me make something very clear: When you graduate, you have to be able to support yourself. As of today, you are more than welcome to come visit us as a guest in our home, but you don't live there anymore."

Those were his words to me at age eighteen, and I knew I had to be able to support myself. I was independent anyway, and I wanted to be able to support myself, so pharmacy had an appeal. I knew there probably would always be a job no matter what form it would take. Even if I had to fall back on retail or hospital, and even if it wasn't my favorite thing to do, I knew I could survive and make a buck, and that definitely fed into how I ended up in pharmacy.

Once I got started in pharmacy, I found the basic science courses, like chemistry, challenging. When we finally started talking about diseases, organ function, anatomy, and physiology, that was when the lightbulb flashed on, and I realized this was perfect for me. Pharmacy school was a really good thing for me.

As I was finishing up my PharmD program, there was a push from the clinical faculty to think about additional training, whether it was residencies or fellowship programs. I had done really well on my clinical rotations and in my PharmD classes, but I wasn't sure what I wanted to do. I decided to go to the American Society of Health-System Pharmacists (ASHP) Midyear Clinical Meeting and visit their placement service area. I was looking through the openings and thought a few of the residencies looked good; there was one at the University of Minnesota and one at the University of Oklahoma.

Bruce Mueller was one of my favorite professors. He mentioned to me that he had a classmate who did a program through Rutgers with the pharmaceutical industry, and he thought I might be interested. He suggested I meet his classmate, Mary Alice, at Midyear, and I said OK. I got there, and he introduced me to her, and she said, "Why don't you apply to the industry fellowship program at Rutgers?" Brian and I met in this fellowship program.

At the time, Rutgers had just started the program; it was only two or three years old, and there were two companies involved at the time: Hoffmann-La Roche and Parke-Davis. Between the first- and second-year fellows, there were a total of six people. I went to interview for the position at Roche, and I was so excited after the interview because I was going to get to do clinical research. I had gotten a little taste of clinical research during my PharmD program because I was always scrambling for money and was paying for my final two years of school.

One of the residents at the hospital where I was working was doing a study on an antibiotic, and he needed help recruiting patients for the study. My job at night was to sit in the emergency room and wait for people to come in who might have pneumonia. I identified the pneumonia patients for him so he could recruit them for the study. I followed the ER doctors around like a vampire at night.

I was excited that I was going to get to do clinical research, help write protocols, and monitor studies, and I knew I would like it. I ended up getting offers from both residency programs and the Rutgers fellowship, but I knew as soon as I got the offer from Rutgers that I would take that one. That's how I ended up in the pharma industry — it was through the Rutgers fellowship.

Roche is where I did my fellowship, and I left the fellowship to take my first job at Parke-Davis. All my advancements and experience within the pharma industry were at Parke-Davis. The R&D job I took at Parke-Davis was in more of a marketing-focused function. It was in what is called Phase 4, which is typically where you are doing studies to support marketing of drugs. These are drugs that are already approved and you might be trying to find a new indication, studying a special population, or trying to help the marketing team out with new claims.

I had two programs that I worked on. When I got there, we were launching this antihypertensive drug. Pretty much anytime people would ask me to do stuff, I would volunteer and do it. The marketing people got to know me when we were doing the launch because there was some controversial data and our regulatory people wanted someone from medical present when they were training the sales team. Nobody from medical wanted to go, so I volunteered. I had a ball. I got to meet all the salespeople and the sales management. I basically gave the same presentation about twenty times; it was really fun, and I became the expert in the room for these launch meetings. That is how I got to know and work with all the sales and marketing people.

I continued in R&D, and then Parke-Davis did a big reorganization in 1994. At that point, I knew I wanted to get into marketing. I first went to our vice president in medical and told him my game plan, and he said it was OK. He suggested I talk to John Montgomery, who was the vice president of marketing. I went to his office and said, "Look, I know there is all this shuffling going on right now, and I just want to let you know I am really interested in getting into marketing. I know I haven't done sales and that is usually a prerequisite, but if you give me a territory I will do it; send me out for someone who is going on maternity leave or something. I just want to know I have a lifeline to come back."

He got up and closed his door and said, "Funny you should come talk to me because we have been talking about you. We thought you would make a good product manager."

I stopped in my tracks and said, "Are you serious?"

He said, "Yes, I would like you to be a product manager on Accupril," which was the blood pressure drug I had been working on. I jumped on it and said, "Yes, absolutely; I definitely want to do it," which is how I got into marketing. I think I was a little bit of an experiment at the time for them, and I assume the experiment worked.

Founding SmartPharma

Brian: After we had several years of industry experience, our company started with a germ of an idea that went all the way back to 1993. Katie and I had completed our fellowships, and we were both working at Parke-Davis. She was doing U.S. product management for cardiovascular, and I was doing global product management for Accupril®, the ACE inhibitor.

I was working on a medical education program and putting a slide kit together for a medical education company. We were paying $70,000 to $80,000 for them to do this, but I was doing all the work. I remember talking to Katie about it and saying we should start our own business doing this because our quality would be really good. We used to joke about that over the years, but then we both went on with our careers and our lives. Katie moved to Washington, D.C., and I went into the agency world. It came down to early 2007 before we pulled the trigger.

Katie: I was working at a startup biotech company, and we were running out of money. It was a terrible time to be raising money. I wasn't getting paid, so I talked to the board and let them know that I would stay on as a consultant. Brian had established the ad agency TRIO at the time, and I think he was looking for a change.

Brian said, "If you are going to consult, let's do what we always talked about; let's do it together, and we will make a business of it." If Brian hadn't pushed that button and said, "Let's do this," it never would have turned into what it is now. Brian has always been the bigger dreamer of the two of us. I certainly jumped on board pretty quickly.

Brian: I had started one company before, except I chickened out. I worked with two very talented creative people, a writer and an art director, and we worked on the same team in pharmaceutical advertising, Novartis was our client, and we had the largest team in the agency with more than forty people. I just hated the bureaucracy. We decided we wanted to start our own advertising agency. We weren't able to swing that financially, so we created a concept and presented it outside of our agency, and, ultimately, we found someone willing to do it with us.

Consequently, the agency we were working for countered and basically said, "You could start that agency with us." I created a concept with two other people to start an advertising agency and I did that and it was interesting, but I really learned after doing it that we were still part of a big corporation, and under a corporation you have bosses, you have rules, and I was really disenfranchised.

When Katie and I had the initial conversation, I had just been told that I had to lay off four people who I hired, four people who were good people, four people that were fully billable in their jobs, but the larger organization was doing poorly, and these were newer employees. So, it was last in, first out. They said, "We can't fire some of these other people; these people have to go."

I went to my boss and said, "How about you get rid of me and fold this agency back into the bigger agency? You are not letting us do what we wanted to do anyway," and I said I would go do something else. At that time, my boss said to me, "Sometimes you don't sound like an agency guy," and I said, "You know, I have been thinking the same thing."

I told him I was going to be resigning at some point in the future, and this was right around the time when Katie was thinking about hanging out her shingle, so we decided to create our own business.

We really didn't know what the vision for the company was, but we knew we wanted to consult for startup companies. I don't think it was much more defined than that, so we set a plan that we were going to start in November. I gave my boss three months' notice, and Katie and I started conceptually thinking about what this business was going to be.

I was already in the service industry, so I was used to writing proposals, doing pitches, and going out and seeking business. I knew what we charged our clients per hour for our services, and I knew most of the industry standards.

Katie: The hardest part of it was figuring out what we were going to start with. I had never put the touch on any of my contacts or anybody to say, "Gee, if I told you I was available to do some consulting, would you have any work for me?" I went up to New Jersey and had lunch with an old business acquaintance to run the idea by him about starting a consulting business. He told me there are a ton of people who would love to tap into your knowledge, and I said OK. The next person I got a call from was his wife. She had a small medical education company, and we were off to the races. Brian and I did not turn down a single project in the first four to six months. We were just trying to keep the lights on. We were probably less directed about the kind of work we took. People heard we were consulting, and if they called and there was a project, we wrote a proposal and we did it.

Katie: Brian had a wife and kids to support, and I had just gotten married. I was more financially stable than Brian, but I was probably the more paranoid one about money. I had this very weird feeling of being detached for the first time in my life from a typical salary position. Therefore, in the beginning, we would just do anything. We started out doing work that was not hugely intellectually challenging. We were helping out with medical strategy or medical education. We put sales and marketing programs together. We found out we knew exactly what needed to be done.

Brian: Our first breakthrough client was a small biotech company out of San Diego called AGI.

Katie: This was our first strategic project for a little biotech, and it came through a guy we knew when he was CFO of Warner Chilcott. He had moved on to AGI, and he had his marketing person call us. They had an interesting idea for a product and they wanted to pressure test it. That was the first time we conducted market research.

We figured out how to do the interviews. Brian and I had sat through or done hours and hours of market research in our careers, but we had never done the back part of it; we usually paid people to do that. Now we were just figuring out on our own how we could differentiate our service versus a standard market research company.

When we did that project, we got some keen insight because we talked with key oncology opinion leaders. We heard one thing from academic oncologists but something completely different from practicing oncologists. Because the practicing oncologists were the ultimate target, it was very eye-opening to the company, and it made a huge difference in how they would go about developing this product.

We realized that all too often, the tiny biotech companies would limit themselves by only talking to the expert thought leaders at the university level. There were services they could use where they would get two experts on the phone and then run off and develop their product based on that small feedback sample. In some cases, they found out that the product that they were developing wasn't needed in the market, but it may have had a theoretical need. The practicing doctors often are very different from the experts. We were able to get at those insights and do it really efficiently because Brian and I were doing the interviews and could probe effectively. We knew the clinical part and the market part.

When we get on the phone and are having a conversation with a doctor, he or she doesn't know who we are. We tell them we are a consulting firm, and we keep everything anonymous as far as the client name. They are open with us; we are able to get into a level of a conversation with them about medicine and about their patients that we know these other companies aren't able to do. We also know when to play dumb. We can ask what sounds like very innocent and naïve questions, but we get interesting answers from them. It's a different approach, and our clients really like it.

Our clients figured that out, and that was our big differentiator out of the gate. We were able to offer all the strategic insight, answers, and research for a lower price than the big guys, and it was much more thoughtfully put together.

Brian: Because I was on the agency side, I communicated with a lot of people I knew in the agency world and let them know that we were available for medical strategy and medical messaging con- sulting. We also started contacting old colleagues.

Katie: I would say that more than 90 percent of our business since we started has come from word of mouth. We have never done an advertisement. We have dabbled and gone to a few industry-type conferences and met people there. We have gotten some leads that way, but almost everything we have ever done has come at the recommendation of somebody who was on the board of a company we did work for, or an investor, or a CEO, you name it. One of our biggest breaks came when one company recommended us to another.

At one time, about 40 percent of our revenue was coming from medical education, and we were hoping to break away from that because the one thing we knew we didn't want to be was a medical education company. It's too much of a commodity, and there are too many people doing it. We thought we could do it really well, but it was not what we wanted to become; it wasn't interesting enough.

Our strength is market assessment and helping companies, whether they're the buyer or seller, decide if they want to move forward on a deal. Until recently, I would say 90 percent of our work was either helping companies put together an assessment that they could take in front of investors, a potential partner, or a buyer to help justify an acquisition or a sale. We were doing the due diligence on every potential acquisition for one company. We have a few clients that are like that today.

Brian: At one point, we had a plan and were thinking of expanding. We created a comprehensive target list of people in Big Pharma, venture capitalists, and investment bankers. We each had a small target list, but we found that it was an inefficient process because people only need our services when they need them, and they usually don't know in advance that they are going to need them. When they are done with us, they don't need us on an ongoing basis.

Katie: If we hadn't done a profit-sharing deal with Napo, we probably would have tried to get on the preferred vendor lists at the Big Pharma companies. We did a little work for some Big Pharma companies, and it is lucrative. We can charge them way more and they don't ask any questions about budget, but getting on their preferred vendor list for us is more work than it's worth because it is a really long process, and you can't charge for any of those hours. In addition, our business model doesn't fit the mold so well in relation to how the purchasing departments look at services like ours.

It was always going to be difficult for us to penetrate Big Pharma, so we found our home with what we call emerging pharma, which are mostly small companies that don't have a product on the market yet; they are in development and are either at a point where they are needing to raise additional funds, go public, looking for a partner, or they are looking to buy additional products. Those are the type of companies with whom we have gotten involved.

By doing that, we have interacted with a lot of their board members who are also investors, and once they have worked with us and experienced the results, they recommend us to others. Brian has always talked about scalability, and I would say that has been a challenge. How can we grow while maintaining profitability and efficiency?

Brian: What we would tell every one of our customers is that if they worked with our company, they were working directly with one of us; one of us would be their primary contact. We had people on our payroll who would do background research or reports, but we are the main contacts with clients. Like Katie said, scalability is a challenge. We tried multiple times in different ways.

Katie: We had to let go one of our very dearest friends and a former work colleague who worked with us at different times. For me, it was one of the hardest things I have ever had to deal with in my career. We had to tell the person that we couldn't afford to keep him on board. To have people at a sufficient level with their compensation, we realized that they needed to generate an enormous amount of business.

Brian: Katie read an article in *The Washington Post* that talked about different types of small companies expanding and paying for health care and 401(k)s, and they had something in there about comfortable living for the owners.

Katie: The article was about a local husband and wife with a business, and they were clearing between the two of them about $350,000 a year after expenses, which is a comfortable living for the owners, but they could never scale the business. Brian and I ran up against that same type of thing where we could do well and we were very comfortable, but every time we tried to bring somebody on who we thought might help us expand, we could never make it work. There were three models that we experimented with over time based on people who had availability, and we could never make it work. The other big challenge we had is all the administrative work that comes with having a business. This includes all the administration for our corporations, the taxes, the workman's comp filing, insurance, all of that stuff. Brian has taken the load on that.

Brian: We have become very efficient, and we do everything virtually. We have a broker who handles our medical insurance, brokers who handle our business insurance and worker's comp and all of those things, and we have a payroll company. It runs pretty smoothly. I handle the accounting and finance, and when we have to get involved with agreements and contracts, Katie does that part.

Katie: If you're interested in starting a company, sit down with a lawyer and get an agreement in place that covers any and all events that could occur in the course of your business. Before we formally started our company, Brian and I met with an attorney in Philadelphia. Brian was in New Jersey and I was in Washington, D.C., so Philadelphia seemed to be a neutral area. The attorney sat across from us in this booth at a restaurant, and he looked at us and said, "You two are friends, longtime friends." We agreed and said we had been friends for years. I mentioned I was in Brian's wedding and that we have known each other forever. He said, "Well, you are going into business together, so your friendship is over." He stressed it again: "I am serious, your friendship is over and done, and you are now business partners."

The good thing about it was we got everything you could imagine in the agreement. We have a management agreement and a couple different agreements that govern our company. Everything is in there: what happens if somebody dies, what happens if somebody gets really sick, and what happens if somebody gets divorced. We went through all of those things with him and talked it through. What if we don't agree? how are we going to resolve disagreements? all that kind of stuff. It was the best advice we have ever gotten. Brian and I have always seen eye-to-eye, but when push comes to shove, we know the agreement is there, so we work it out and don't tend to get into big spats about the company.

Brian: I highly recommend it. First of all, you have somebody who makes you contemplate things that you would never ever imagine.

We had to experience one when I went through a divorce, and you find that some of these things that you had in place were good to have. Our attorney would always say the same thing when we discussed some of our business arrangements: "A contract is not for when things are going great; it's for when it goes to hell that it becomes important."

Katie: We have an LLC and an S Corp, and I laugh because it is just the two of us and we have this very complicated financial structure, but it is all there to help us from a tax perspective and to give us a lot of flexibility with how we can compensate different people who work with us.

We have had clients that wanted to give us part of our compensation in stock, and, in some cases, that might have been a good idea, and in other cases clearly not, but we formed a holding company to put the stock into.

That side of things I never would have anticipated; it would have scared me in the beginning, and I have often said that on my own I could never have built this company to where it is now and with its longevity if I didn't have Brian.

Brian: We took a major turn a year ago and are about nine months into a three-year contract with our new gig, so we decided to try something different. I would say it is an extension of what we were doing. We used to pick winners and losers, and people would take our work and advice and acquire a product or a company and make millions. We helped them make decisions in products and in raising capital.

We had an opportunity with a company where we knew more about the drug than we thought anybody else did, and we believed it was a winner. We felt it could be really successful, so we decided to throw our hat in the ring and put our money where our mouth was.

Katie: We are not charging any fee right now; we are 100 percent at risk on the Napo deal. We get paid off with net sales of this little drug. The name was even changed and it's now called Mytesi. It's an antidiarrheal drug.

As goes the sales of the drugs, so goes our fortune. I made a comment to Brian that if entrepreneurs knew how long everything was going to take and how hard it would be, nobody would ever start a business, and this is exemplary of that. We are probably six months behind where we were hoping to be, and there have been some bumps in the road. Things have been much harder to get going than we anticipated, and the things that we don't have control over are, of course, the most frustrating things.

In pharmaceuticals, people will often tell you that manufacturing is the most complicated part of it, and we are definitely living that. Even though it is not our responsibility, it affects us. The good news is we think we have this drug on an upturn and are going to find out what the potential of the drug is. If it does half of what we think it can do, this will end up being a really lucrative deal for us.

The dream is to make the Napo deal work and then scale this business. Napo wasn't in the position to raise substantial launch capital, so we have done this at a very low cost. Our partners at Mission are at risk on this deal; we are at risk on this deal. If they were paying an agency for the amount of work we are doing for them to get all the advertising and get everything done for the sales team and do all the things we are doing, they would be several million dollars in the hole, and they don't have that money up front. We are doing this much more efficiently than any agency ever could hope to do it.

We have a lot of help from contractors and, believe it or not, our PharmD students who come through and rotate with us. If we can make this work, we think we can package it into a real value-added package to biotech companies that need marketing and launch help.

With the small biotech companies, they are all looking to get bought. They all want to get bought before they have to commercialize. They would like to get bought after phase two, but the fact of the matter is the big, big money for a really significant deal from Big Pharma isn't going to come until you are approved. Big Pharma doesn't want to take the risk, so they will buy stuff really early or they will buy really promising drugs that have multibillion-dollar potential, but these drugs that are maybe $250 million to $500 million in potential sales tend to languish. What that means is that these companies have to go out and launch the drugs on their own.

What we have found is that these little biotechs have these failed launches all over the place because they weren't prepared, they don't really know what they are doing, they don't have the staff. They throw themselves at the mercy of a contract sales organization that charges them all kinds of silly money and doesn't deliver, and they dilute the heck out of their shareholders by raising millions for a launch. We think we can break that business model. We joke about being the Uber of pharmaceutical launch, but that is what we would love to be.

Brian: There is one thing that is a little bit different because we worked on a lot of products over the years, and there are a lot of products that we have evaluated that we would never, ever do this for. We would have to pick the product before the company picked up because the only reason we are willing to commit on this drug is because we are the ones who did the forecast, we did the market research, we believe in everything we evaluated companies for over for the last eight or nine years. When we look at this drug, it meets all the conditions that would motivate us to offer a positive recommendation to invest in it.

Katie: If we are successful and this drug starts to take off, somebody will buy Napo. If someone has the cash to put into developing other indications, we think this drug could do a billion dollars, so they will get acquired. The other thing we have done is to make an exit palatable for a buyer. If they wanted us to exit, we have some residual in there, but it is not such a long tail or onerous tail that it would chase a buyer away, and we did that on purpose.

We would do this model with anyone if the product is right. We have one small Chinese company that has some products that we really like, and Brian has been working with them for a couple of years. The CEO has already told us that if we show that our model works, to sign him up. That's the big dream.

Exit Strategy

Katie: I think about an exit strategy all the time because I want to retire early. There is certainly one scenario here where if this Napo deal took off beyond our wildest expectations, we could cash out. The other extreme is that if it doesn't even hit the minimum expectation, then we may have to fold up the tent and go home—or at least go back to our more traditional consulting. I would say our realistic moderate expectation puts it in a place where it is a very lucrative thing for us, and it provides that building block to scale and to go to other companies to launch their products.

Brian: We would have to hit a homerun for this to be an exit strategy in itself. Going into this, I thought two things. One, we would be able to demonstrate a model that we could reproduce. We have contacts at the big agencies, people who we have worked with over the years who could come in and help us make this bigger and keep us around for two to three years to help them build it.

Second, if it works and Napo gets bought, our contract gets bought out, and it would give us some time to think about next steps. We learned that there are very few individuals who know as much about doing all of it as we do now.

With entrepreneurship, if you are going into it to be rich, that's a really bad reason because you end up working really, really hard, and there are no excuses; there are no shortcuts. You certainly can do quite well if you do the right things and you get a little lucky, but I always say to people that doing what we do is like riding a bike uphill: Once you stop pedaling, you don't coast; you go backward.

I don't know if I have a pure exit. First of all, I don't know if there is enough that I have an interest in doing, so I could see this lead to some other avenue for me, at least for another ten years.

Katie: Another idea Brian and I have discussed is our list of drug products; not NCEs but viable drug products. If we could demonstrate to an investor that we know how to get this done with investor backing, we think we could take several drugs all the way through to approval and launch. That is another one that is a little bit fantasy, but crazier things have happened. It is something we don't ever rule out, because we always wanted to have our own product that we control.

You have to have an offering in which somebody needs to come to you instead of someone else. It's not like you have to be totally unique and nobody else is doing it, but if it is something somebody else does, like our business was, you have to be better at it in some way. Just being cheaper won't get it done.

Brian: You have to get your hands dirty and put your money where your mouth is; walk the walk and talk the talk. We aren't looking for an answer; we are looking to give the *complete* answer. We always say what we do has to be perfect; it has to be really high quality because if you make some tiny mistake, the client may see the tiny mistake, but they also think that other mistakes are in there somewhere, too. If you think that you are going to be the brains and sit back and let other people do the work, that is going to be a tough one.

Katie: I can't imagine going into a partnership like this with a stranger. It's true that it's like a marriage, and you're going to need a prenup. I could never have done this if I didn't know enough about Brian to know that we have generally shared values, the same expectations in terms of ourselves and the level of work, what we both consider to be acceptable or not acceptable. Not just with the work, but ethically and morally. We have had people ask us to do things and we have had to say no. Just recently, Brian had to deal with this because he had somebody trying to pump him for information because they are bidding on something that they know Brian has information about and Brian is not about to tell them. They are definitely looking to swing a favor, and we just don't operate that way. I know Brian would never do that.

You have to trust the person because there are just too many times when we are running fast, and I have to trust Brian and he has to trust me. When I say we are good to go on this, or this contract is fine, Brian trusts my judgment. There are lots of times when we like to see what the other one is doing as much out of curiosity as anything, and neither one of us is afraid to have the other one look at the work and provide comments. We find errors and contrasting thought in each other's work all the time. It's such a luxury when we get to look at each other's work.

Brian: Yes, it makes it better. I have always felt that. The one thing that would get scary is if we became so busy that we wouldn't have the opportunity to put it in front of the other person. I know if I do something, Katie will look at it with a fresh eye and will make the work better. Trust is critical, and that's the basis of a lot of it.

CHAPTER SEVEN

Lloyd Myers

Co-founder of CECity
University of Pittsburgh School of Pharmacy

Simone Karp

Co-founder of CECity
University of Pittsburgh School of Pharmacy

This brother and sister team were willing to take a risk by investing in a business model that put continuing education on the internet with a multidisciplinary approach. They formed the industry giant CECity and continually adapted and improved the business as technology advanced.

Lloyd and Simone are admittedly different in skill set. Lloyd is the older brother by three years and Simone was two years behind him in pharmacy school. Lloyd has strong entrepreneurial skills in administration, operations, and technological areas, whereas Simone is brilliant in sales and marketing.

Together they formulated an idea to put continuing education on-line using the internet, then seemed to always improve this model ahead of the competition. By the time they sold CECity to Premier Inc. for $400 million in 2015, they had built a market-leading health-care solutions provider that specialized in performance management and improvement, pay-for-value reporting, and professional education. Here are their insights.

SIMONE'S STORY

We grew up in Pittsburgh, born and raised in an area called Greenfield. Our father worked in a furniture store in West Virginia for thirty-five to forty years, and he drove back and forth an hour each day to pay for us to go to college and become professionals. He was a great man.

I started at Penn State in pre-med and transferred to the University of Pittsburgh. Once at Pitt, I was trying to decide on a major and was looking at what the university offered. I had always been somewhat entrepreneurial and forward-thinking. I wanted something with flexibility, and as I learned more about the pharmacy program, I saw opportunities inside and outside of healthcare. I was interested enough to pursue it.

After the first day, I was hooked, because pharmacy had a connection to my interests, which included science, math, and interacting with people. The interaction with people was important to me because you don't always get to experience that in different health-care sectors, so it allowed us to interact on the patient side and on the collegial side.

When I was in high school, I had an AP chemistry teacher who I really liked and found out that her background was working as a pharmacist. I found it fascinating that she had a pharmacy background, yet wanted to teach high-school-level chemistry, and I admired her for that. She was a great woman.

What made even more of an impression on me was the corner drugstore we visited growing up. Everyone would treat the pharmacist like he was their doctor. They would stop by and ask him questions, and they had such admiration for this gentleman and his brother.

My sister's father-in-law was a pharmacist, and he and I used to sit for long periods of time and I would ask him questions about what it was like to be a pharmacist in a community pharmacy. He would talk about the pharmacy part of it, but also the business aspect of it because, as he said, community pharmacists were true small businessmen. That was the part of it that was fascinating to me, that you could be in health care but still run a small business.

A lot of people hand down the retail community pharmacy store from father to son, and they share the learning that comes with running a retail store. There was a visiting professor named Stan Cohen who taught the only business course at the pharmacy school at Pitt. It wasn't like he taught multiple courses, but he taught "The Business of Pharmacy," and for me it was the most fascinating course in pharmacy school.

He was very candid, and he would tell these humorous stories about how he interacted with people in the insurance business and all the different interactions in the retail world. That was about the only exposure we had to the retail world, but it was an important part of the educational process.

Interning at West Penn Hospital was great for me because I was also able to work there while still in school. Like Lloyd, I worked all the way through pharmacy school. My interests were in two areas: the neonatal unit and oncology. I did a rotation at a children's hospital in the oncology unit, and that's what really set my path in this area.

LLOYD'S STORY

My first job was in retail with People's Drug, and I moved to the Washington, D.C., area and lived in Alexandria, Virginia.. I worked in Langley Park, Maryland., so I had to take my boards in Maryland, which included a wet lab. Simone went with me, and it was a memorable trip; I passed that wet lab.

When I was in school, I also worked retail and hospital. I started working at West Penn Hospital in Pittsburgh. My education took place inside and outside the classroom. I really enjoyed working and getting my hands into pharmacy. I loved the education, but if you had to compare and contrast Simone and me, she sat in the front row, and I sat in the last row. For example, I am not going to tell you that I loved organic chemistry. There were certain classes that really interested me and turned me on to various parts of pharmacy. We had really good professors in Pharmacognosy, and I found all the weeds and seeds discussions interesting. The professors did a good job of figuring out how to interest the students and really hook them.

Simone talked about our corner drug store in Pittsburgh growing up and how we treated the pharmacist with such respect. Here in Maryland where I worked, they literally called you "doctor" and came to you with anything and everything medical. You were truly doing triage and ER visits in some cases; it was an interesting place.

I cut my teeth there, and I learned what it was like to fill 300 scripts on my own with one pharmacy technician, and what retail was all about from a business standpoint.

I stayed there for about a year-and-a-half, and an opportunity came up in Pittsburgh at a place called Stadtlander's Pharmacy. The Perelman family owned it, and Greg Perelman was looking for a pharmacist. Somebody knew me and reached out, and I ended up moving back and working there, where we were primarily doing retail and ostomy back then.

We had the good fortune that Tom Starzl moved to Pittsburgh and started the transplant program at University of Pittsburgh Medical Center (UPMC), and as a result of that, people started coming into the store with post-transplant prescriptions or for other programs like infertility, HIV, and AIDS. These prescriptions were for really large dollar amounts, and we would tell people we needed their credit cards for $5,000 or $10,000. It was the start of the first specialty pharmacy business in the country.

So, we did that together for a while, and then I decided to start my own business. I ended up at the corner drug store that Simone talked about--Murray Pharmacy. I worked the retail side, but also in a very bootstrappy way created other programs.

Where Stadtlander's was engaged in transplant and HIV, Murray Pharmacy got more into oncology, infertility, and some transplant. For the most part, we competed in similar products and services but for different disease states in the same city.

Interestingly enough, because of our work in oncology, what happened next was Murray Pharmacy's rise to become the largest provider of Neupogen® that Amgen had in the country. It all emerged from this little corner drugstore, and it was all based upon the methodologies and approaches we had built. We then decided to start teaching people around the country this business model, and we made a few other stores very successful in Chicago, New York City, and Florida. These pharmacies became regional centers for specialty pharmacy, which is something I always look back on and feel pretty good about.

We worked with Amgen and created a program, and then we did something similar with the American Pharmaceutical Association (APhA). It became a whole series, and it took people step-by-step through creating a specialty pharmacy and taught them how to start thinking about pharmacy beyond just the dispensing service. What we know today as specialty pharmacy — how to deal with patients, managed care coordination, financial services, and everything else wrapped around it — we didn't know all that in the beginning, but it kind of evolved and spread, so I am pretty proud of that as well.

Stadtlander's sold and then we sold, and this is when specialty pharmacy went more corporate with CVS and other big players. I was basically looking for the next thing to do.

Simone: I was very fortunate when I was still in pharmacy school to come across this whole concept of working as a pharmacist within the pharmaceutical industry, and I asked a friend if I could shadow him for a week. He worked for a company called Lederle Laboratories. I shadowed him and was really excited about this whole other part of pharmacy that we did not learn about in pharmacy school. With my interest in oncology, I realized there were only two companies that had an interest in oncology at the time — one was BMS and the other was Lederle Laboratories.

Lederle Laboratories was starting to put together an organization that would solely focus on oncology, so I started there in the early years and helped in the oncology division. I helped launch a couple products while there and market them. I worked there for about five years.

When Amgen was starting to launch their first products, I was recruited to help launch some brand-new biotechnology products into the market, including Epogen® and Neupogen®. At the same time, Lloyd was on the specialty pharmacy side establishing that type of business model.

People did not understand these new classes of products at all. They were large proteins that required injections. People wondered why they had to be refrigerated. During that same period of time when Lloyd was trying to figure out his next thing, I was trying to figure out my next thing. We started to discuss CE City.

Lloyd: We kind of stepped into it. Simone and I were looking at what came next because Amgen started to change, and I had sold the business, and we knew we always wanted to do something together. Simone is brilliant in sales and marketing, and I had more of the administrative vision and operations side of things skill set. I also had a strong interest in technology. We started in consulting and worked with the different partners we knew.

Then, this miracle thing called the internet started to emerge, and we were interested in that and learned a lot about it, and we kept exploring it. Simone had been doing education for Amgen, and we wondered if we could create something on the internet that would allow us to scale out the education process. That's how we got started. The third leg of our story ended up being our brother-in-law, Andy Rabin, believe it or not, who was an engineer from Carnegie

Mellon and who was doing healthcare technology. We bounced stuff off of him and worked out how to do it, and that's how we got started.

We saw healthcare education and continuing education changing from a funding standpoint, and new payment models were emerging. We decided we were going to move way ahead of these changes. Simone had some experience going around the country and educating folks about products and services. We weren't sure if anybody learned because there was no way to measure the impact. There was also no way to scale it except for putting people into airplanes and sending them all over the world.

We thought that the relationships we had with the American Pharmacists Association, National Community Pharmacist Association, University of Pittsburgh, and others created an opportunity to white label a platform that they could leverage for their constituents. We did not create the content; we basically supported the platform and connected both the users and the content developers. That's how we set up our business model.

Simone: One thing we decided early on was that we were never going to develop content, so we wanted to work with thought leaders. The thought leaders typically connected either in the medical specialty society space or in the academic space. So, we partnered with medical specialty societies and medical centers so we would have access to subject matter experts for content development.

We also partnered with contacts in the pharmaceutical industry. Back then, the regulations around continuing medical education for healthcare professionals were quite different than they are today. Nonetheless, we were able to build a model in which we were able to get content developed and accredited by some of the leading organizations in the country.

We thought it was imperative to have a multidisciplinary approach to the education, so we would have content accredited for physicians, pharmacists, and nurses. We moved away from having it available only for pharmacists or just for physicians. I could see we were really starting to collaborate as teams to understand the newest and most innovative treatment options for patients. We also used the technology to make sure people got the appropriate CE/CME credit based on their profession.

Lloyd: Initially, CECity was primarily focused on education, and then we pivoted to a business model in which our customers were not just industry, so we had to create value for customers like hospitals, practices, payers, and other customers. It was a significant shift, and that moved us into the next phase. What we created at CECity is this notion that we can connect education to gaps in quality measurement, and, therefore, performance, to create a learning healthcare system. That was the underpinning of what we ultimately created at CECity, which is a learning healthcare system technology platform, which is being deployed now.

Simone: People would say to us that we should change the name of our company once we started to connect quality, measurement, and assessment to how you are going to improve, and then link it to education.

However, you don't only want to show somebody they have gaps in care; you want to educate them to close those gaps. It all ties back to education. We wanted to be able to take that same education and pivot it and send the right people to the right education at the right time. So, we never changed the name.

Lloyd: That is true from an operations standpoint and a mission standpoint. The key to our success is that we over-delivered on our promise and people trusted us, and we built the business around that trust. That was the key; it wasn't like we sold something and walked away from it. We would always be there and cared about the people we worked with on both sides of the table.

If you look at our model from a 40,000-foot view, the lesson is we continually sought out something that interested us which was tangential to what we had just learned, but we were always looking for a new learning opportunity. We also wanted to take advantage of what was developing in the pharmacy world or the broader healthcare world beyond that.

That's the thing I see a lot now, especially in large companies, is people look straight ahead at their computers or business units and don't really consider how the dots connect or how they can leverage what they have learned or what they need to learn to take it to the next level. That is probably the biggest difference between being entrepreneurial and just having a job.

We were on the edge at least two or three times to the point where you start to question whether this is worth the risk, especially because we bootstrapped the whole thing and were self-funded. We started to grow quickly because we were the leaders in quality measurement and reporting in the ambulatory space, and there was a question of how we could do that and the decision of whether we needed to take on external funding. There were days when we wondered if we were going to make it; could we make payroll, could we survive? We were very resourceful and found ways to grow and to manage through that.

There were probably two or three times when a market shift occurred that concerned us. Eli Lilly, for example, used to support continuing education in a much more significant way, as did other pharma companies, but that changed in the early 2000s. We were looking at it, saying we have the wrong business model for a changing world. Fortunately, we were able to pivot because of the way we were looking at the landscape not as purely educational also connecting quality and education.

Luckily, I have a supportive spouse, and you need to know that there are going to be days when you're afraid that you have made a huge mistake. It's a rollercoaster, as my wife says: "You buy your ticket, and you take the ride." It's not for the faint of heart. We self-funded all the way to exit, which was challenging, but we were able to do that.

We thought about it along the way. The problem with taking investor money is it has pluses and minuses. We thought the biggest issue would be that whoever came in would want to turn the business in the direction that only focused on the revenue and the earnings before interest, tax, depreciation, and amortization (EBITDA) instead of the purpose and mission we established.

Without that balance, you have a short-lived opportunity. If you are in it just to get in and out, then maybe, but that was not for Simone, Andy, and me. We saw that if we did the right thing, the money would follow. We knew you had to be smart, lucky, and be in the right spot, and we were fortunate that it all worked out. We never had to compromise the reason that we were doing things, and people respected that—and it differentiated us, too.

Exit Strategy

When it came time for an exit strategy, it started with being approached. Throughout the five or six years leading up to that time, people noticed us because, not only were we leading in the education space, but we were leading in the ambulatory quality and reporting space, too. This was forming the underpinnings for the new payment models, which today is the Medicare Access and CHIP Reauthorization Act (MACRA) for physicians.

We had venture capital and private equity ask us if we needed help, but we said we were fine. Then we started having strategics call in from a variety of parts of the business, some purely educational, some purely quality and reporting. Some of the larger strategics started to come in that had very broad businesses too.

We got connected to Premier Inc., which eventually acquired us, when we started doing work with them. As we started bumping up against each other in the marketplace, we boosted our reputation with their team, and that ultimately led to the transaction. There were a number of folks who were looking at us in a number of strategic ways, so once we had the serious discussions, we sought out support and more professional help.

Going back to MACRA and value-based payment, pharmacists need to understand the way the CMS payment model is going to change. This is a whole new economy that is completely turning the payment model of fee-for-service on its head. I don't know that pharmacies and pharmacists really get that yet because they don't have a direct relationship with CMS due to the part D measures and part D billing, which are kind of indirect to pharmacy.

Putting Value in Value-Based Payment

In the physician space, there have been a number of surveys conducted that have found that physicians don't really understand MACRA. Only about 50 percent of physicians have even heard of it, but they are going to get paid going forward based on quality measures and their outcomes as opposed to the number of procedures they have done.

Does pharmacy have enough of an understanding of what the new payment models are, where they are going, and how they are going to impact pharmacy? That's the first step — to really educate people in pharmacy.

One of the programs I am getting engaged in at the University of Pittsburgh School of Pharmacy is a new pharmacoanalytics education and training program built around population health, measurement, and performance. That's going to be an important part of population health, whether it's in the physician practice or the pharmacy. The large organizations, including CVS, Walmart, Walgreen's, etc., clearly understand that population health is a piece of their business and an important part of pharmacy going forward. I don't know that it has trickled down to pharmacists yet, and it hasn't touched much of the payment system directly, which is why I think there is a long way to go for pharmacy in terms of opportunity.

Simone: If we think about the history of pharmacy, we were never paid for our consultation time, if you will, but if you go to a physician, there is a time-based fee that you are charged. Going back to the beginning of this discussion, that corner drugstore that I admired, I never got a bill for however long the pharmacist spent with me; pharmacists were never paid for their services. We gave them away and charged more of a transaction fee. This new economy that we are in opens the door for pharmacists to show their value as part of that multidisciplinary healthcare team, and as a result of that, it even changes how pharmacy is paid.

Lloyd: For those who may want to capitalize on this and other trends, the first thing to consider is how big of a thinker are you? If you want to be able to do anything, you have to think beyond the job description. How do all the dots connect? How does what you do affect the people around you and the people on the other side of the counter? Then are they like concentric circles? What are the payment models? What are the standards of care, etc.?

It's all about educating yourself and being self-directed. It's not just what people are teaching you, but what you can learn, whether it's technology or whatever it takes to expand your education far beyond what you learned in school. What you learned at school is the solid foundation. It's like one of our professors said, "We are going to teach you how to find things in the library, but it is your job once you graduate to go out there and look them up. That would be the start. The second thing is, are you comfortable being entrepreneurial? Some people aren't. If you are and you don't mind taking risks, then whether it is on your own as a business or within an organization, don't be afraid to make suggestions and say, "This is how I think we can grow the business."

The question is, who are the students who will benefit from reading about being an entrepreneur? Not all of them will, because not everyone wants to be an entrepreneur. It's funny because Simone and I are brother and sister and are complete opposites. We took personality tests in the early days of our business and found that we are in opposite quadrants. She reacts differently when under stress than I do. It also helped us understand that we aren't in the same quadrant as our accountants. You go to accounting school and find that they are even less entrepreneurial than pharmacy students. That's the issue.

We went to the University of Pittsburgh School of Pharmacy and worked with a group that wanted to build apps to solve all these problems. They self-selected who the entrepreneurs were within the class; there was a subgroup of them. If you could help identify people who are entrepreneurial, then you could nurture them along a track that is specific to being an entrepreneur, and other people will be very happy not doing that because they aren't that type of risk-taker.

There are students within each pharmacy class who are potential entrepreneurs. There are people like Simone who would be wonderful at sales; her personality lends itself to that. If you could help identify all these varied traits for people, I think they would make better career choices.

Simone: We have an array of students going into pharmacy school, and we have for many, many decades. Lloyd is a visionary, and you need a strong vision of what the future will or can be to be an entrepreneur. We saw the pharmacists who were entrepreneurs go into business in the community drugstore that we talked about earlier. We saw that those who weren't entrepreneurs were probably going to work somewhere where they were more like employees, maybe a hospital pharmacy, for example.

This goes back to admissions in the pharmacy schools and making sure that we are not just looking for the politest kids or the brightest kids with the best test scores or the best grades in high school.

Do they have that entrepreneurial skill set mixed in with the other personality types you typically see in pharmacy schools?

As Lloyd said, we see problems in pharmacy today because we see a lot of pharmacists who don't want to get out from behind the counter to counsel patients, and it's because it's not in their personalities. Personally, I want to jump over the counter and hug the patient who just walked in. It all starts there.

CHAPTER EIGHT

Erin Albert

Founder of Pharm LLC and Yuspie LLC
Health Economics Pharmacist, Myers & Stauffer LC
Author and Podcast Host
Former Associate Pharmacy Professor

Should we work at one company full-time, or should we combine several interesting career paths? Erin Albert may have figured out the ideal career path for a subset of graduates. She works four days per week at Myers and Stauffer, the Medicare and Medicaid experts, as a health outcomes pharmacist, and she devotes the rest of her life to entrepreneurial passions, including her two career development companies, as well as writing books, podcasting, and advocating for women.

Albert believes in non-stop learning, so it's not surprising that she obtained her bachelor's in pharmacy from Butler University, an MBA from Concordia University Wisconsin, a PharmD from Shenandoah University, and a JD from Indiana University's Robert H. McKinney School of Law with a concentration in healthcare law.

She has written fifteen books, including *The S(He) Says Guide to Mentoring; Multipationals; PlanC: The Full-Time Employee and*

Part-Time Entrepreneur. She has written a series of children's books targeted at boys and girls from five to nine years old to introduce them to the languages and career paths in science, technology, engineering, and math (STEM), called *The Amazing Adventures of the Princesses from Planet STEM.*

I sat down with her prior to a signing for her latest book and realized that pharmacy students, young pharmacists, and faculty needed to hear her story and her philosophy. I also learned terms I hadn't heard before, such as *intrapreneur* (i.e., entrepreneurial thinking within a traditional job) or *multipationals* (i.e., people with diverse and multiple occupations that occur simultaneously). Her idea is that you can work in a traditional pharmacy field but do it three to five days per week. The remainder of the time is spent establishing businesses and/or following other life or career passions, whether or not they are in healthcare-related areas.

It may not be for everyone, but it surely is for many. Who knows? Maybe society and the pharmacy profession benefits too. Here is her story.

BIRTH OF AN ENTREPRENEURIAL SPIRIT

I grew up in the cornfields near Crumstown, Indiana, just outside of South Bend with one other sibling who is my Irish twin. Right now, he and I are the same age, which happens once a year for exactly one month. My parents did not have the good fortune of attending college, so it was always their intent for my brother and me to attend college. We did.

While I was growing up, my parents flipped houses. My dad was a tool-and-die maker, and he worked second and third shift, for the most part. My mom worked for trucking companies as a billing clerk, and she usually worked second and third shift as well. I don't know how they worked on minimal sleep, but we would fix up houses during the day on weekends. We would buy rental properties, and my parents would pay us to clean them up. We learned how houses functioned and how to remodel them. We were lucky enough to gain our first exposure to hustling at an early age.

Another thing my parents taught us was the value of working hard for a paycheck. My brother and I had jobs after school, and we worked for others when we were of age. In college, I had at least one, if not two or three, part-time jobs, even though I was going to school full-time. I was working full-time when I went back to business school at night. I went back to pharmacy school to get my PharmD, and when I went to law school, I worked. I always had a job. That kind of mindset rubbed off on us at an early age. Even though it was never the plan for me to be an entrepreneur—it was an accident on my part—but that mindset was instilled early, thankfully.

I feel fortunate to have parents who had an entrepreneurial spirit. Even though my parents mandated that my brother and I go to college, and that came to fruition, they were also entrepreneurs and instilled that in us. There is literature that supports the idea that entrepreneurs beget more entrepreneurs, so if you are lucky enough to grow up in an entrepreneurial family, you adopt many of the behaviors and habits of entrepreneurs early. Not everybody has that luck, however.

We also had the luck of choosing our own career paths, and I chose pharmacy for several reasons. In high school, I was struggling to choose between medical school or something else in allied health care. We had a career day my sophomore year of high school, and a pharmacist came in and talked about the benefits of being in pharmacy. I was impressed. You still get to do things in STEM in pharmacy, like science and math, but you are also helping people.

Candidly, I never wanted to be married to one career either, and I felt medicine would have committed me to that. I liked the flexibility of pharmacy, and that led me to this path in my career. By the way, I call a career path a career lattice these days; it's not just a linear or vertical career path anymore.

FINDING YOUR MOTIVATION

It's important to understand who you are as an individual and what motivates you to find the right career. Ever since I was a little kid in kindergarten, one of my favorite things to do was go to the library and check out a big stack of books. A lot of women who go into STEM loved reading as kids. I was always into reading, writing, music, and all kinds of after-school activities, so for me it wasn't about just picking one thing; I love doing a lot of different things.

I went to Butler University for my undergraduate degree; I chose it because my parents wanted me to remain in state. There were two pharmacy school choices at that time — Butler and Purdue. I visited Purdue, and it was overwhelming to me. It's a state school, and for a 16-year-old it was very large and intimidating.

My first job out of pharmacy school was at a Kroger Pharmacy in Plymouth, Indiana. I later decided to go back to school to pursue an advanced degree. It was in the late 1990s, I was working at Centocor, which is now part of Johnson & Johnson, and I had my bachelor's in pharmacy. I was struggling between choosing an MBA program or a PharmD. My boss at the time, who is still one of my dear friends today, recommended that I go back to business school to get my MBA because I already knew the language of pharmacy and drugs, but the language I didn't know was business. She said if I was going to stay in the industry, I needed to know both languages, so I decided business school was for me at that point.

I later ended up earning a PharmD as well. I was working as a medical science liaison (MSL) in the industry at the time I decided to return to school to earn my PharmD, and most of the pharmacists in the MSL role were PharmDs. With PharmD being the primary degree when I entered the market, I had to compete with people coming straight out of pharmacy school. I chose Shenandoah University because it was one of the few programs that would allow you to finish your PharmD flexibly if you had a bachelor's in pharmacy. I went through the program at night while working full-time during the day.

PANOPLY OF OPPORTUNITY

One of the rotations I did during my PharmD led me into law school. It was a customized rotation that I did inside the industry, but it focused on pharmacy law. At that point, I had the opportunity to see how much law is in everything we do in biopharma. I worked with the general counsel at Sepracor in this rotation, and it really opened my eyes. That was another seed planted for me to move on to law school. Learning experiences seem to lead to other learning experiences down the road.

Another unique experience I was led into was podcasting. I tried podcasting in 2006 when it first came out because I was coaching individuals who were getting into the pharmaceutical industry as an MSL. I had a couple of episodes about that specific role, but then I stopped doing it because it was time consuming. Then, Todd Eury, who is the wizard behind the "Pharmacy Podcast," approached me to be a guest back in 2015, and I was reignited by that. He asked me to join his group, which I did in 2016 as a co-host focused on career development.

Podcasting is another channel to communicate with a group of people with a shared common interest, but it is a unique channel because the audience is captive and it's a somewhat intimate medium. Most of the listeners of the "Pharmacy Podcast" are commuters, or they are working out on a treadmill. Those are the key times in the day when reading a book or a blog isn't practical. My podcasts tend to focus on career development for pharmacists because that's what I do as a coach.

We have achieved a win-win with the podcast, and now we are taking it to professional societies and creating a longtail experience from those meetings by recording our conversations with thought leaders while we are live at meetings. Afterward, we edit the content and put it out after the meeting. We create this long tail for a lengthier discussion on that topic beyond the live event, which our listeners love, and we love them!

We have more than 64,000 listeners for the "Pharmacy Podcast" now. Eury is the brainchild behind it, and he started it back in 2009. A lot of the co-hosts have niche areas that they cover. I can't think of many radio or television opportunities for pharmacists to talk about the business of pharmacy, and with the "Pharmacy Podcast," we get the opportunity to do this every day and share it with our listeners.

Podcasting has applications for so much in health care. I'm personally curious about the world of healthcare IT, and the "Pharmacy Podcast" offered the opportunity to be recorded live in a booth at HIMSS 2017. There were 42,000 people at this conference this spring—it was overwhelming! But what I love about podcasting from big events is that we create a portal for people to go back and review content from the meeting later on, even after the meeting. It extends the conversation about topics at a meeting, convention, or event beyond the live event itself. When organizers of conventions and events are pouring millions of dollars into exhibit booths and live events, why not capture the content or a conversation with the thought leaders at that event and share it later and in different places to maximize it? The "Pharmacy Podcast" already attended a McKesson convention and will be heading to Cardinal's RBC meeting soon to record podcast episodes at the conferences. Smart organizations are finally seeing the benefit to this medium and are engaging customers and listeners in a new, exciting way.

I also like talking about the career options in pharmacy. When I was an undergraduate, I was basically told about two options: retail or hospital pharmacy. Today, with the world of health care being so complex, there are so many more choices! Of course, those two choices are still the primary ones for many pharmacy school programs, to the point where there is some criticism of this practice. But the fact that pharmacists can choose so many different career paths now is a win for those of us who get bored easily, like new challenges, and want to be creative within the profession. Moving forward, health care and drug therapy are only going to get more complex, but this allows for more creative career paths.

In addition to these pursuits, I have had the opportunity to teach. The course I taught to pharmacy students had three major components. The first component was getting the students to know themselves better. They must know themselves to be successful. What motivates them? What do they value? What are their interests inside and outside of pharmacy? They took a battery of self-assessment tests, including *StrengthsFinder*, Myers-Briggs, etc. There is a *StrengthsFinder* test for entrepreneurship now, too. I had the students go through multiple tests and then create a personality CV for themselves.

The goal was to look for trends in the data, including what was consistent, and how each student could maximize her or his individual strengths. Also, marrying their values to the company's values where they work is important, too, because it makes for a happier and more satisfied employee or entrepreneur.

The second component of the course was for them to come up with a business plan and pitch it in a "Shark Tank" fashion with real-world entrepreneurs in health care and IT at the end of the semester. That was the bulk of where their course credit was earned. Most pharmacy students never built a business plan before, so this experience was ongoing during the semester, and students worked through the process of building a plan from scratch.

The third piece of the course was bringing somebody in from the real world each week as a guest speaker. This person had to be a pharmacist entrepreneur, healthcare entrepreneur, or someone who helps healthcare and pharmacy entrepreneurs. The students had to prepare questions for these individuals in advance, and it was a conversation between the students and the professional who came into the room every week. The entrepreneurial mindset is what I tried to get the students thinking about when we brought one of these speakers in.

I was glad to see the new Accreditation Council for Pharmacy Education (ACPE) guidelines for pharmacy schools that require discussion about leadership and entrepreneurship in all 140+ pharmacy schools under Standard 4, which is great.

ENTREPRENEURSHIP AND THE IVORY TOWER

Historically and philosophically speaking, pharmacy used to be very entrepreneurial. Graduates went home and ran Mom and Dad's drugstore; they were all traditionally owners. Now, we have moved toward clinical pharmacy, with board certification being the gold standard. Like it or not, a lot of the faculty in pharmacy schools have walked down that career path. They worked in hospitals, and maybe they are board certified in a therapeutic area, but they are not necessarily entrepreneurial.

If you are going to work for a hospital or big health system, most of those people aren't really that entrepreneurial in the true sense of the word. I am encouraged by our guidelines changing now to talk about entrepreneurial behavior and leadership; but we must find faculty who have the entrepreneurial mindset, too, which is a lot rarer. Ironically, there's a chance that the students who are coming in are more entrepreneurial than the faculty.

That's why I started the elective course I taught, and that's why I think it's important to bring the real world into the ivory tower. I have criticized academia about this; they don't bring enough real-world practitioners in clinical pharmacy and the business of pharmacy into the classroom. Ironically, most entrepreneurial programs in business schools today don't have faculty with real-world, direct entrepreneurial experience.

Many faculty members may have PhDs in entrepreneurship, but they have never had to make payroll, worry about cash flow, or run a business. My criticism of academia aside, pharmacy is a business, period. We need more entrepreneurial and intrapreneurial pharmacists out there moving the profession forward, and without these mind sets, I personally think other allied healthcare professions will chip away at pharmacy and take the newer practice areas if we don't seize opportunities.

Most of the faculty in academia graduated from the top of their pharmacy school classes, went the residency route in general medicine, got their specialty residency in PGY2, and then they went into teaching. If most pharmacy practice faculty took the route I just described, that may be the only route they know; therefore, they are pushing that route as the "gold standard" or best route for students. I'm here to declare it's not. There are many routes.

During the six years I taught the elective course, it attracted two types of students: what I call the "social chairs," or the gregarious, bubbly students who were always trying to network and were involved in a lot of clubs, groups, and activities outside of the classroom. They didn't always have the best GPAs, either; they were usually 3.0 or 3.2 GPA students, but they had the charm and charisma to be interested enough in taking this elective to make new contacts and to work in a team on their business plans.

The other group of students were what I would call the challenging students, in that they in some cases were struggling within the pharmacy program overall, to the point where some of them probably did not fit well in pharmacy. But, for some reason, they really embraced this class, and for the most part, they did a pretty good job.

The students embraced the concept of entrepreneurship, but my personal pet peeve with entrepreneurship in the media is that there is a false perception that "true" entrepreneurs must be full-time. Or, that a part-time business of one's own in addition to a day job is "less" than a "true" entrepreneur. You don't have to be a full-time entrepreneur or a full-time employee—you can do both. I personally haven't sold a $5 billion company yet, but I have a nice little cottage business on the side that still feeds me creatively and that I can manage around my near full-time day job. I love doing both.

One of my favorite books of 2016 was Adam Grant's *Originals*. What I loved about this book was that he was the first academic guru in publishing to finally come out and say that not only is it OK to have a full-time day job and a part-time entrepreneurial career, but it might be *better* to do it that way. The risk is more calculated this way, and his example of the Warby Parker founders is spot on for pursuing entrepreneurship part-time.

The literature and the mass media are finally coming around to this viewpoint—that you don't have to do all one or the other; in fact, there may be strengths and assets in doing both. This intrapreneurial mindset is something pharmacy should be embracing and backing up with faculty, guest speakers, and visiting faculty who are living, breathing examples of this.

I wrote a book called *Multipationals: The Changing World of Work, and How to Create Your Best Career Portfolio*. It is almost a safer bet now to have multiple careers going on simultaneously rather than just one, and I call this "multipationalism." I studied these folks who have multiple jobs simultaneously because I wanted to understand them better. As I studied them, I found a few commonalities among them, myself included. We had all been laid off from a job in the past, and it had been devastating. Being laid off from a job fundamentally changes your brain and how you approach work. Today, companies will lay off hundreds or thousands of employees and not even think twice about it. What are the employees doing to prepare themselves to move toward an intra- and entrepreneurial mindset in this age in which the workforce and technology are changing so rapidly?

Past generations had a 9-to-5 mentality along with the mindset of working for one company their entire lives, retire, and get that gold watch. That is over. One way to insulate yourself in terms of career development is to be a Jack or Jill of all trades.

CONTINUING EDUCATION

Speaking of that topic, I completed my PharmD in 2005. After being an MSL in the pharmaceutical industry, I moved into teaching and started working as faculty in a college of pharmacy in 2006. We didn't have a full-time pharmacy law professor at the time, so I approached the dean and the department chair to whom I reported that I had this idea about attending law school so we could have a joint PharmD/JD on faculty full-time. They were both supportive of this idea, so I took the LSAT and became embroiled in the wonderful world of law.

I went to Indiana University's Robert H. McKinney School of Law, and that law school was founded as a part-time night program for working professionals, which I really appreciated. As an aside for all schools, programs that allow working professionals to return to graduate school will win in the future. Purdue purchasing Kaplan is the perfect example, and President Daniels is smart for doing this. The growth in higher education is not in training undergraduates — it's in training and retraining already working professionals for coming technology changes. Pharmacy schools that adopt this mentality will also win in the future.

Author Daniel Pink says, "Persistence trumps talent every time," and I completely agree with this statement. If you have a struggling student who never gives up, I would probably hire that student before I would the 4.0 GPA student, because a lot of the 4.0s want the answers. They like it black and white; they want to know what's going to be on the test. The entrepreneurial world will never have a rubric; many times there are no black-and-white answers. You must figure it out on your own. If you don't have the "jump in and figure it out" mindset, you'll never be a successful entrepreneur.

Part of being an entrepreneur is capitalizing on opportunities as they arise. As I mentioned, I was an MSL for years, and I loved that job. It was one of the best jobs I ever had! I loved it so much, I wanted to start studying it across the pharma and biotech industries. I started benchmarking across the industry with an annual job satisfaction survey. I was sitting on about five years worth of data, and I was really struggling to find a publication that would print what we wanted to publish. We had the piece submitted and it was accepted to a journal, but they were sitting on it for months.

I became frustrated with that, so I pulled it and decided to publish a book about it rather than wait for the green light or permission from some other journal. That book was *The Medical Science Liaison: An A to Z Guide*, published in 2007.

After that, I got hooked on the process. I got on this Ferris wheel of, "Hey, let's go study this subject," and let's take people on the journey with us and publish a book about it. I have tried to commit to publishing at least one book per year, and I did that, except for in 2012 when I was graduating from law school, trying to pass the bar, and working full-time.

Back in my teaching days, one of the things that I wanted to teach pharmacy students about was book publishing. I found colleagues with this passion in other colleges on campus—education, business, and the arts—and they helped identify students across campus who were interested in working on small teams to publish children's books each year as a final-year project. Most were children's books focused on public health topics like vaccines, diabetes, or asthma, just to name a few. One year, students wrote a children's book about pharmacy titled *Pharmacy and Me*.

The first year of student book writing and publishing included a book for adults called *Prescription to My Younger Self: Lessons That I Learned After Pharmacy School.* The students went out to the pharmacy rock stars and approached them to write letters from their current-day selves to themselves on the day that they graduated from pharmacy school. It was about the life lessons they learned about themselves and their profession after pharmacy school.

Meanwhile, horrific data came out and continues to come out about women not choosing STEM careers. As I dug into the data, the one commonality of all women who chose STEM was a love of reading as children. So, when I was on sabbatical back in 2013, I wrote a children's book to engage girls in STEM careers, and then I started a crowd-funding campaign to give enough copies away to cover all the libraries in the state public library system, which we succeeded in delivering. Children's books for me were inspired by teaching my students how to write them—they taught the professor!

Erin Albert

WOMEN IN LEADERSHIP

I continue to advocate for women's issues. This year, I am president of our local chapter of the Healthcare Businesswomen's Association (HBA) Indiana, which is an international organization of about 8,000 members across the globe and has about twenty to twenty-five chapters and local affiliates. We have been around now for about fourteen years as a chapter; the organization has been around for about forty years. Our focus and mission is to get more women into leadership positions within healthcare and life sciences. This year, I am focused on getting men into the conversation about gender parity and getting more women sponsored and into leadership positions.

As you probably know, two-thirds of pharmacy school students are women, and women have been the majority in pharmacy since the early 1980s. However, when you look at the leaders of pharmacy and healthcare organizations, they are nearly 100 percent men. I track these data and share them broadly—the numbers don't lie. What is happening that is derailing the majority within the profession—women—to opt out of leadership positions?

It is important for those of us in leadership positions to spotlight women at the helms of organizations, and also include men in the conversations about how we can get even more women involved at the highest and most senior levels of healthcare organizations, because right now, men are the leaders of these organizations. What is truly ironic is that women are making all of the healthcare decisions in their families, as well as major purchasing decisions, yet men are making all the decisions at the helms of healthcare organizations. This is a huge disconnect. Smart companies that have diverse leadership teams and board diversity will win in the future because they'll understand the customer.

I borrowed an interesting term from Ivy League business schools. Young <u>men</u> enrolled in business programs are starting organizations called "Manbassadors" where they bring men <u>and</u> women together to have conversations about achieving gender parity. I love this concept because this is Generations Y and Z stepping up, and men are being proactive about the gender parity conversation.

Also, women can talk to women all day long about gender parity, but if they don't involve men in the conversation, they are only reaching half of the audience. The problem of diversity will never be solved with only half of the population engaged in the conversation. So, we are creating a Manbassador panel with all men to have tough conversations about how men and women can step up and mentor/sponsor more women to get them into the C-suite.

Mentoring and sponsoring, by the way, are different, and women lack sponsors. Sponsorship is when the mentee and the mentor both work for the same company and the mentor or sponsor is the one who fights for the mentee when the mentee is not in the room — for promotions, new assignments, and projects. Women are good at finding mentors, but they still lack sponsors, and sponsors are key to moving up within, and even sometimes outside, an organization.

My best advice is to be around the people doing the work that you want to do or that you aspire to do. I hate the term "pick brains" because people are busy. Don't waste their time and potentially their money by picking their brains! Offer something of value to them in exchange for their time. What are you a superhero at? Everyone can learn something from others, so be sure that the learning is asked for and also offered.

Mentees always have more power than they think they do, but the conversation and relationship must be a two-way street. You need to be strategic about how you approach networking, but at the end of the day, like author and speaker Jim Rohn said, "You are the average of the five people you hang around the most, so choose carefully." He is right because if you can get close to people who are doing the work that you would love to do — just like my parents did with entrepreneurship when I was a kid — it rubs off on you.

There was a recent publication which supported the theory that hanging out with others with big minds and ideas literally changes your brain for the better. So, be judicious about who you choose to be around, and choose very carefully, because these people will have more effect on you than you will probably ever know. Another great book about the power of who's in your life is called *Connected: The Surprising Power of Our Social Networks*, by Nicholas Christakis, MD, PhD, MPH. It basically demonstrates that if you hang around four other smokers, you are much more likely to smoke. If you hang around people who are obese, you are much more likely to be obese. Again, choose carefully. This is my best advice.

CHAPTER NINE

Navneet Puri

Founder of Nevakar Inc.
Rutgers School of Pharmacy

Some pharmacists are strategic opportunists. Navneet Puri wanted to go into the healthcare field and started pharmacy school thinking that if he didn't like it, he would enroll in business school or medical school. Along the way, he realized he really liked pharmacy and understanding how medicines are discovered and their mechanism of action.

After pharmacy school, he joined the pharmaceutical industry and worked in production planning long enough to know that he didn't want to do that the rest of his life, and knew he needed more education to get to where he wanted to go. While completing his master's, he had the chance to do a summer internship at Syntex, which is now part of Roche Biosciences, and he realized a PhD was the best route for him, allowing him to think and debate at the appropriate level regarding product development.

While completing his PhD at Rutgers, he started to form the management philosophy that has made him successful in building two companies. Puri believes strongly in cross-functional collaboration and building teams with strong individuals—letting them make decisions and contribute independently. He has a strong will and is known for his perseverance and persistence, traits he learned and honed in graduate school.

After experiences with several companies, he concluded that he enjoyed product development more than drug discovery, and pharmaceuticals more than biotech.

As is the case with many entrepreneurs, they often find that working within a corporation may not let them get things done fast enough; the decisions take too long and frustration can build. Puri decided to leave Baxter to form his own company, Innopharma. It was an injectable-focused development house that developed the Abbreviated New Drug Application (ANDA). Short-term they outlicensed it; longer-term, they kept the ANDA asset for themselves. Innopharma sold to Pfizer in 2014 for $225 million with an earn-out potential that could bring the total to $360 million.

Although he was enjoying working within Pfizer as the vice president of worldwide R&D, he discussed options with them and determined he wanted to start another company. He raised $55 million from investors and formed Nevakar, a company that develops novel formulations of existing approved drugs in the injectable and ophthalmic areas.

I've known him since Innopharma was formed and I was president of Bioniche Pharmaceuticals. Dan Robins, PhD, vice president of R&D for Bioniche, was the first executive hire for me, and his eye for talent was obvious because he wanted to visit Innopharma and Puri at his New Jersey office.

We were impressed with Puri and the team he was building, and this led to signing a development deal with them for an injectable product to supplement our own R&D efforts. I was impressed with Puri then, and I'm even more impressed with him now; he is one of the brightest healthcare entrepreneurs we have. His story is another roadmap of how to build a pharmaceutical company and create value for shareholders, and also how to manage and lead people.

CHOOSING PHARMA

Growing up, I was an average student, like many kids who are focused on one step at a time and not thinking too far ahead — which is probably not that unusual for that age group. I had the opportunity to get into pharmacy school, and, frankly, I had no idea what pharmaceutical sciences were — I really wasn't even that sure what pharmacy was — it was all about being somewhere in healthcare. I was in India, and there was no clinical pharmacy discipline; the majority of students went into the pharmaceutical industry upon graduation.

In healthcare, most of the attention goes to physicians, of course, so when I got into pharmacy school, I figured I would explore the area. I would see how I did, and if it didn't work out, I would go to medical school the next year.

To my surprise, my first year in pharmacy school was quite interesting. It turned out to be a lot more interesting than I thought it would be in terms of how they discover new medicines, what the medicine does, and its mechanism of action. All of those things added up to something that was exciting for me.

I finished pharmacy school, and went to get my first job. I went to interview for the job of an associate scientist, and while I was being introduced by the head of R&D, another office colleague joined them from the production planning and material management department. He sat in on the interview in a casual manner. When the interview was over, I received an offer from the R&D side, and then the production planning guy came to me and said, "What are you getting paid? I will pay you a lot more than that; join my department," and I said OK.

That's how I started my first job right out of pharmacy school; not going into R&D, but going into production planning and material management. All I knew was I would still end up interacting with R&D and the manufacturing departments. After about three months, I realized that this was mostly logistics and was just following procedures or protocols that others had already come up with. I wasn't going to be using much of my brain in this job. I had an undergraduate degree in pharmacy, but I thought I needed more education and decided to go to graduate school. I wanted to have a higher level of understanding and get involved in decision making, especially in a cross-functional manner.

This was in 1990-1991, and in those days Baxter was the biggest company in India, and if I couldn't see my future there, it was doubtful I was going to be able to see it anywhere else. I called myself a strategic opportunist.

At that stage, I spoke with a lot of people. This included people who had studied for their PhDs, those who stayed in India or left India, and who pursued careers beyond pharmacy — maybe on the management side. I had a few months before the next school year started, so I decided to take entrance exams for different areas. I took the Graduate Aptitude Test (GAT), a science and engineering test in India, and that was the test you had to take for graduate school in pharmacy. I then took a test for entrance into an MBA school in India, and I took the Graduate Records Examinations (GRE) along with that. I figured I would take all the entrance tests, gain admission, and then I would make my decision. As you can see, I was very opportunistic at that point in time.

Fortunately, I received admission in all these areas. I had admission to a couple of business schools in India to do an MBA, admission to go to any school I wanted for my graduate studies, and then I received admission in the United States for two schools. I picked the one that offered me a scholarship, and that was the University of Mississippi, known as Ole Miss. They offered me a fellowship, so I decided to come to the United States in 1992. That was the second inflection point in my career.

While there, I studied pharmaceutics. My interest always has been in development, formulation, and pharmaceutical sciences, and I did my master's with Dr. Kristie Willett. I also had an opportunity to do a summer internship at what was then Syntex Research, which was acquired by Roche and became Roche Biosciences. That was my first foray into industry. When I started my master's, my mindset was that I was going to finish it and go for a job in industry. But I took the internship, and Syntex was a very R&D-intensive company. It was not a very successful company, but it was an intensive R&D company. Some very successful and accomplished scientists worked there.

After the internship, my thought process changed. After earning my undergraduate degree, I went into industry and left because I could not see myself contributing in the way that I wanted to. I then went into the second industry environment during an internship, which was so R&D-focused or scientific-focused that I realized that my master's would not be enough for me. I needed to get my PhD to think at a level and debate at a level in which I could genuinely contribute. My mindset had been to finish my masters and get a job, but that's when I decided to go for my PhD.

While I was finishing my master's, I went back to India and got married. I came back to the United States with my wife, Reema. I started my PhD, and she stayed with me for a few months at Ole Miss. She told me, "Either we get out of this place, or we're going to have issues," which was my incentive to look for options.

We decided that for my PhD, I was going to explore other options and look at bigger schools in more metropolitan areas. At that time, I didn't apply to a lot of schools, but I knew somebody who was finishing up her PhD at Rutgers, and she introduced me to the school. I met Patrick Sinko, who was to be my PhD adviser. We talked about my research interest, and he was impressed. I joined the school and got admission there, and that's how my PhD started.

PhD Philosophy

When I started at Rutgers, I was fortunate enough to get two other internship opportunities while I was doing my PhD. I went for one internship at Amgen and another at a small biotech company in Montana. Again, these were great experiences that gave me exposure to all different kinds of work, including development of small molecules, peptides, large proteins, and different methods of drug delivery.

I chose to work on microparticulate mediated sustained drug delivery, and this was to be non-oral. It was completely out of my adviser's comfort level because he has always been more of a transfer mechanism across the GI tract kind of guy.

He had no idea what I was doing, but he was open enough to allow me to work in the areas that interested me while I continued with him. He was open enough to say, "You're doing your own research, so you have to find other mentors besides me who can better guide you, too." I thought that was pretty big of him.

I wandered the campus at Rutgers and built collaborations within the school of medicine and the schools of environmental health sciences, chemistry, and biochemical engineering. I knew a friend from Syntex and asked him to be on my thesis committee. Basically, I built a cross-functional advisory board for my PhD thesis and defended it that way, which was very unusual, at least at that time.

I always looked at pharmaceutical science as applied science, so you have pure physics, pure chemistry, and pure biology, three basic sciences, and then you apply those in different manners toward the whole process of new drug development. I have always been a fan of asking around and being curious, as well as building cross-functional collaborations to keep learning from different people. That was part of the reason why my PhD project was so extensive.

My adviser was known to be a tough professor and a tough personality, but I found him to be a great mentor for me during those years. He was tough, absolutely, but he could also see where to open up, where to let go, and where to encourage me. There were times that we disagreed, and he encouraged that as well.

Every Saturday, he would call his entire group to the lab, and from 9:00 a.m. until 3:00 p.m. he would pick one person who had to present his or her research topic. It was almost guaranteed that by the end of the day that person was going to cry, because Professor Sinko used to grill that person so vigorously. His philosophy was that it was better to be grilled within the university and not let the real world make you cry, and that stayed with me. I remember the first advisory board meeting that we had at Nevakar. I made the point that I wanted to improve myself and my team internally and not let the market tell me that I was wrong.

Professor Sinko was in my office recently, and I showed him the small token of appreciation that he gave me when I graduated; it was sitting with my other awards. That was a beautiful thing. It was a small picture of a stream flowing through a rocky area, and on the bottom of it is written, "In the confrontation between the stream and the rock, the stream always wins—not through strength, but by perseverance." He saw the quality in me that I refused to give up.

I never shared this before, but I failed my qualifiers the first time I took them. Under normal circumstances, people would usually say, "You are not cut out for this career path," and the thought of quitting came to mind. School was taking a big toll on me, and I was going through some very difficult personal issues. My mother had passed away and I was very close to her, and I couldn't get back to India in time.

My mind was not in the right place, and I told my adviser, "Look, I am just too shaken up right now, and I just flunked my qualifiers, and I am not really sure I am cut out for this." I remember every word he said: "Look, you are going through a lot right now. Go home, sleep on it, take the weekend, and come back on Monday morning. If you still want to quit, I will help you find a job. But remember one thing: I believe in you. I think you can do it; I strongly believe that you can do it."

I went home, and the whole weekend I just cried. On Monday morning, I came back and told him that I found it very hard to quit, and I was going to give it all I had. He said, "Look, this lab is open for you, my door is open for you, and I believe in you." After failing my qualifiers, I finished my entire PhD in three-and-a-half years at Rutgers, when it usually takes five or six years—mainly due to my strong will.

After much introspection, I realized that once I decide something, I do it. I know that failing is part of life, and I have failed enough; I failed way more than I ever could have imagined, but I think once you have failed, you come back a lot stronger.

CULTIVATING A CAREER

My first job was at the Ohmeda division of Baxter. This was a straightforward R&D job in injectable product development located in New Jersey. About a year-and-a-half into the job, I got a call from Amgen that they had seen my research papers that I published in the journal *PhD*, and they were interested in having me interview for a group they were hiring that focused on microparticulate mediated sustained drug delivery. Here was an opportunity to go into the discovery side in a drug delivery area, which is where I felt I wanted to be, so I thought, "Let's take a chance with Amgen."

That was a great job in a wonderful company. They wanted me, and I beat out a person from Stanford for the job, which made me

Navneet Puri

feel good. I could relate joining Amgen to my experience at my first job. I joined Baxter out of pharmacy school, which I quit after a few months because I could read between the lines and needed to get my master's degree. Here, I was taking my first job at Baxter's Ohmeda division after grad school and leaving to join Amgen because I felt I wanted to do drug discovery more than product development. Then, after about two years at Amgen, I realized that the entire group was focused on finding patents and publishing their own work.

I would ask about the methods they were developing and suggested we talk to the tech transfer group. I asked, "What about the operations group?"

I wanted to understand what they would like to see for scaling this up, for optimizing this, and they would just laugh at me. I would say, "What is wrong with you guys?" and they said, "We just do our work and let those groups pick it up when it is time."

I said, "Why not be proactive?" If you see potential, why not talk to the business lead and the program manager and try to build a collaboration within a few different departments? But that did not fly because it was a very hierarchical environment.

I was not willing to spend my life or my career in one building and go out of the building only when there was a meeting scheduled, so I had to spread my wings. I told my boss at the time that this was getting very restrictive and although I love research, I wanted to see whatever I do result in a product. We were not able to see eye-to-eye.

While that was going on, Baxter kept calling me back. I was getting phone calls that "the group is growing, we are doing very well, our

~ 175 ~

sales are increasing, we understand that you like to work in a lot more collaborative, cross-functional manner." They said they were open to giving me other opportunities as well, and that sounded good to me.

My boss at Amgen realized I wanted to get more involved with cross-functional work, so by the end of my time at Amgen, I had several options, but I decided to go back to Baxter. The main reason was because the opportunity was good, but there were two other compelling reasons. The first was that whatever I did, at the end of the day I wanted to see it become a product. This made me realize I was more of a development guy and not a discovery guy. The second option was that when I worked at Baxter, it was a more conventional molecule, classical pharmaceutical sciences company, and Amgen was a biotech company.

My thought was to always work the biotech side of it, and I realized that I wanted to grow my career in pharmaceuticals and not in biotech. This was the way I looked at myself. To me, the West Coast was not the place for the pharmaceutical industry, at least in those days. To grow my career in pharmaceutical sciences, I had to come back to the East Coast.

All the dots were connecting, and I had to follow my gut. I worked for one-and-a-half years at Baxter, I came to Amgen for one-and-a-half years, and now I was going back to Baxter. I had to settle down because I didn't want to be looked at as somebody who keeps hopping around; but at the same time, I always listened to my gut, and all these experiences were teaching me something. They were making me realize and decide what I really want to do; what I am good at. Wherever I was, I was never happy with the status quo. I always wanted to question things regarding how to make it better, and how to think bigger. Baxter was kind enough to give me those opportunities.

When I went back to Baxter, although I was in R&D, they gave me opportunities to look at the development aspects of every project. My issue was when we got a new product, I wanted to see a financial model. I would see a financial model, see the numbers, and I would go to the marketing group and challenge their assumptions. In turn, they would get ticked off. Then I would go to the accounting department, the finance department, and go over the financial model with them, and they would remind me that I was an R&D guy. I said, "Yes, but I still need to know this."

I'd see a manufacturing site was getting rejected because of an audit, and I would go to the quality department and start questioning them. On one hand, they were impressed that I was taking an interest, and on the other hand, they were wondering, "Why is this guy all over the place?"

Soon, they said I would lead teams with a mandate that I had to look for in-licensing opportunities. We would look for those opportunities and evaluate them in a cross-functional manner with support from all departments, including marketing, accounting, finance, manufacturing, and R&D. We had to make recommendations to the team to see where it went.

That was a wonderful experience, and I give Baxter a lot of credit for opening up like that and creating that kind of a matrix environment. Baxter was a business-savvy company, so we knew that the projects would make money and have a value proposition. That's how I got involved in the business development effort, and, of course, one thing leads to another.

We used to come up with opportunities, and I learned a lot during the entire process. Although I was primarily in R&D, the team had a dotted line to present it to steering committees. The committees would meet once a month, and some key decision-maker would not show up that month, and then it would get delayed and dragged out. Often, the opportunity would become unavailable when the decision was not being made within one or two months.

We worked hard to identify companies that would be able to work on those opportunities, and there were limited numbers, so we could not take months to evaluate the decisions. The second was indecisiveness because of excessive bureaucracy, and that was giving me hesitation about the decision-making process.

I evaluated it this way: First of all, there is a supply-and-demand imbalance. There is a segment of products that people are not able to develop because these are scientifically, technically advanced and challenging; but there is a real market where people really want those products.

I felt that I could do that with my background and network. In addition, I was not satisfied with the overall decision-making process; it was taking too long. I could just do my job, be happy, come home for dinner, and hope the decision gets made, but, again, that was not me. If I work on something, I want to make sure I follow it through to the decision-making process.

So, fast-forward to 2005, and that was after about six years for me at Baxter, and I was very much at peace with myself. I said, "Look, I really want to take things into my own hands now, and I want to make a much bigger impact than what I can achieve by working as an employee."

When I was leaving Baxter, the president of my division came to me and offered me a one-year sabbatical. He said, "I know you want to do this thing, but if things don't work out, my doors will be open for you."

I said, "That's awesome, and I really, really cannot thank you enough, but I have to decline because if I do that, then I am going to jump with a rope tied to my hip, and I will never give it all I've got, and I really want to give it my best shot."

I decided to leave and start InnoPharma to focus on complex generic injectables. I knew that area, and the science was the part with which we were the most comfortable. The rest is history, and that's the way we grew InnoPharma and the team.

INNOVATING WITH INNOPHARMA

I was clueless when I started InnoPharma, and I didn't even know how to get a confidential disclosure agreement (CDA) done. I knew products, I knew the science behind them, I knew what it took to develop them, but I had no money, I had no infrastructure, and I had no guidance, so it was really learning from the ground up for me.

I studied the databases and the publications to see where the opportunities were and what makes an opportunity difficult. I looked at the fundamental issues that needed to be solved to take it to the next level. At the same time, I knew I didn't have an infrastructure, team, money, or anything, so I had to build collaborations.

The first challenge was to work on those products, and that's when I spoke to multiple development and manufacturing companies. I said I would bring some opportunities, and what I ask is that we do a risk share. Allow me to use your infrastructure, allow me to generate the data in your lab, and allow me to get it manufactured at your facility, and you share that risk, you incur that cost, but the idea is mine. I am going to drive the entire project from the scientific, project management, and business side of it, and if we are able to succeed in it, we do a profit share.

I left Baxter as an associate director, so those kinds of arguments for someone who had not proved himself and who didn't have a whole lot of credibility were hard to make. Nonetheless, people liked what I had to say. I knocked on the doors of dozens of companies, and out of those eventually several were open enough to allow me to start working by utilizing their infrastructure at their cost.

Of course, along with that, I had to travel, and there was a cost involved on my side. I did this for about a year and a half, and during that time, whatever money I had was gone. I took out a second mortgage on my home, and I ran out of that money as well. It was Sri and me at that point, and he was a long-time friend with whom I shared my ideas. He liked what I was doing and was willing to roll up his sleeves.

THE BIG BREAK

I came across Dan Robins, head of R&D at Bioniche, and he liked what I was doing and the way I was doing it, and that was my first break. He gave me feedback that what I was doing was great, but I didn't have control over my destiny. He wasn't convinced that the products were going to be developed, manufactured, or have any controls. His suggestion was to try to control our fate and start developing products in our own lab.

Another break was a deal with GeneraMedix for several projects that got us going. All of this was leading me to the fact that I needed to have my own infrastructure, but I was completely broke. I knew that this was where I needed to go, and that's when I started raising money from angel investors, friends, and people I knew.

I raised a small amount of money—the first time was about $800,000—and that was my first source of money to start establishing a lab at InnoPharma. I then raised money from individuals for about four years after that. Every year, I had to raise money because we grew very gradually. For me, everything was a new deal. Whenever I picked a new project, it was an incremental expense, a new risk, and I had to convince people to join my team. It was very gradual growth at InnoPharma from 2005 until I raised my first venture capital money, which was in 2011, so we went six years with a gradual, slow-growth approach.

I would do minimal work initially, and develop it, and license it out because I could receive milestone payments. I would get milestone payments, and then I would gain a share of the sales revenue.

Prior to our raising venture capital (VC) money, one of our investors came in and said, "You guys are doing great work, you have a very scientific way of thinking. You've got a very good selection of projects, but you are creating value for somebody else. You have a source of revenue, but you have no assets. You need to start retaining your own assets so you can create the value for the shareholders as well as for yourself."

That's when we decided to raise money from the VC firms and start retaining our own assets. It was very gradual growth at InnoPharma.

The first phase was to outsource and complete development, with me managing everything. We did a complete risk share/profit share model with my development partner. Then we did a profit share with the marketing partner, and I then split that profit with my development partner.

The second phase had us developing the product at the InnoPharma labs, but we still did not have funds for manufacturing — so we did a risk share model with the manufacturing partner. We then would license the product to the marketing company and split the profits with the manufacturing partner.

Eventually, we stopped doing the risk share with the manufacturing partner when the VC money came in. It is also when we stopped licensing any products. We were now keeping all the products and profits for InnoPharma.

When the VC money came in from Thomas McNerney and Partners, we could afford to sponsor our own manufacturing. After that, we stopped licensing products, and that's when we started building value. I would say from that point on, we had an exponential growth curve.

We had numerous challenges during the initial five years of InnoPharma, and money was one of the biggest ones. The second was that I was outsourcing far too much, whether it was development or manufacturing. Many things happen with third-party manufacturing sites, and if you are not resourced enough to have sufficient oversight, that can lead to some not very good outcomes, and things happen. We got burned quite a few times, and there were a lot of lessons learned from InnoPharma. Even after we raised VC money, we still were relying on the manufacturing companies, relying on the contract research organizations for a turnkey approach, and we were still dependent on manufacturing facilities for product stability.

They would take full responsibility for all of those services, and I would take their word for it based on agreements. That was another learning experience, because it rarely happened in the way it was originally promised or written in the contract.

Today, we take all those experiences and make sure there are no assumptions made. We require strict oversight, and we all know we will outsource something, so whenever we do, we have to make sure our vigilance and our diligence goes up in terms of oversight.

I followed my gut feeling and common sense, which I will call my 'logical approach' because I didn't go to business school. I didn't hire a CFO until after the TMP money was raised. I did not hire a business development person until the last year of InnoPharma. I did all those deals myself. I licensed close to thirty products. I did what I felt was right.

I had a friend who was a CEO of a smaller marketing company, and I told him my concerns about all the deals I was doing. I told him I don't like to sell fluff, so my proposals are based on fact, and I will not propose anything I can't defend. I told him I am putting all the cards on the table, showing them everything, and I wondered if I was being taken advantage of by partners. He told me to never change, and I asked why. He said to remember that a classically trained business development person or a marketing person, with all due respect, is known to combine software with hardware with vaporware, but when you are talking to people directly you establish credibility; people trust you. They know that whatever you are offering you can defend it; they know that you have integrity and that you are going to take it all the way to conclusion. In the short term, maybe you don't get enough value for your assets, but you are building credibility for the long run. I replied, "OK, then I am going to continue the way I'm doing it."

I wished I learned it from the street, but I learned it from my own setbacks and my own success. Most importantly, I learned from the team that was around me and all the partners that I licensed products to; and all the companies with whom I did my profit-sharing and risk-sharing approach. Whatever I learned was along the way and while wearing multiple hats as an entrepreneur, and it was an awesome experience.

If I hadn't done all of this, I would not appreciate what a CFO does when he or she comes in, or understand what kind of oversight I need to have for a particular department, or what a BD person does for licensing in or licensing out, or what kind of a deal structure is needed, or the negotiations. I'm familiar with the terms in a typical agreement because I had to look at each and every agreement inside and out. I used to read each and every line of it, which used to drive the lawyers crazy, but that was me in those days, because I did all that myself. I did work with all the manufacturing facilities. Because I did all of this, it gives me appreciation for these functions, and it can make you a much better manager and reader. This is why I count my blessings, because of all these experiences.

I would attribute my success to being very open and sharing the vision in a very general manner. People saw that I gave up everything I had for this particular vision: I gave up my job at Baxter, I gave up whatever savings I had, I took a second mortgage, people listened to all of that. People knew that if I was completely in, they had a sense that I was not going to abandon it along the way.

People have to eventually buy in and become convinced. They will want to know: do you have a clear vision, can you articulate it enough, do you really believe in it, and are you open enough? I was very open with people, and I said, "There are no guarantees of success, but the one thing I can assure you is that if it is successful, everybody is going to benefit from this thing." That really clicked with people, not only then but even now.

At Nevakar, we are a lot more fortunate in terms of resources and the network that we have, but to get good people on the team, they look at me, they look at whether I really have a clear vision, and do I really believe in it, and that goes a long way.

After the recruitment is done, the retention is, of course, another crucial aspect of it, and my thing is that I am surrounding myself with people who are better than I, who are smarter than I, and after I hire them, I trust them. I tell them, "Look, this is the reason why you are here; you bring in a complementary skill set, you bring in your experience--which is what makes you the leader in that particular area. Then you have to trust them and empower them, but at the same time you have to lead them.

If I let everybody go their own way, it will create chaos. So, to bring focus to the chaos, the leadership plays a very important role, and that is where the retention aspect comes in. I must make sure you are open in terms of your own vision, are articulate and convincing enough, and you have to be genuine. Your communication has to be frequent, and you have to know how to relate to people.

It was an evolving process because whenever I would pick some ideas and talk to people, they got scared and said, "This is too complex, and these are the issues." My reply was, "This is why I am picking you."

When we sold InnoPharma, we had eleven product approvals, and nine of them had either zero or one competitor on the market.

Along the way and as we started getting FDA approvals, we identified our assumptions in terms of the issues and the barriers: was the market evaluating it, and was it really working, starting from the first, second, or third approval? We found we picked good products, and we predicted the market penetration really well, too. We had to maintain the same thought process and the same diligence in terms of execution because it was all about execution, and that is how we just kept working it.

In terms of exit, I would bring it to the same investor who came to me originally and I'd claimed, "We are creating value and giving it to somebody."

His advice was, "Keep it yourself, with your shareholders, and the company by not licensing things."

This was key advice that led to an eventual exit. That's when I raised more money, and after that, we started working more toward increasing the value of the company.

If I look at how the exit occurred, we would meet in our board meetings with all the usual quarterly hiccups, but we saw a good pattern of growth. In our board meetings we agreed to keep growing the company, and maybe we would think about an exit in a 2016, 2017, or 2018 time frame. In December 2013, our two VC board members from Thomas McNerney & Partners (TMP), who were both very financially driven, commented, "There is a lot of liquidity in the market right now, it is a hot M andA market, and we at least want to have a market check to see what is going on. No pressure; the team doesn't have to get engaged, but let's do a market check."

As always, I was open to ideas, although I strongly believed that we were growing InnoPharma, and we were going to grow it much bigger than what it was in December 2013. I took their feedback, and we hired J.P. Morgan to do a market check. They came back after two weeks and said, "People like what you do, and there is definitely an interest."

That's when we made it a full-blown process, and the results were great. However, we were not ready for it; it was not planned. That was another learning experience. One lesson is that you plan your life, and the other is that you always have to have these channels of input from external variables. And make sure you are willing to let things go sometimes and recalibrate your plan.

In December 2013, my board members drew in an input about the external financial environment, about the M&A market, and we tested the waters. The result was awesome. That was another experience in which you should always have a channel for external input from not just a financial perspective, but from all kinds of perspectives, and I brought that lesson to my own team.

If you see the way I grow my team, it is based on what could go wrong and where it could go wrong. What could be required to grow the business the way that I envisioned it to grow? In the areas that we work in at Nevakar right now, nobody is coming in and telling me what kind of an organizational structure should be there and what kind of skill set there should be because it is a unique model. I still look at this as an evolution; I started with one thought process, and it has been evolving.

I receive gratitude for the board of advisers, consultants, lawyers, accountants, and the team internally. You have to keep your eyes and ears open, and you learn so much. The day that we say, "I am not going to listen," and, "I think I know best," we stop growing ourselves as does our organization, and the team around us as well.

MAKING THE ACQUISITION

Then Pfizer acquired InnoPharma for about $360 million in 2014. December 2013 was a market check, and then we geared ourselves up in the first quarter of 2014. We started making our presentations around March or April, and by May we were done. By July, we had multiple interests and eventually three offers. At the end of July, we were pretty much done with our deal, but the closing happened in September because of the Federal Trade Commission (FTC) issues. They had some questions about some products and some non-compete evaluations were going on, but the closing was in September 2014.

Coming back to the initial statement I made, I am a strategic opportunist. I went to Pfizer with my mind completely open. We had a great exit not just for the shareholders, but for the team as well. Pfizer acquired us for a very good strategic intent. I wanted to continue to grow the business within Pfizer and learn along the way, and I thought maybe I would retire from Pfizer. Maybe I would be happy in a big company environment with a lot more resources.

I went to Pfizer with my eyes wide open and my mind very much open, and Pfizer was very accommodating. In my typical way, my intent was to make sure I was able to connect the dots and find out who all the stakeholders were. It didn't matter whether they were in Groton, Connecticutt, New York City, Kalamazoo, Michigan, or Australia, but I wanted to find out who at Pfizer could benefit from this acquisition, so I kept traveling and meeting people. I kept educating them about what they just acquired so the integration could be done in a meaningful and productive manner and as practically as possible. It was a good thing that I had met so many people because integration progressed in a seamless manner, and within a few months. Along the way, I learned more and more about the environment at Pfizer.

I had a dual title; I was vice president of R&D, reporting to the head of R&D at Groton, and then I was president of InnoPharma, which was a wholly owned subsidiary of Pfizer. As time went by, I was involved in the evaluation of new acquisition opportunities and part of the integration planning for the hospital market when it happened. I realized more and more that my role was evolving more toward global leadership and a lot more into creating and managing processes, and I found myself not very excited about that.

I took a few days off to do some introspection: what is it that really excites me? When I started my career, I went into development, but I really wanted to go into discovery. When I went into discovery, I realized what excites me is making my research my work product, and that is the reason I came back to the product side of it. Then I realized that I like to work in a cross-functional environment where I am connecting different dots to make the bigger story; that's just the way I am. If I get confined to one specific mold, then I start feeling restricted, and I realized at this stage of my career, I get a lot more motivated and a lot more excited by creating new value and by creating value that can be sustainable over time. I was not going to be able to do that within the boundaries of a large company like Pfizer.

I was open with my thoughts to my immediate supervisor and to other people in the management team at Pfizer, and I give a lot of credit to Pfizer, as I did to Baxter. They were very open, they were very receptive, they provided me with full support, and they were very understanding. I told them now that the integration is done and the team has found a good home, I have to think about what really excites me, and I want to make sure I am motivated every day when I come to work. What really motivates me is creating new value, and that requires a nimble environment, which comes with an entrepreneurial setting, not a large company setting.

That's when I decided to leave Pfizer. I left on very good terms, and people were supportive. I knew I was not going to go back to a generic mode. I was going to do something that was differentiated, but, again, differentiated so as to provide a meaningful value and differentiated in a way that the value is sustainable. It had to be in a patient setting and be overall healthcare-centric.

After I left Pfizer, I took a month off, and that's when I thought about the business model for Nevakar. I started the company a month later. Nevakar is a combination of two words: "Nev," which means new, and "akar," which means form or structure. That aligns with what I am doing, which is giving new forms to existing molecules and giving new structures to existing drug products.

If you want to be an entrepreneur, make sure you understand you. Why is it that you want to do what you want to do, and what is your motivation? Those are the most important questions. If your motivation is not crystal clear, then you are not doing yourself justice, because this is going to take a toll on you personally and professionally.

Once your purpose is clear, you can address the "what." Focus on "what" you want to do, and this is where the planning aspect comes in. Then look at the "how." How are you going to do what you want to do? That's where the overall resource and logistics aspects come into play. Many people may be thinking about starting a new business, but they need role models. The motivation has to come from within, and they need to be inspired.

I have three additional tips for young entrepreneurs: The first is to be visionary. The second is to build fundamental pillars for creating, growing, and managing value. Those three pillars are team, products, and infrastructure. Finally, the third is to be resilient.

CHAPTER TEN

Gordon J. Vanscoy

Founder of PANTHERx Specialty Pharmacy LLC
University of Pittsburgh School of Pharmacy

After a successful career in both academia and business, Gordon J. Vanscoy founded a specialty pharmacy business called PANTHERx, focused on rare diseases and exceptional customer service for patients and their families. The lesson: It's never too late to reinvent yourself.

Vanscoy grew up in Pittsburgh, where his dad inspired him with his work ethic and his family helped nurture a competitive spirit, but the hunger for learning and success was all his. He was admitted to the University of Pittsburgh at age sixteen and obtained a pharmacy degree, followed by a PharmD degree from Duquesne University. He returned to the University of Pittsburgh to earn his MBA.

Vanscoy built his experience level in clinical practice but also in business during his career, and he was continually thinking of new business ideas or clinical applications. After "retiring" to Naples, Florida to fish and golf, he realized he still wanted to stay involved with business ventures, and not just through his funding company,

RxELENTLESS Capital. He formed PANTHERx Specialty Pharmacy LLC in 2007, which is a specialty pharmacy focused on rare diseases. It is frequently recognized as the premier specialty pharmacy and is an annual recipient of patients' choice awards.

I met Vanscoy for a cup of coffee in a shop called BadAss Coffee. His penchant for high-octane coffee, fast cars, and airplanes made me realize he will never retire and will live up to his billing as a serial entrepreneur. He is high-energy and full of ideas.

His story will inspire all of us who have ideas and don't pull the trigger — maybe because we think we might be too close to retirement or some other excuse. In this case, it shows that an entrepreneur can make a move earlier or later during his or her career and be successful.

BLUE-COLLAR UPBRINGING

I was born and raised in a Pittsburgh suburb, and I came from a blue-collar family as the youngest of four. My dad had an eighth-grade education, was a veteran, and worked in the mills for thirty years, but he rose to the level of superintendent at the mill. My mom never graduated from high school.

My dad was involved in several businesses, and I learned the value of hard work from him. What he learned from running his businesses was the importance of relationships, being true to your word, and the importance of return customers — and I learned a lot from him.

I started working at a nearby carwash and gas station when I was twelve, and I stayed there throughout high school. I would work from 6:00 p.m. to midnight four days a week during high school, and the owner trusted me enough to have me manage the business for him.

My parents saw that many professionals were successful, and they realized how valuable education was for me. My brothers and sister had not pursued higher education, and I was committed to it. Back in ninth grade I took the college boards, did well, and I ended up leaving the comfort of high school and entering college when I was sixteen.

There was a lot of competition among my siblings, and we clearly saw our father always working so hard, and those two traits followed me through my adult life. Growing up in a blue-collar family benefited me because it made me strive for success. I think Millennials and Generation Z today have much more than I ever did, but it may be at a deficit because they never have had a hunger, desire, or the necessity to succeed; for me it wasn't optional.

Entering college early was difficult, and, quite frankly, I didn't know there was a college other than Pitt. Pitt was *the* academic institution. It was the one that my parents admired, and I quickly grew to admire it and wanted to go there. I did well on my college boards the first time I took them and received a partial scholarship to Pitt. Several of the reasons why I wanted to go to Pitt was I was bored in high school, I could continue to work, I could stay at home, and at that young age, I wasn't seeing the value of living on campus.

My parents always wanted me to go into medicine; they wanted a doctor in the family. However, the person I remembered the most from my childhood was the local pharmacist because he was accessible and would help treat colds, flu, and upper respiratory infections.

I completed two years of my undergraduate degree, and when I was trying to figure out what I wanted to do with my life, I was able to talk to people in the medical and pharmacy schools. The interaction with the pharmacy school went well and was very practical. I liked the treatment side of medicine, and I could go two more years and find out the chances of getting into medical school, or I could start pharmacy school right away. I entered pharmacy school and never looked back.

At Pitt, it was a four-year program. There were about 100 students, close to where it is today, and it was mix of 40 percent commuters and 60 percent on-campus students. It was science-laden, which I really enjoyed, but I wanted more clinical work. I heard rumblings about Pitt starting a new Doctor of Pharmacy program, but it wasn't going to happen soon, so I knew I would head to Duquesne University after pharmacy school for my PharmD degree.

When I was in pharmacy school, the big retail chain in the area was Thrift Drug. They had a student aid program where they would assist financially with your education, but you had to work for them afterward to have the loan forgiven. I interned for them in one of their worst stores in Clairton, Pennsylvania., but I learned a lot along the way at that store and several others that I rotated through. They started a clinical team that went out and did blood pressure screenings. I thoroughly enjoyed it and the whole clinical component of it. I never spent the money they provided in the form of student aid; I banked it and planned to pay them back if I didn't go to work at Thrift as a registered pharmacist.

I liked the retail store setting, especially when I would go to a remote store in some of the more economically depressed areas. I had a great clinical experience; however, I did not like some aspects of retail pharmacy, such as the front-end merchandising and the stocking of shelves. I gained a respect for community pharmacy that I never had before.

At the end of the program, I decided to forgo working at Thrift Drug to attend Duquesne and earn a PharmD degree. It was a prestigious two-year program; the first year was therapeutic and the second year was a residency. I was a teaching assistant, which helped pay for some of my tuition. It then transitioned in year two to the American Society of Health-System Pharmacists' (ASHP) accredited residency program at Mercy Hospital.

I wanted to stay in Pittsburgh, and at the last second a faculty position opened up at Pitt to create clinical ambulatory programming at a local Department of Veterans Affairs (VA) Hospital. It was the craziest thing to come back two years after I left Pitt, especially because my old professors became my peers.

I was involved with one of the first anticoagulation clinics in the United States, and I was working with physicians and prescribing for patients. The clinic was borne out of nuisance. We were constantly needing to change coumadin dosing for our patients and had to chase down the physicians to get the approvals. Pretty soon, it became clear that we needed to get everyone on board with the fact that the pharmacist needed prescribing privileges for this specific action. We started a traineeship with the support of DuPont, so we brought in physicians, nurses, and pharmacists to train them how to manage anticoagulation. We eventually got Category I clinical privileges, broad prescribing and refill renewals, and we formalized the structure of the clinic, had all the reporting and quality assurance, and it became the beginning of a clinical practice at Pitt. We weren't just recommending changes to physicians; we now had the responsibility and authority to do that.

Specialty Pharmacy

An alumnus came to me about a medication adherence problem he had with a retail pharmacy called Stadtlander's that got into a mail-order business for transplant patients. They needed some assistance on the research side. That morphed into building clinical programs for them, and then I joined them and built a clinical division of thirty employees.

Initially, they were a local retail store. Stadtlander's went national because so many transplant patients got transplants from the medical pioneer, Dr. Thomas Starzel, in Pittsburgh. Then, patients would return home and could not get the drugs, initially cyclosporine, at their local drug stores. Dr. Starzel was considered a godfather of transplants. Stadtlander's filled a void by delivering those products to patients via the mail and by providing a clinical bridge to their physician in Pittsburgh.

The need for specialty pharmacies grew out of the demand of the patients not having access to drugs, or they couldn't afford the drugs, they needed counseling, or they needed social service assistance. Stadtlander's may have been the first large-scale specialty pharmacy in the country, and I was fortunate enough to be there at the beginning.

Stadtlander's was riding the wave of the transplant business, the use of cyclosporine, and the launch of ProGraf (tacromilus). It was also the beginning of the HIV/AIDS epidemic in the 1980s and the early 1990s, when all the new HIV therapies were coming out.

We launched Crixivan® for the entire country as an exclusive provider; it was the only place you could get it. Prior to Crixivan®, there was AZT, but therapeutically, it wasn't even close. Crixivan® was the entity that saved people's lives. It seemed that every person with AIDS, including celebrities and sports figures, got their medicine through Stadtlander's.

As the business grew and became somewhat commoditized, it made sense for one of the big healthcare distribution giants to acquire this platform. Bergen Brunswig eventually acquired Stadtlander's.

After the acquisition, I was promoted. Steve Collis became the president of Stadtlander's, and I got along well with him, initially managing the clinical division and then becoming the interim chief operating officer. The irony is that Collis is now the CEO of Amerisource Bergen, one of the big three drug wholesalers with sales of more than $100 billion.

Eventually, the margins fell out of the business and the book value of the company went down. We had a good run with transplants, HIV, and other disease states, but competition was getting fierce and reimbursement caught up with us. We downsized the company and then put it on the market. It ultimately sold to CVS ProCare.

The margins fell mainly due to the insurance companies and the federal government tightening things up. At one time, in the glory days, reimbursement was wholesale acquisition cost (WAC) plus 50, then it went to WAC plus 20, and then it eventually became average wholesale price (AWP) minus. The whole sector became very competitive, and patients were able to get their products elsewhere. It became a dilemma for the company because our revenues dropped 50 to 60 percent, and the margins dropped even more. We had sold the company to Bergen for more than $400 million, and when we sold to CVS, it was for about $140 million.

Continuing Education

My next career move was continuing education (CE) programs. While working at Pitt and Stadtlander's concurrently, I was responsible for national education programs for the school of pharmacy. I used to do a lot of continuing education programs on the cardiology and anticoagulation side, which generated a lot of revenue for Pitt. I saw that as a business opportunity and started my own Accreditation Council for Pharmacy Education (ACPE) accredited company, which was called University Pharmacotherapy Associates (UPA). We were one of the first independent companies to have ACPE grant accreditation.

Ultimately, I had to decide whether I was going to become a full-time CVS executive or leave CVS and pursue UPA full-time. If I left CVS, I was going to have a long non-compete agreement, so I decided to continue with the university and go full-time with UPA. We created one of the country's biggest pharmacy CE organizations.

At one time, we were probably doing 600 to 800 live regional programs a year. There was another Pitt alum, Lloyd Myers, who was working on an internet company doing education online called CECity, and we were the first to partner with them. They became a tremendous success and eventually sold to Premier Inc.

Path to PANTHERx

I bought a home in Naples, Florida., as a vacation property, but I decided to retire there after three years of back-and-forth travel to Florida. I was still part-time with the University of Pittsburgh, and my plan was to golf, fish, and spend time with my wife. I became bored quickly, and my wife knew I missed the action of running a business.

A couple of my former students wanted to meet and talk about a business idea. One of the students had three retail stores, another was working for Accredo, and the other was working for an independent. They asked if I could help them with a business plan and maybe do something in specialty pharmacy at retail. I looked at their business plan and we discussed where we could truly refocus on patients and bring clinical and true value to society.

We looked at two models. One was working with large chains or independents to create a specialty pharmacy offering for them. The other was focused on the rare disease market. Those were our two possibilities going into this, but we knew we had to create a core specialty business to prove ourselves. We saw such a change in the industry. The three or four mega entities really dominated specialty pharmacy, and we saw a good deal of consolidation and commoditization. This triggered the thought process of: Is there a new niche opportunity in specialty? What started the ball rolling was what we saw emerging from the orphan drug act and the pediatric voucher system. I thought there was going to be an orphan drug niche opening up that didn't really play to the strengths of the big players in the field.

The three partners and I sat down and I explained that this model dates back to when specialty pharmacy began, but with a twist—it is focusing on rare diseases in small populations. If we could establish a specialty pharmacy that could focus on this space and leverage a renewed focus on white glove patient care, we could build a good business. That was the birth of PANTHERx Specialty Pharmacy.

I had no desire to go into business and reassemble a traditional specialty pharmacy with folks who had been in the industry for years. It was these young, ambitious, talented people that intrigued me—individuals who did not know how to fail and didn't have a significant background in specialty pharmacy.

So, we all met at Eat'n Park, which is an iconic restaurant in Pittsburgh, for breakfast, and the concept of PANTHERx Specialty was born. We even chose the name at that breakfast because all of us were Pitt Panthers. We knew it was going to be a long haul.

One of the partners who was heavily involved on the retail side had three retail stores, and he had a conduit through which to gain part of a national payer contract because specialty at retail was becoming a popular item back then. We got business the old-fashioned way. One of the original partners would go out to physician offices to get one patient at a time. That's how it all started.

One thing I learned when I worked at Stadtlander's is that we grew very quickly, and sometimes with uncontrolled growth you lose focus. When you grow too fast, you don't necessarily hire the best people because you don't have the luxury of time. I learned the value of controlled growth and the importance of ensuring the quality of the individuals you hire as you grow.

Another thing I learned from my Stadtlander's days is I created an academic partnership with Pitt. We were the first in the country to start these managed care residencies and specialty certificate programs. We also started partnerships with industry, and I brought all that back to PANTHERx.

I learned the importance of medication compliance at Stadtlander's, too. We knew we had a much higher-risk population. If they weren't adherent, they either rejected an organ, or, in the case of HIV, became resistant, so we knew the stakes were higher. We brought the concept of adherence over from Stadtlander's. Finally, the approach to managing providers and patients with white glove service was brought over to PANTHERx. I learned a lot at Stadtlander's.

We started PANTHERx via bootstrapping. I had a company called RxELENTLESS Capital, which is an angel investment firm. Along with several very successful retired non-healthcare executives, we began starting and feeding several healthcare endeavors and start-ups. The idea was that all the PANTHERx limited partners would get in the game, but RxELENTLESS Capital was going to be on the back end of that to support this endeavor in the event that they needed any substantial funding.

Over time I loaned the company money in an attempt to get the other partners to understand my commitment to them and this company. I did not dilute them with RxELENTLESS Capital. because we knew that we would get much more out of the company by having personnel completely vested in the company versus diluting them out. RxELENTLESS Capital was in the background, and my personal financing, as well as with investments from the other partners, made the company work. Every dollar that we made was reinvested in the company.

When we were working with the angel investors, many of them had seen specialty drugs on TV. Many knew or had an appreciation for how important these new therapies were becoming. All had a keen interest in their own health or their families' health, so the interest was there.

Our elevator speech was, "We see a niche of drugs that presents an opportunity. If we are able to establish PANTHERx as a traditional specialty, and at least get a core base, then we can leverage some of our relationships and get the company going in this niche area."

The most important thing I mentioned to them is that there are more than 7,000 rare diseases, and less than 5 percent have any type of therapy. Ninety-five percent have nothing. The FDA pipeline for these products is robust, not only with orphan drugs but also with the concept of personalized medicine. This is where the future of medicine is, and by the time we got through those three or four sentences, they were completely engaged.

Fortunately, one of the partners had a background in community pharmacy and knew what was involved with state inspections, so he understood the basics of starting a very small business. Another partner had a couple years of experience working with one of the large specialty pharmacies, so he knew the nuances of specialty pharmacy at that time. The third partner, a recent pharmacy school graduate, brought a technology aspect to the company.

We had our basic skill sets needed for running a small company, with the addition of the three operating partners. We also had the ability to create web apps to get on the internet and look much larger than we were. Finally, I brought the contacts, reputation, and the experience base of the past. That was the recipe for the beginning of PANTHERx.

As I mentioned, we initially got patients one at a time. Then we started getting some relationships with small to mid-sized payers where we were either exclusive or semi-exclusive for very small plans that wouldn't get attention from the big guys. Once we got some of those relationships (and they were absolutely critical to us), we delved into a couple of other areas to build up our core base. We started looking at ways to build up our core business in the corrections industry and in 340B business.

Initially, we had to look at other opportunities to build our core platform, not just the rare disease space, so we would be looked at as a legitimate and fiscally sound player. We knew we got there when we were awarded South Carolina's AIDS Drug Assistance Program (ADAP) and won a competitive bid from one of the big specialty pharmacies that was the incumbent.

Still, we were such a tiny entity, nobody knew about us. The biggest issue was keeping morale up for the individuals who had left jobs to come work for us, and the other partners were concerned about making payroll. It was about keeping them optimistic and looking forward. It was easier than I expected because these weren't professionals who had been out for thirty years and had thrown themselves into a risky situation. These were pharmacists who were so young that I don't think they had failure on their minds.

Another issue was dealing with the lack of access to limited distribution drugs (LDDs) where the drugs are very expensive and have a very narrow network. A lot of the oncology drugs are like this where you can only get them at a dozen pharmacies or a couple dozen specialty pharmacies. LDDs were a big challenge for us. We were trying to get providers and payers to understand that even though we didn't have direct access to all the drugs, we were still a complete solution. When we included an LDD supplier in the mix as a partner organization, they sometimes tried to cherry-pick the patient away from us, too. This was a big hurdle for us, and it was nice once we were able to get that behind us and focus on the orphan drug market.

Then our focus was on hiring new employees. Specialty pharma is a high-revenue, low-margin business, so imagine how much revenue you have to make to be able to afford a $100,000 pharmacist. It's pretty amazing; it's millions of dollars. For years, one of the senior partners and I basically volunteered our time. I didn't take a dollar from that company for three or four years to be able to get a foothold.

GROWTH STRATEGY

After seven years of being in business, about 20 percent of our eighty employees are pharmacists or have pharmacy backgrounds, and the rest are more technical or call center in nature. We started an internship immediately and started channeling students through the business, and people became aware of PANTHERx. There are so many specialty pharmacies in Pittsburgh; our talent pool in the area is tremendous, and we have that talent at PANTHERx. We look for individuals who are hard-working, and that's part of being a Pittsburgher, that hard-working mentality. Our goal was to foster that culture to give them the work ethic construct and reinvest in them through training, opportunity, and reward. That's why we have so many satisfied associates. In fact, we were recognized by *Modern Healthcare* as the No. 4 company in terms of employee satisfaction for 2016.

Everything starts with the patient, who receives the product. There is a personal piece of the business, a clinical piece of the business, and a financial piece of the business. If your patients love you, payers, providers, and the orphan drug industry will take notice, and you will grow. Our biggest award to date is that we were recognized as the winner of the Specialty Pharma Patient Choice Awards during the 2017 Asembia Specialty Pharmacy Summit in Las Vegas. No other measure or national recognition could mean more to us.

The rare disease market is primarily manufacturers launching orphan products where it is in everyone's best interest to have a limited or exclusive distribution network. The patients, payers, providers, and the pharmaceutical industry benefit because you have one source of data. A specialty pharmacy partner that can react rapidly to changes in the environment is essential. There aren't thousands of pharmacies where their patients are spread across the country, and it is almost impossible to collectively understand what is going on in that patient base and interact with them in a meaningful way. It's because of this unique relationship that patients and providers are directed to us, because if a patient needs a certain drug or therapy, we are the only source or one of a few places where they can get it.

When a pharmaceutical company launches a product, we are on the phone with all payers to introduce them to this new product, even though they may not have a patient at that time or may never have a patient who needs it. We are educating them clinically and giving them access to this information. When they eventually get a patient, we contract with them so we are in their payer network.

We have become experts in understanding everything surrounding our patients' needs. This includes how to work with payers in terms of what their processes are, getting drugs on formulary, and getting prior authorizations approved for the patient and doctor. We understand the clinical requirements and the evolving standards of care in this patient base. We also understand the organizations like the National Organization of Rare Diseases (NORD), which is an example of a rare disease patient advocacy group, and the financial support they may be able to provide for patients.

We also understand co-pay programs for these patients. If there is a financial shortcoming, we work to understand options for the patients. We work on behalf of the patients to get their medications covered, and if there is a co-pay, then we work with any co-pay program or organization to help. These drugs are so expensive that any component of the cost would financially devastate most patients.

The cost of these life-saving drugs is calculated into the pricing of insurance plans. Insurers have actuarials that derive their mix of patients. If you think about the distribution of patient financial intensities, they anticipate that a select number of patients are going to be at both extremes — some who don't cost them any money and some who are very expensive, and this is built into their rates.

On the other hand, there are so many new orphan and rare disease drugs coming out that we have to be conscious of the fact that it is not an endless resource. We work with payers in that capacity, and we work with providers to educate them about the financial complexities for the patient. There may be ten specialists in the country for a certain disease, and these patients go back home, and we may be the only constant contact with them, so we are constantly discussing the patients' care with the provider.

We are utilizing our resources to let payers know what is coming. They then typically react by granting temporary status, permanent formulary status, or manage it one patient at a time. Again, we collect all of these data on small populations under one roof so we can quickly have statistically valid information about what is happening with patients. We report data back to the pharmaceutical company, a data hub if needed, and sometimes the FDA if there is anything concerning. It works out for everybody.

If a drug is approved for a rare disease and we have a relationship with the biotech partner, we go to payers for approval, find resources for the patient, educate the providers who then provide us with the scripts, get them out flawlessly, and continue to manage the patients and collect data.

Prescriptions most frequently go to the patient, but there are certain drugs that go to the physician's office for the first dose; we are not into the hospital market where we would ship to hospitals. It depends on the drug and what the requirements of the drug and the patient are.

Our target is to be a multi-billion-dollar company by 2022. We are big enough to matter but small enough to care, and that is one of things that is very important to us. We don't have these complex phone trees, and the person you talk to may often be the same person each time you call. You get personal interaction and close follow-up. Infrastructure costs are pretty extraordinary, and our margins are very, very thin, and that is because of the business we are in—and we are constantly reinvesting.

RIPE FOR ACQUISITION

We have been approached hundreds of times for acquisition. Honestly, it happens three or four times a week, believe it or not.

Our position is we are not for sale. We keep an open discussion with the banking industry; you always keep the industry close at hand and keep them generally aware of what's going on, but the big players fully understand the PANTHERx approach. For us to sell at this point doesn't make any sense because the real value that we bring is still to come.

In trying to be a great company, sometimes you lose sight of the fact that you have a business. There have probably been one or two situations in which we made decisions that limited our growth, and we didn't take some risks due to having such a long-term vision in place.

One of the things we decided not to get into was the distribution of any of the scheduled drugs. There are numerous drugs coming out on the narcotic and pain relief side in which we have had opportunities to be a major specialty pharmacy partner. I fully recognize that if you are in cancer pain or chronic pain, it can be devastating. On the other hand, there has been much written about our narcotic abuse epidemic. It has led to an equal amount of regulation, which is probably warranted, but the cancer patient may suffer in all this. We decided not to go down that path because there were too many landmines.

PASSION FOR PHARMACY

I don't have an exit strategy because I do this more as a passion. I have been with the University of Pittsburgh for thirty years, and I love working with young, talented individuals. My goal with this company was to give the individuals I work with an opportunity that they couldn't get anywhere else. In terms of an exit strategy, it was more about them. However, in developing PANTHERx, one thing I learned from starting a half-dozen companies is the best way to be successful in a business is to build it like you are building it for a sale, because if you are building it for a sale, that means you are doing all the right things in the business world. You are reinvesting in your company, you are building an infrastructure, you are growing smartly and are scalable, and you are doing all the right things that make it attractive to the investment world or to other big players.

The reality is that I have no intent of doing a quick sale of the company. We also have a commitment that until we become a billion-dollar company, we won't even bring it up at a board meeting. However, there may be an opportunity to gain some efficiencies by being part of something else. I am not saying we won't entertain that idea, but we will be very discerning about it.

Another way we add value is by making sure we are not a big box corporate culture and are empowering every employee, using their talents, and making them feel good about themselves. It is kind of the Steve Jobs philosophy of hiring talented people to run the business and not telling them what to do. That is what PANTHERx is about. It is a group of individuals without strict borders and boundaries. It's not an organization that makes decisions based upon the hierarchy of a title.

We were named as the fastest-growing company in Pittsburgh in 2016 and 2017 by the *Pittsburgh Business Times*. On a national level, *INC* magazine ranked us as the ninth-fastest growing company in the country in 2016 and the fastest-growing healthcare company. With growth comes the need for a dynamic business environment and a constant focus on our strategy. That is what we deliver.

Again, it is keeping true to our core mission, which is to be focused on rare diseases and other devastating conditions. There will continue to be new therapies for devastating, rare diseases. We need to focus on continuing to get either exclusive or semi-exclusive relationships in which there is a steady flow of patients who have high-cost therapies.

PREPARING FOR THE FUTURE

Early in my career, in 1991, I finished my MBA at Pitt while I was on faculty and saw the extreme value in understanding the business side of the world. I saw an immense opportunity for the development of leaders in the business of medicine, but we were doing a terrible job at it.

All the time I was at Pitt, we worked with the business school to try to create a dual degree program, but from the way the academic calendars and scheduling worked out, it never made financial sense because we were never able to shave off a term of tuition doing a combined PharmD MBA

It was the students coming out of the PharmD program that I would have in some of my entrepreneurial business classes. I encouraged them to earn an MBA. Two of the people I started PANTHERx with went back and got their MBAs, but I knew there was a better way to do it. I got together with my colleagues in the business school and we started brainstorming. I got together with industry leaders who were my friends, like Larry Merlo from CVS, as well as a half-dozen other accomplished individuals, and we all discussed that it would be great to create an executive pharmacy business administration program where we use the best of the graduate school business and pharmacy programs, all grounded in the practical applications of the business world. We agreed to put something together that was feasible; a one-year program, something for individuals who had enough experience to have the context to understand the concepts.

The business part of the curriculum would have a twist with medicines, and the pharmacy side of the curriculum would have the discipline of business. We would allow for personalized tracks, including specialty pharmacy, which was near and dear to my heart. The other was community pharmacy, which was near and dear to Merlo. So, we started the Master of Science in Pharmacy Administration (MS-PBA) program. Dean Patricia Kroboth was open-minded and supportive about it, giving me the room to do it the way that we wanted to do it, which isn't typical in academia.

We built the one-year MS-PBA program as an executive program, launched it, and graduated our first class of seven students in 2016. We didn't want to pattern it off of anyone else's program, and no one else was doing anything exactly like it. Instead of a "push" recruitment strategy of pushing our credible graduates out and having them find jobs, we used a pull strategy in sending the founder's employees to the executive program then having them return to our organizations as our future leaders.

We just launched our institutional track, which is a hospital pharmacy leadership track. We have additional tracks planned, too. It was a collection of experiences that told us to create something that we knew we needed, and it was so simple in concept and no one was doing it, and we were fortunate enough to have the environment in which to create it.

The first class was all pharmacy students, as is the second class. However, we are not limiting it because as you know, most people in the C-suite aren't pharmacists, so anyone could be part of the program. Recruitment for next year looks good because we have our first class out and helping to recruit for us. We are probably looking at 30 percent of the class next year being non-pharmacists. We don't consider any applicants unless they have been in the working world for three years. We want to set up students for success, not just to pad our enrollment.

LEADERS

My Favorite Quotes About Leadership

1. Leaders aren't born, they are made—and they are made just like anything else, through hard work, and that's the price we'll pay to achieve that goal, or any goal. —Vince Lombardi

2. Leadership is the art of getting someone else to do something you want done because he wants to do it. —Dwight D. Eisenhower

3. Great leaders are almost always great simplifiers who can cut through argument, debate, and doubt to offer a solution everybody can understand. —General Colin Powell

4. Never tell people how to do things. Tell them what to do and they will surprise you with their ingenuity. —General George Patton

5. No man will make a great leader who wants to do it all himself, or to get all the credit for doing it. —Andrew Carnegie

6. A leader takes people where they want to go. A great leader takes people where they don't necessarily want to go, but ought to be. —Rosalynn Carter

7. I start with the premise that the function of leadership is to produce more leaders, not more followers. —Ralph Nader

8. The nation will find it hard to look up to the leaders who are keeping their ears to the ground. — Winston Churchill

9. Leadership is the capacity to translate vision into reality. — Warren Bennis

10. Education is the mother of leadership. — Wendell Wilkie

11. If your actions inspire others to dream more, learn more, do more, and become more, you are a leader. — John Quincy Adams

12. Lead and inspire people. Don't try to manage and manipulate people. Inventories can be managed, but people must be led. — Ross Perot

13. Leadership is unlocking people's potential to become better. — Bill Bradley

14. Not the cry, but the flight of the wild duck leads the flock to fly and follow. — Chinese proverb

15. A good plan executed now is better than a perfect plan executed next week. — General George Patton

LEADERS

Their pathway to success and career
fulfillment using their pharmacy degrees
*with words of advice
from each leader*

CHAPTER 11

BECOME THE CEO AND LEADER OF A
PROFESSIONAL PHARMACY ORGANIZATION

Paul W. Abramowitz

CEO of ASHP

I grew up in Cincinnati, Ohio, and therefore consider myself a Midwesterner. My parents instilled in me the desire to attend college, and I graduated with a double major in biology and chemistry. It was not until later that I developed an interest in pharmacy and obtained BS Pharm and PharmD degrees, thus establishing my career path.

Prior to becoming chief executive officer (CEO) of the American Society of Health-System Pharmacists (ASHP) six years ago, I worked in hospitals and health systems for thirty-four years. I served as associate hospital director for professional services and chief pharmacy officer at the University of Iowa Hospitals and Clinics, and professor at the University of Iowa College of Pharmacy. I also held prior positions as director of pharmacy and associate professor at the Medical College of Virginia and the University of Minnesota.

I am often asked by students and residents what led to my current position as CEO of ASHP and if I set my sights on this early in my career. My response is that the thought of becoming ASHP CEO never entered my mind until many years later. However, an early mentor of mine encouraged me to become active in ASHP as a volunteer. I credit ASHP with instilling in me a strong desire to not only do my job, but also to creatively seek ways to do it better. Having the good fortune to have excellent mentors, I was advised to take on new opportunities and additional responsibilities when possible, which I readily accepted.

As time went by, I found that I had a strong desire, not only to provide patient care, but also to develop new and innovative ways to justify and expand clinical pharmacy services. I then spent much of my career trying to do just that. My mentors also taught me that you should try to multiply your effectiveness by contributing your ideas and successes broadly to the rest of the profession. Thus, I and my teams have always tried to actively combine practice, teaching, and research that focused on improving outcomes of care and reducing cost through quality pharmacy care, developing new care models, reducing adverse drug events, and expanding comprehensive pharmacy care to the ambulatory setting.

My advice for new graduates and residents is as follows:

- First and foremost, put extensive effort into your practice, keeping the patient at its center.

- Take the time to observe what is going on around you, and take on additional responsibilities by increasing your efficiency.

- Become a part of great teams of individuals and contribute to and benefit from their wisdom.

- Be creative and innovative, and look for ways to share what you are doing across the entire profession.

- Find and seek out mentors who can impart their knowledge to you, and find others whom you can mentor.

- Never be satisfied with the status quo, and continually look for ways to enhance your professional activities to improve care.

- Give back and become part of a professional organization.

CHAPTER 12

BE THE FOUNDER AND LEADER OF A
PROFESSIONAL PHARMACY ORGANIZATION

James G. Alexander

CEO and Founder, Industry Pharmacists Organization (IPhO)

"Once a pharmacist, always a pharmacist." This is one of my favorite quotes from a long-time friend and mentor Joseph D. Williams, a Remington Medal winner and highly successful pharmaceutical industry CEO. Like Mr. Williams, I consider myself to be a pharmacist first in everything I do, even though I never practiced in traditional pharmacy.

A long time ago, I chose to apply the valuable skills I learned in pharmacy school to other exciting professional endeavors. Among other things, in my career I have been a pharmaceutical executive, an academician, a general manager of an online CME company, an author, an entrepreneur, the CEO of a professional organization, and an executive recruiter. They don't teach you how to fulfill any of those roles in medicinal chemistry class. But, as it turns out, the

PharmD degree is so versatile that you can accomplish just about anything if you put your mind to it!

I held down three different pharmacy jobs simultaneously during pharmacy school in Nebraska, one of them under the employ of Daniel Moravec, Sr., who first introduced me to pharmacy. I liked them all, yet I found myself searching for other career alternatives. In that search, I applied for a summer internship with a major pharmaceutical company, and it changed the course of my professional and personal life. That internship represented the beginning of my amazing journey into alternative career paths.

After graduating from pharmacy school, I became one of the first PharmDs ever to participate in an industry fellowship. At that time, the PharmD degree was still new, and pharmaceutical company employers were unsure about the different roles we could play within industry. The program springboarded my industry career, and in just ten years after my fellowship, I rose to the level of vice president at Warner-Lambert, which at the time was a Fortune 100 company. Our company developed and launched Lipitor (atorvastatin), and during an incredible run it became one of the most successful pharmaceutical products in history. This did not escape Pfizer's notice, and they decided to acquire our company.

Although Pfizer made me a great offer to stay with the company, I wasn't eager to return to corporate life, so I decided to pursue a road less traveled. That led me back to the Rutgers Fellowship Program, where I had gotten my start in industry. During ten years as the first director of the Rutgers Pharmaceutical Industry Fellowship Institute, I trained 400 PharmDs who now work in industry, founded two elective courses, wrote fifty publications, and taught/mentored thousands of future pharmacists. It will always be remembered as one of the most rewarding periods in my career.

At the time, it occurred to me that there was still no home in the profession of pharmacy for pharmacists working in industry. As a result, I decided to found the Industry Pharmacists Organization (IPhO), and in just a few short years, it has become a very successful organization. It has been amazingly rewarding to create an online, virtual organization like IPhO starting with nothing but an idea and a blank piece of paper.

Although IPhO's journey is just beginning, as of this writing we have fifty student chapters, a national community encompassing 450 PharmD fellows, and a following of 10,000 pharmacists working in the U.S. pharmaceutical industry. Co-authoring a book about industry fellowships has been just one example of my unique experiences with IPhO.

I am also active in executive-level search, helping to place professionals into senior-level positions in the pharmaceutical industry. As executive vice president of Strawn Arnold & Associates, I continue to follow one of my passions by helping others identify and pursue their professional journeys in the pharmaceutical industry.

Although my path has been a non-traditional one, I have remained a licensed pharmacist for more than thirty years. Who knows, maybe one day I will complete the journey and engage in direct patient care! But even if I don't, I will have enjoyed an amazing career as an entrepreneurial pharmacist. I know that what I do every day helps patients, just as I was trained to do in pharmacy school; I am just doing it in my own unique way. After all, "Once a pharmacist, always a pharmacist!"

Two tips for student pharmacists:

- "Life moves pretty fast. If you don't stop and look around once in a while, you could miss it." As it turns out, Ferris Bueller's famous line applies to professional life, too. Don't get caught up in the exam-to-exam life. There are a lot of things you can do with a PharmD degree if you take the time to look around.

- Put yourself out there. After many years, you can comfortably look in the rearview mirror and reflect upon the experiences that shaped your life—the decisions you made, the people you met, which of the roads less traveled you took. But early in your career you are only looking out of the windshield, so experience everything you can get your hands on. Many experiences will have little yield, but some of those encounters will mean everything to you. You just can't predict which ones!

CHAPTER 13

BECOME AN EXECUTIVE WITH A
PHARMACY BENEFITS MANAGEMENT (PBM) COMPANY

Jody H. Allen

Vice President
Express Scripts

My job did not exist when I went to pharmacy school at the University of North Carolina at Chapel Hill (UNC-CH). If someone had told me I would become an executive with a large pharmacy benefit management (PBM) company, I would not have known what a PBM was or what kind of business a PBM conducted. I was determined to be a clinical pharmacist—to work in academia or an acute care setting with physicians and other clinicians. I was a "clinical cowgirl" and wanted to use my pharmacy knowledge to improve patient care. So, after graduating from UNC-CH, I headed to Virginia Commonwealth University (VCU) in Richmond, Virginia., to get my PharmD. My graduating class size was four students!

After graduating from VCU, I was one of the first PharmDs to practice in an acute care setting outside of an academic teaching hospital in Virginia. We worked to decentralize the pharmacy, put pharmacists in patient care areas, and move them out of the basement. I became involved with local and national pharmacy organizations and served as president of the Virginia Society of Hospital Pharmacists, served as a delegate to American Society of Health-System Pharmacists (ASHP) for many years, and was appointed to several committees at ASHP and Academy of Managed Care Pharmacy (AMCP). I found active participation in professional organizations rewarding and made some lifelong relationships in pharmacy.

After practicing in acute care for twelve years, I began to think about my next step. Did I want to move into an administrative position in acute care or do something else in pharmacy? A colleague contacted me and asked if I would be interested in a position in managed care, using many of the same principles from acute care with drug utilization review, formulary management, and clinical consultation for health plans. So, I began the next step of my career—working at a pharmacy benefits management organization.

I worked hard, formed new relationships (including with programmers), developed a clinical call center, and worked on sales strategies and client relationships. It was a new world. I learned by doing and sometimes by making mistakes, recognizing them, and learning from them. I stretched outside of my comfort zone, learned new skills, and entered leadership roles. I moved from my original PBM, First Health Services, to another PBM, Medco, which was later acquired by Express Scripts.

As a result of hard work, staying current on practice, having passion for clients, and leading others (teamwork), I was able to become the lead for the clinical team and was eventually promoted to vice president, clinical account management. Along the way, I was also fortunate to be appointed to the Virginia Board of Pharmacy, where I have served for seven years, including as chairman of the board.

When I speak with students or other new pharmacists about working for a PBM, they ask, "What pearls do you have for success?" My pearls are as follows:

- Find your professional passion and get involved, not as a member, but in active engagement. You will make new friends and develop lifelong professional relationships, which will serve you well in your career.

- Be open to new opportunities and consistently network with others.

- Prepare yourself by taking on varied and challenging assignments to develop new skills; you will find this develops confidence.

- Whatever you do, do it well. Always come prepared to work or to meetings, and no matter how many presentations you have done, practice every time.

CHAPTER 14

BECOME THE CEO AND LEADER OF A PHARMACY FOUNDATION

Stephen J. Allen

CEO
ASHP Research and Education Foundation

Do you recall those times growing up when you were dreaming about which career would be "something that you wanted to do the rest of your life?" I'll admit that as a child I wanted to be a sanitation worker so I could hang on the back of the truck. As I grew older, I wanted to be a pilot, but my fear of heights and eyesight issues stymied that dream.

Ultimately, working in a corner drug store for a wonderful man who was a pharmacist sold me on a career in pharmacy. Neither of my parents had a college education or could afford to pay for college, and yet I selected a career that required more than five years of education that I would need to pay for myself.

Very determined, I set my sights on my education and quickly realized that I wanted to practice pharmacy in hospitals. I sensed that

I was suited to lead a pharmacy team rather than become a clinical pharmacist, so I chose graduate school and a two-year pharmacy residency after my pharmacy degree to pave the way for my career path.

At twenty-four years of age, my first job was an assistant director of pharmacy position, and that set me on a path to become director of pharmacy for a twenty-year period where I led pharmacy practice in a tertiary care children's hospital, a community hospital, a university teaching hospital, and in a managed care organization. Along the way, I was involved in professional organizations at the state and national levels, networking, and showcasing my ability to team with others and to lead endeavors that would benefit those committed to transforming pharmacy practice into a patient-centered profession.

So, how does one make a radical change in one's career to leave active practice to become an executive of a nonprofit research and education foundation? The simple answer is that opportunities arise for those who work hard, showcase their abilities to collaborate and lead, and who have a vision for advancing their profession. Each position I had in the hospital setting had unique challenges that enabled me to team with others, and that was also the case with my professional association work.

When you lead with a caring, collaborative, passionate style, and your results are evident to others, doors open for you that you might not necessarily anticipate. In my case, leaders of the American Society of Health-System Pharmacists (ASHP) organization determined that my experience and professional approach would be ideal for expanding and transforming the ASHP Foundation, an organization dedicated to helping pharmacists advance practice.

I've been blessed with the opportunity to spend the better part of twenty years raising funds and securing the support of individuals to give back to the pharmacy profession.

As you tackle the issues in your career in pharmacy, I recommend you consider some of these perspectives gleaned from my experiences:

- Realize and embrace the notion that your pharmacy education is just the base for a commitment to lifelong learning. You must continually invest in expanding your knowledge and learning new skills to be more effective in both life skills and professional roles. When you do, new opportunities arise, because people are watching!

- If you ever begin to view your employment as "just a job," then you need to reconsider your circumstances and reinvest in the activities that will re-energize you or lead you to move in a different direction where you can pursue your passions.

- Remember that the more you give, the more you will reap. Get involved in professional organizations, mentor those who work for you, and commit to teaching pharmacy students and residents. The personal and professional rewards are immeasurably magnificent.

- Be resilient, because challenges will inevitably confront you. It is equally important to react with patience, poise, and commitment to plan your actions in responding to these challenges.

What you accomplish in your career, the relationships that you establish along the way, and the lessons you learn set the stage for the wonderful opportunities that evolve when you transition from full-time work to part-time engagements or retirement. You are setting the table for new professional engagements and/or engaging with those special people in your life with whom you wish to spend your time, many of whom will be colleagues. Please know that if you think I can help you by sharing additional perspectives or insights, feel free to contact me. I am committed to giving back whenever I can because I have been so blessed in life and in my career.

CHAPTER 15

BECOME THE DEAN OF A SCHOOL OF PHARMACY

Jerry L. Bauman

Dean
University of Illinois at Chicago College of Pharmacy

Despite having no experience or relatives in the profession, I chose pharmacy instead of medicine or chemistry because, respectively, I have a touchy vagal reflex around blood, and I had broken nearly every piece of glassware in organic lab. During a successful (grade-wise) but aimless time in undergraduate pharmacy school at the University of Illinois, I happened upon (or they happened upon me) two very influential mentors: Dr. Henri Manasse and Dr. Richard Hutchinson, who saw potential and ambition in me where I did not.

Both encouraged me to continue my education via differing routes without apparent worry about my empty wallet. This was during the early days of clinical pharmacy, and through my experiences at the University of Illinois Hospital during "clinical" rotations, I found my passion.

Dr. Hutchinson, through varying methods, essentially forced me to return to not only get my post-baccalaureate PharmD, but he demanded that I attend the University of Missouri at Kansas City (UMKC). At this time, the UMKC PharmD program was rigorous (to say the least) and attracted some of the top pharmacists in the nation. I loved (almost) every minute of it; anyone who went through that program will attest to the unforgettable and valuable education and overall experience.

There, too, I found mentors and role models who helped shape my thinking and career forever.

I returned to Illinois to begin my first academic tenure track position, not realizing that being on the tenure track required substantial research productivity and funding. I had little to no research training, but I liked to write and enjoyed the thrill of publishing a paper and making a contribution.

At Kansas City, I developed a keen interest in the treatment of arrhythmias, and, fortunately at Illinois, there was an internationally recognized group of arrhythmia physician scientists led by the late Ken Rosen, one of the fathers of invasive electrophysiology. I'm not sure they ever figured out what a clinical pharmacist was, but I'm not sure they cared as long as you could keep their hours, contribute to the care of their patients, and do meaningful research. So, I learned clinical research methods on the job, with their great patience and assistance. I developed a unique (at the time) interest in drug-induced arrhythmias and published several visible papers in this area.

This initial success led to other projects and an increased sophistication in my methodology, including a few influential works on cocaine-induced arrhythmias/sudden death. I was promoted and tenured, and other opportunities in the profession, such as national committees and positions, ensued. Young, talented pharmacists wanted to come and train with me, and they went on to have successful careers. These days were probably the most personally rewarding of my career.

Just about the time I found the need to retool and was considering a sabbatical to learn new methods, I was asked to be a department head in the college. Due to the faculty we recruited and retained, the department thrived both in terms of clinical pharmacy practice and research.

After nearly a decade as head, I was asked to be dean. Based on observing past deans, frankly, this was a job that I didn't aspire to, but I also didn't want anyone else to do it! After a decade as dean, I have thrived and our college has done well and is highly regarded. During these ten years, I have also served on an interim basis as provost and vice chancellor for academic affairs at the University of Illinois at Chicago (UIC) for a year and vice president of health affairs for the University of Illinois system for more than two years. As I came to find out, being dean is the best academic administrative job in a university, so I decided I wanted to return to it after experiencing these opportunities. I have some advice for those who want a career in pharmacy academic administration:

- First and foremost, hire good people and surround yourself with those who are smarter than you. People drive the success of an academic unit. They need to be loyal and people whom you respect and trust to be able to tell you when you are screwing up — and you should listen to them.
- You must say "yes" to opportunities despite insecurities about whether you can succeed. As you can see from my

career, I was not trained to do most of these jobs except that of being a clinical pharmacist.

- Create a workplace environment where employees like to come to work; there has to be some fun in the place, right? Happy people are successful and productive people.

- In academic administration, you must put the organization first—not parts of it—and certainly not your personal desires. Time to give up pursuing personal successes. Remember, it's the faculty and students who drive the place.

- Play nice with others. Ever notice how the jerk in the group struggles to do well? In my opinion, social skills and the ability to work easily with others and in groups is often more important than your knowledge and technical skills.

- Manage down first. Academics is not like working for IBM—almost nothing can be done dictatorially. You have to have the troops behind you to get things done. Obviously, you want to have the support of your boss, but if the college faculty are behind you, you are in a strong position.

- Work closely and collaboratively with the dean of the College of Medicine and its leadership. There's no mistaking that they are the big dogs in a health science center.

CHAPTER 16

COMBINE A PHARMACY CAREER WITH ENTREPRENEURIAL VENTURES

Katasha S. Butler

Veterans Health Administration
Founder, The Conciergerie for Events
Founder, Social Event Venue

Growing up, one of my favorite games to play with my sister and my cousins was "Office." The house we lived in had an enclosed front porch with large windows that pushed out. The porch was the "office" and the "customers" would walk up to the windows with their requests. It is such a fond memory — us acting like professional adults, shuffling papers and answering phones, attending to our non-existent "business." As I reflect on those times, two words pop into my head: organization and imagination. I had both of those in spades, and it foreshadowed what I would be doing as an adult.

I chose pharmacy as a career as a sophomore in high school. My mother told me recently she always thought I was going to be a judge — apparently, in fifth grade that's what I told her. I was in a gifted program for most of my primary education, and everyone thought medical school was my destiny. But bodily fluids and I could never be friends, so I knew that was out. I chose pharmacy and stuck with it. I excelled in math and science, but I also liked home economics, where we could design and sew our own clothes.

In pharmacy school, you could often find me sitting in Therapeutics class flipping through the latest *Martha Stewart Living* or *InStyle* magazine, or planning a classmate's wedding and designing invitations. Still, I had no idea that my future would call for me to eventually start an event-planning agency and open an event venue. I planned my first full wedding for complete strangers when I was doing my clinical rotations.

My love of fashion, design, and parties led me to voluntarily plan events for the many civic organizations of which I was a part. This was an important step because it allowed me to hone my skills. It took the encouragement of a dear friend to challenge me to take the leap and make it a real business. He challenged me regarding how I talked about what I did and how I needed to start charging money for my work. At that time, I was in a high-pressure corporate job in the managed care sector with lots of responsibilities and travel; it was during that time that I built my first business. I recall staying up until 5:00 a.m. creating my own website and then going to work at my "real" job at 8:00 a.m.

Being a pharmacist helped me finance my dreams. I didn't have to worry about how I was going to pay my bills while still growing my fledgling business. I didn't take any loans, even while gutting and remodeling the event venue to make it operational and pretty. Due to my successful career, I could ride out the highs and lows of a startup. I'm not sure that if the circumstances were different I would have two businesses today—as I said, it takes perseverance and money to ride out the startup phase. I may have become too risk-adverse to open the banquet hall if I weren't working.

I'm also not sure I would ever quit working as a pharmacist. It is a career that I enjoy immensely—especially in my current environment—and, frankly, it took a lot of work and elbow grease to get here. However, I am a serial entrepreneur who always has something in the hopper, so who knows if my next big thing will take me out of pharmacy for good. Right now, I love promoting the practice of pharmacy as a PGY1 residency coordinator, a member of the Butler University College of Pharmacy Board of Visitors, and the occasional pharmacology and entrepreneurship lecturer.

Seven is the number of completion, so I have seven tips for pharmacy graduates who want to combine a pharmacy career with an entrepreneurial business venture:

- Entrepreneurism and working for yourself is considered very "sexy" these days. Don't let the advice of others cause you to quit your day job in this hard-earned pharmacy profession.

- Take full advantage of the flexibility that a pharmacy career offers. You can work days, nights, weekends only, part-time, etc., to support yourself and work on your dream business endeavors.

- When you are thinking about starting any business, you must constantly ask yourself, "Is what I'm doing or want to do adding value?" If people don't see the value in your product or service, they won't pay for it.

- Mind your pennies. When starting a new business, it's common to want all the associated collateral: logo shirts, pens, magnets, and folders! That is a colossal drain and waste of your financial resources. In time, it will all come.

- Everyone is not your customer. Sometimes, I price myself out of business to avoid headaches down the line, and it's OK. Time is worth more than money.

- I'm a sucker for innovation. "Keep moving forward" is my mantra. Others may not understand your new business right away, but trust that they will eventually catch on.

- There will always be a gaggle of people who won't like you or your product or service for no apparent reason at all. Don't let the desire to be liked guide your decisions. No one will be happy about it in the end.

CHAPTER 17

BECOME A MEMBER OF CONGRESS

*The Only Pharmacist in Congress, Proudly Serving
Georgia's First Congressional District*

Earl L. "Buddy" Carter

**Congressman
The United States House of Representatives**

My dream in high school was to be a star athlete. However, the cards were stacked against me: I was short and slow. My junior year of high school I told my dad that if a football recruiter from Nebraska or Oklahoma didn't come to see me, I would look into a new career. Unfortunately, those scouts never showed up for me, so I started looking for jobs around my hometown of Port Wentworth, Georgia. I landed a job as a delivery driver at a pharmacy and immediately knew that I wanted to have a career in pharmacy as a pharmacist. I then went to school to pursue this dream. I graduated from Young Harris College and then earned my bachelor of science degree in pharmacy from the University of Georgia.

People often ask how I became interested in public service with my background. With my extroverted personality, I have always felt a need to be involved. In high school, I held leadership roles in my church, and in college I was the president of the freshman class at Young Harris College. When I first opened my own pharmacy in a small community in 1988, I became extremely involved in the community government. I served as a member of the city council and eventually as mayor of Pooler, Georgia. From there, I became involved in state government, serving two terms in the Georgia House of Representatives. I was then elected to the Georgia Senate and served until I was elected to the United States House of Representatives in 2015.

My personal experience as a pharmacist for more than thirty years has been of great advantage to me in Congress because healthcare issues are always prevalent. I am able to draw from the experiences of my patients, good or bad, when it comes to making healthcare decisions because I have seen firsthand how the healthcare system works in real life. Being the only pharmacist in Congress also helps me to be an advocate for my fellow pharmacists because I know the value of our profession. I often say the pharmacist is the most underutilized and undervalued profession in the United States. We must advocate so this is no longer the case.

When I have the privilege to speak with pharmacy students, who are the future of our profession, a few words of advice I always share include:

- Be involved! You are among the best and the brightest students, and we need you to be involved on all levels. Whether it be a neighborhood association, a school council, a city council, or even in Congress — we need you!

- Choose a pharmacy career path that you love, because you will be doing it the rest of your life. Whether it be hospital, community, or an atypical pharmacy career path, try everything and find where your passion lies. Pharmacists are in a unique position to make real differences in health care. I challenge you to find your niche, put 110 percent into whatever you choose to do, and be agents of change.

CHAPTER 18

BECOME THE EDITOR OF AJHP

The Road to Becoming a Journal Editor

Daniel J. Cobaugh

Editor of the *American Journal of Health System Pharmacists*
(AJHP)

Community. Retail. Hospital. These were the predominant, prac-tice-based career options for pharmacists when I was completing my bachelor's degree in pharmacy at the University of Pittsburgh in the mid-1980s. Clinical pharmacy, at that point not much beyond its adolescence, offered a limited number of opportunities because it hadn't yet developed into what it is today. Confronted with this landscape of limited options and not yet having discovered my passion, I struggled to envision my future in the profession.

Everything changed in fall 1985 when, on an extraordinarily ordi-nary day, an energetic young faculty member, Edward Krenzelok, PharmD, bounded into our fourth-year drug information course to lecture about clinical toxicology and poison centers. His energy and passion were palpable, and I was transfixed. Soon after, I contacted

Dr. Krenzelok with a formal letter, as was the standard approach in those days before email, and he promptly responded with his own letter. The result was a three-month internship at the Pittsburgh Poison Center in the summer of 1986, which was career-altering.

That internship drove my decision to pursue a PharmD degree and a hospital pharmacy residency with an eye toward a clinical toxicology fellowship. Soon after starting the fellowship, I met the poison center's medical director, Sandra Schneider, MD, who, like Dr. Krenzelok, would become a lifelong mentor and friend. After the fellowship, I took a position with Dr. Schneider as the coordinator of the toxicology treatment program at the University of Pittsburgh Medical Center and as a faculty member at the University of Pittsburgh School of Pharmacy. In 1993, when Dr. Schneider became the chair of the new department of emergency medicine at the University of Rochester, I joined her there to oversee the emergency medicine research program and to become the director of the Finger Lakes Poison and Drug Information Center. I was living my dream of being a pharmacist and a clinical toxicologist.

I didn't recognize or completely understand them at the time, but I had at least three characteristics that were affecting my career choices. First, I had an interest in pursuing answers to questions. I recall a casual conversation I had in the poison center with one of the emergency medicine residents, a brilliant young physician named Jim McCabe, about the mechanism and treatment of tricyclic antidepressant toxicity. "Since these drugs affect the sodium channels, might hypertonic saline serve as a better antidote than sodium bicarbonate?" Off we went to the lab to test our question in a pig model. On a similar note, Dr. Krenzelok and I debated the pharmacokinetic differences between oral and intravenous ethanol when they were used to treat methanol and ethylene glycol toxicity. An absolute bioavailability study comparing the two administration routes ensued. This desire to answer questions through research — whether innate or learned through my exposure to talented clinician scientists — was pivotal in my professional choices.

Second, I recognized the importance of information dissemination as a means of changing practice. This took the form of serving as a faculty member in education programs for various types of health professional colleagues, presenting poster and platform research presentations, and authoring journal articles and book chapters.

One example that stands out is our work at the University of Rochester to establish one of the first emergency department (ED) research enrollment programs in the United States. This program was the foundation for many successful ED-based research initiatives at the University of Rochester, but my colleagues and I recognized its greater potential to change the face of emergency medicine research.

The obvious next step was to publish a description of the program in an emergency medicine journal. Imagine my delight when, during a recent visit to the ED at George Washington University Hospital for a wrist fracture, I was approached by an "emergency medicine enroller" to participate in an ultrasound study — almost twenty years after that article was published! Our efforts made a difference. This deep desire to facilitate the sharing of knowledge and experiences has been a common thread throughout my career, and although it was not a consideration in my early career plans, it is the bedrock for journal editors.

This leads to the third characteristic that has influenced my career decisions: a strong desire to channel my energy into meaningful activities that will truly make a difference for patients and healthcare professionals as they provide care for their patients. One of my most profound professional experiences was my service on the University of Rochester's Research Subjects Review Board (RSRB), which was the university's investigational review board (IRB).

During my time on the RSRB, we were confronted with some of the most challenging situations that an IRB could encounter, including the tragic death of an undergraduate student during her participation as a volunteer in a medical research study, and the review of the research protocols for RU486, later marketed as the abortifacient mifepristone. These experiences as an IRB member helped me understand the critical role of these committees in protecting human subjects in the research process and subsequently informed my actions as a grant officer and as an editor.

While at the American Association of Poison Control Centers — my next career stop after the University of Rochester — I was responsible for implementing the nationwide toll-free telephone number for poison control centers and leading the development of guidelines for the pre-hospital triage of poisoning victims. Consistent with my desire to make meaningful contributions, I believe these activities made a real difference in others' lives, and they provided me with experience, knowledge, and insights that I've called upon in my role as an editor.

Upon joining the American Society of Health-System Pharmacists (ASHP) staff, advancing the research and publishing aspects of my career wasn't top of mind. Instead, I focused on supporting ASHP members as they worked to provide the best possible care for their patients. Nonetheless, within six months of joining ASHP, opportunities to participate in two transformational practice changes — improving medication-related continuity of care and advancing pharmacy practice in the ED — presented themselves.

While working on these initiatives, I drew heavily from my experiences with research, guideline development, education programs, and journal publishing as we used multi-pronged approaches to achieve our goals. About two years after joining the ASHP staff, I had the opportunity to become the director of research for the ASHP Research and Education Foundation, where during an eleven-year period I oversaw a practice-based research grant program that awarded more than $3 million in research grants and focused on new investigator development through numerous educational offerings.

In January 2015, I became the fifth editor in chief of *AJHP* in its almost seventy-five-year history. My experiences as a researcher, research program director, IRB member, association staff member, and grant officer uniquely prepared me for this position. In 1985, as I was struggling to find a professional identity, I couldn't have imagined the circuitous path that would lead to this opportunity of a lifetime. In retrospect, I recognize the common elements that guided me throughout my career. As you begin your professional journey, I hope the following tips will help guide you to a passion-driven career in pharmacy:

- Be reflective and introspective about those professional activities that bring you the greatest fulfillment and ignite your passion for your profession.

- Identify individuals who can become lifelong mentors and trusted friends, because they will be critical to your development, both professional and personal.

- Recognize professional opportunities and pursue them with vigor.

- Don't be afraid of change; embrace it. You will be enriched by even the most difficult experiences.

CHAPTER 19

BECOME AN EXECUTIVE AT A MAJOR DRUG WHOLESALER

Christopher T. Dimos

Senior Vice President, Strategy and Business Development
McKesson Corporation

I was blessed to be born into a family of entrepreneurs. My great grandfather, grandfather, and father all owned and operated our family restaurant business. As Greek immigrants, it was a fantastic way to be able to provide for our family and be an integral part of the community.

Sometime between second and third grade in elementary school, I began my restaurant career. I was an official greeter and the cleaner of all things close to the floor. This gave me a great opportunity to interact with the patrons who frequented our restaurant, including the owners of other nearby local businesses. I was exposed to several different occupations. The ones who really caught my attention were the two independent pharmacists who operated pharmacies on the opposite corner from our restaurant.

During the next twelve to fifteen years, I had the opportunity to cook their breakfasts, lunches, and dinners and get to know them on a personal level. When I was contemplating my career choice, my grandfather gave me great advice: "People will always be hungry or sick." Because I had extensive experience with the "hungry" side, I chose the "sick," or health care, path.

Unlike several students in pharmacy school, all my breaks and part-time work were in the restaurant business and not the pharmacy business. When I graduated from the Purdue University School of Pharmacy and Pharmaceutical Sciences, I chose to take a dual career path and explore the fields of nuclear pharmacy and community pharmacy. These experiences quickly showed me that my passion was human interaction and the rewarding experiences of changing people's lives.

The community practice offered me great experiences. Through the influence of incredible mentors, I could explore not only the practice of pharmacy but several of the support functions, including procurement of product, managed care negotiations, IT responsibilities, and broader business responsibilities.

Building on these varied experiences, I could combine corporate business opportunities with my entrepreneurial spirit. I helped to develop a pharmacy dispensing application, a robotic prescription-filling device, one of the first classes of trade purchasing organizations, and many other innovations.

Most importantly, I was part of a team that had a positive effect on the health and well-being of many people. My pharmacy experience taught me how to learn, highlighted the need for continuous improvement, and challenged me to do more than I ever thought possible.

Through hard work, dedication, and quite a bit of luck, I was able to retire at age forty-nine. Little did I know that it would be my first failure. After nine months, I failed at being retired. I was blessed to be able to re-enter the industry in a different place. I went to work for a global healthcare company where I had the opportunity to influence the lives of people around the globe.

The skill sets I gained in pharmacy school, business school (yes, I did the hardest thing for a Boilermaker and attended Indiana University for business school), and through business experiences laid a great foundation. But, it was my commitment to continuous learning that allowed me to start this next chapter and be able to have a meaningful impact both from a business and a human perspective.

As you embark on your professional career journey, keep these things in mind:

- Be courageous. Never underestimate the power of one: A single individual or a single idea can have great impact.
- Never compromise your integrity. Your "brand" matters.
- Commit to continuous learning. We are all works in progress.

CHAPTER 20

BECOME THE CEO OF A WORLD-CLASS CHILDREN'S RESEARCH AND CHARITY HOSPITAL

William E. Evans

Former CEO of St. Jude's Children's Hospital
Pediatric Cancer Researcher

When I turned sixteen, there were two exciting consequences: I could get my driver's license, and I could get a job to pay for the car I desired. It was serendipitous that my first job was as a delivery boy for Warren's Apothecary. Had I become a delivery boy for my girlfriend's father, who owned a very successful plumbing supply company, I might have become a plumber. But that didn't happen, and as luck would have it, Charlie Warren showed me what it was like to care for patients as a pharmacist. He had a flourishing clinical practice in the 1960s, before it was en vogue to put "clinical" and "pharmacy" together, and he made it clear to me that I should forget about medicine and dentistry and focus on pharmacy. So, I did.

The second serendipitous moment was when I applied for a pharmacy technician position at St. Jude Children's Research Hospital during my second year of pharmacy school. Like my first job, this was motivated largely by the need for cash. I had no grandiose plans of spending my entire career at St. Jude or of establishing an independent research program as a St. Jude faculty member. And there was certainly never the thought of one day becoming the CEO of St. Jude. Yet, in the end, all of these things happened.

After joining the St. Jude faculty in 1976, I was told that National Institutes of Health (NIH) research funding was a *sine qua non* to become a successful faculty member, so that became the first step in my St. Jude career path. Forty years later, that grant was renewed through 2020, providing a bit more runway before I headed to the Côte d'Azur full-time.

In 2004, when I was asked by the faculty and the board to become the fifth CEO of St. Jude and take on the leadership of a billion-dollar enterprise, I decided to give it a go, despite having taken no management courses, no business courses, nor any finance courses in college. In fact, I often joked that my only "C" in pharmacy school had been in "Pharmacy Administration," a course I had trouble taking seriously. When I decided to leave the CEO position in 2014, my reason was somewhat selfish; I wanted to go back to the frontlines of discovery and clinical translation to improve pharmacotherapy for children with leukemia. That is when I started my career at St. Jude, and that was where I had hoped to finish it.

My advice to pharmacy graduates, which I have repeated in various commencement speeches over the years, is that their pharmacy education has provided them with a solid foundation upon which they must continue to learn and upon which they can pursue a wide array of career opportunities down the road.

All four of my predecessor CEOs at St. Jude had been physicians, as is my successor, but that did not deter the board or my colleagues from asking me to take the helm. I tell new graduates that there are some things in health care that their degree has not prepared them to do, such as being chief of surgery, but there are many more things in health care that they are as well prepared to take on. Some of my tips for anyone who takes on these leadership responsibilities include:

- Be ready, be creative, and be confident.

- Surround yourself with smart people, and ensure these are not just people who always agree with you. Strong input from multiple perspectives is important when making decisions that have enterprise-wide implications.

- Developing a strong institutional strategy is absolutely critical, but "culture trumps strategy." A strong institutional culture will accelerate progress toward achieving organizational strategic plans. A weak culture will slow progress, or, in the worst case, preclude it.

- Culture cannot be faked. A CEO who says that the organizational culture is important and espouses compassion, collaboration, innovation, and quality as the culture, and then makes autocratic decisions that largely reflect his or her own interests will quickly be seen as an imposter and not a leader who appreciates the value of everyone and believes in the importance of organizational culture.

- Make the board one of your critical partners, yet maintain the distinction between governance (board) and management (senior leadership team).

- There is no substitute for doing your homework and being prepared. Anticipating questions is often a good way to prepare for challenging moments.

CHAPTER 21

BECOME THE NATIONWIDE EXPERT ON DRUG SHORTAGES

Erin R. Fox

Senior Director, Drug Information and Support Services
University of Utah Health

During pharmacy school, I decided to complete specialized training in drug information because I could never decide on one central interest. I loved solving problems and researching new drugs, so drug information was a natural fit for me. I never expected to become an expert in anything, let alone drug shortages.

In 2000, I was the newest staff member of the Drug Information Service and volunteered to lead a project around providing drug shortage information nationally. The work involved was the least glamorous you could do at the time, and it included making lists of National Drug Code (NDC) numbers and calling companies to see what products were actually available. Our service had always maintained a standardized way to communicate drug shortage information to our clinicians, and our director was successful in selling the idea to our group purchasing organization and the American Society of Health-System pharmacists.

When I volunteered for this new task, I had no idea that I would end up spending most of my career working on drug shortages. By working to minimize the impact of drug shortages on patients every day, I have developed an incredible passion for solving this public health problem.

I have had amazing opportunities to advocate for our patients by serving as a media resource. I spent time with our public relations department learning how to craft a message and picked up other tips on working with the media. I have had tremendous opportunities to contribute to the discussion about drug shortages by participating in and presenting at the FDA public meeting and multiple summits. I frequently speak to physician, lawyer, nursing, and pharmacy groups to not only educate about how to minimize the impact of drug shortages for patients, but also to help advocate for changes needed to the system.

Most recently, I have become an advocate for change on another issue that affects patient care—high drug prices. In my view, this is simply another type of drug shortage. High prices can make drugs unavailable to patients, and hospitals must use many of the same strategies they use to manage drug shortages to manage high drug prices. By speaking with the media about high drug prices, I have been able to help move the advocacy discussion along. In 2015, I testified for the Senate Aging Committee regarding how high drug prices affect hospital systems and force hospitals to change the way care is provided to patients when prices increase to unsustainable levels.

My goals have been to make sure clinicians understand how they can minimize the impact of drug shortages for their patients and to advocate for change by manufacturers and the government to ensure consistent drug supplies at an affordable cost.

My tips for grads are as follows:

- Volunteer for new opportunities; you never know where they may lead.
- Be willing to work hard at tasks that may not seem very fun.
- Identify an area of interest and learn all you can.

CHAPTER 22

BECOME A LEADER AT THE FDA
A Career in Protecting Public Health

Beth F. Fritsch

Deputy Director
Food and Drug Administration (FDA)

I was raised in Connellsville, Pennsylvania., in the 1970s and 1980s as an only child. My father worked in a factory after serving in the United States Army during the Vietnam War. My mother was a homemaker and attended beauty school. I lived in a blue-collar neighborhood that was home to many military veterans.

The largest city near my home was Pittsburgh, and it was quite a sports spectator town. During the spring, we watched the Pittsburgh Pirates play, and during the fall, we watched University of Pittsburgh football and our beloved Pittsburgh Steelers. In 1979, when the Pittsburgh Pirates won the World Series and the Pittsburgh Steelers won the Super Bowl, it didn't get any better than that for a Pittsburgh sports fan.

When I was in high school and exploring career opportunities, I knew I wanted to enter the medical field. I excelled at math and science and considered medicine, nursing, and chemical engineering. I settled on pharmacy perhaps because when my dad spoke of his Army assignments, he told me that he served as a pharmacy technician. When I researched the pharmacy profession and learned that job placement was near 100 percent for graduates, I was convinced that this was the best path forward for me.

I applied to three pharmacy schools: the University of Pittsburgh, Duquesne University, and West Virginia University. I decided on the University of Pittsburgh because I was guaranteed admission into their pharmacy school program provided that I maintained a certain grade point average. I was not much of a risk-taker back then, or even now.

Attending Pitt was the right decision. As I was nearing the completion of my pharmacy degree program I developed an interest in pharmacy law, so I took the Law School Admission Test (LSAT). I planned to work as a retail pharmacist part time and earn a law degree. As I met other law students and learned about the competitiveness of the field and that many of the starting salaries were less than my pharmacy salary, I abandoned that career path. I would eventually return to college twice, to earn an MBA and a doctor of pharmacy degree.

After abandoning my law school aspirations, I realized that my true interest was at the intersection of health care, science, and policy. I met a few officers who were members of the United States Public Health Service, spoke with them, and applied for a commission.

My first assignment in July 2000 was to the Food and Drug Administration (FDA) in the Office of Generic Drugs. I learned about regulatory requirements for generic drugs, allowable amounts of inactive ingredients for generic drugs and patent challenges, and strategies that innovator companies used to delay the introduction of generic drugs. After spending three years in the Regulatory Support Branch, I accepted a position with the Division of Bioequivalence. In this position, I gained knowledge of the pharmacokinetic, pharmacodynamic, and dissolution testing requirements of generic drugs.

In 2008, I left the Office of Generic Drugs for an opportunity in the Office of Special Health Issues, which would later become the Office of Health and Constituent Affairs, in the Office of the Commissioner. One of the attractions of working in the Commissioner's Office is the exposure to a wide range of FDA's regulatory involvement. I worked on outreach activities to health professional, patient, and consumer audiences related to food (menu labeling), veterinary medicine (judicious use of antimicrobials in animal agriculture), biologics (H1N1 vaccine), devices (surgical mesh adverse events), drugs (drug shortages, MedWatch), and tobacco (the Real Cost Campaign).

Pharmacists generally associate the FDA with drug approvals, but there are many other aspects of regulation in which the FDA is involved. For example, during the H1N1 outbreak, personal protective equipment (e.g., masks) and flu-detection kits (i.e., determining if the H1N1 flu strain is present in the blood) are regulated by FDA's Center for Devices and Radiological Health. Vaccines (e.g., H1N1 vaccine) are approved by the Center for Biologics Evaluation and Research. The Center for Drug Evaluation and Research approves drugs (e.g., antiviral drugs) and manages drug shortages.

Based on my experience, my tips for grads are as follows:

- Upon embarking on your pharmacy career, join at least one pharmacy association. This could be a local pharmacy organization (e.g., Maryland Pharmacists Association) or a national pharmacy organization (American Society of Health-System Pharmacists).

- Network! Attend conferences and meet others in your field of practice. Outside of my first position at Rite Aid Pharmacy, when I was directly recruited from the University of Pittsburgh, an acquaintance/friend within the organization in which I aspired to work facilitated my job transition.

- Keep learning! The only constant in pharmacy is change. In 1995, only nine states allowed pharmacists to immunize. Today, pharmacists have authority to administer immunizations in all fifty states, the District of Columbia, and Puerto Rico. Recently I obtained my Board Certification in Pharmacotherapy. It was a great learning and networking experience.

- Give back to your profession by precepting and mentoring students. As your students blossom in their career paths, a great sense of pride is experienced, knowing that in some way you contributed to or influenced their careers. I've written many letters of recommendation for pharmacy students who are pursuing residency or fellowship opportunities. When the students are selected, I feel a great deal of gratification.

- Early in your career, volunteer for new opportunities. I became involved in the United States Public Health Service (USPHS) Pharmacist Professional Advisory Committee. I led the University Point of Contact Initiative that identified

USPHS pharmacists to interact with each of the pharmacy schools in the United States. The initiative became a successful model for recruitment.

- Get outside of your comfort zone! My career growth and satisfaction increased as I changed positions and gained additional knowledge. It is easy to stay in one place and be comfortable, but you really grow when you seek out new learning opportunities and move outside of your comfort zone. One of my former directors and mentors challenged her staff to identify at least one activity each year that was deemed "outside their comfort zones." Each year, this activity was discussed during employees' annual performance appraisals.

CHAPTER 23

BECOME A LOBBYIST

Lobby Departments and Agencies of the United States Government on Behalf of Companies of the Generic Pharmaceutical Industry

David R. Gaugh

Senior Vice President, Sciences and Regulatory Affairs
Association for Accessible Medicines (AAM)

I have been very fortunate in my professional life to experience four different career paths, all of which were afforded to me because of my education and training in pharmacy. I grew up in a family heritage of pharmacy; in fact, I am a fifth-generation pharmacist. My family owned two retail pharmacies, and I began my work-life experiences managing the inventory in the stores, a.k.a., stocking the shelves and reordering product. That experience, while seemingly menial, was critical to the success of the stores, and it taught me to strive for excellence in every task I undertook. Those early lessons carried me through pharmacy school and every position I undertook thereafter.

I always knew I would go to pharmacy school, and I also always knew I wouldn't work in retail pharmacy, at least not long-term. Once I graduated and received my license, I immediately went to work in hospital pharmacy; direct patient-care was my interest. After several years there and after rising to the director of pharmacy position, I began to realize that my interests were on the business side rather than the patient care side.

My experiences as director of pharmacy provided me with the foundational skills of leadership, strategic planning, and financial management, and they ultimately led me to the business of pharmaceutical contracting with a major group purchasing organization (GPO). At the GPO, I led the pharmacy contracting team in negotiations, relationship building, and marketing.

These experiences, and the associated professional/personal networking, opened the doors to pharmaceutical company opportunities, where I became the general manager for a leading generic injectable pharmaceutical company. My previous skills and experiences allowed me to build on new areas of interest, including business development, product development, regulatory, and marketing. It also allowed me to develop skills I hadn't even thought about, like political acumen. This acumen developed unexpectedly due to the drug shortage situation in the United States, and I found myself spending more and more time on Capitol Hill and at the FDA.

My next stop was Washington, D.C., and the Generic Pharmaceutical Association (GPhA), now known as the Association for Accessible Medicines (AAM). Today, I am lobbying departments and agencies of the United States Government and several foreign governments on behalf of companies in the generic pharmaceutical industry.

David R. Gaugh

My key message is that there is a world of opportunity awaiting you once you have completed your pharmacy education and training. I have a few tips for you:

- Work hard and smart, and strive for excellence in everything you do.

- Always be in learning mode; everyone you meet can teach you something new.

- Be goal-oriented, both short-term and long-term, and have a vision for your future.

- Develop strong networks and even stronger one-on-one relationships.

- Be open to new opportunities and experiences.

CHAPTER 24

BECOME THE CEO AND LEADER OF A MANAGED CARE COMPANY

Nancy Gilbride

CEO, Envolve Health, and Senior Vice President, Centene Corporation

I grew up in Racine, Wisconsin, as an only child. My parents owned their own business—a large grocery store—and I began working for them when I was fourteen. I started out bagging groceries and ascended to the highly coveted role of cashier. My parents always encouraged me to go to college, hoping I would graduate with a business degree and return to Racine to purchase and run the store for them, allowing their legacy to continue in our small family.

I had other ideas, however. As an only child, I was fairly sheltered and not very confident, but I knew I wanted to explore my options. Because I was a bit intimidated by larger colleges, I started out at St. Norbert in DePere, Wisconsin, in computer science and math, simply because I was fairly skilled at math. However, my complete inability to understand and thrive in a programming-based world, which I learned about two months in, led me to meet with my career counselor to find my passion. After several tests suggested a strong affinity for health care, I decided to transfer to the University of Wisconsin-Madison to pursue a degree in pharmacy.

While I was in pharmacy school, I took advantage of every opportunity to get involved in student pharmacy associations to expand my leadership skills. As a result, when I graduated I had a very well-rounded understanding of options for pharmacy graduates. I knew that I wanted to be a future leader and to shape and influence the profession on a broader scale, so I decided to pursue the master's residency program in hospital pharmacy administration at the University of Wisconsin-Madison Hospital and Clinics.

It was by far one of the best decisions I have made in my life. I was blessed with many strong mentors who exposed me to multiple paths. I began my career in managed health care twenty-four years ago with UnitedHealthcare in a little-known pharmacy benefit management (PBM) subsidiary named Diversified. The PBM world was very young and a little risky, and was focused on implementing solutions to help manage pharmacy cost and quality for all types of payers.

During the next twenty-two years, I remained in the PBM industry while that sector experienced explosive growth. I never had a plan; I simply focused on building my strengths and following my passions. I came to Express Scripts with their first acquisition (ValueRx) when the combined companies had $3 billion in revenue. By the time I left Express Scripts after nineteen years, they had become a Fortune 22 company with $100 billion in revenue. I learned as much as I could, raised my hand for every opportunity that presented itself, and got little sleep. As a result, I worked across all market sectors (health plans, state government, employers, federal agencies) in multiple clinical (clinical product development, managing the clinical programs for payers, and managing clinical teams) and business roles (leading teams of account management professionals responsible for customer retention, satisfaction, and profitability) and sales.

When I left Express Scripts, I was one of four presidents responsible for all of the PBM business; my sector was the Federal Pharmacy Division, and I ran the P&L for the $10 billion unit. Every role I held always faced our customers, which was very important to me because service is in my DNA, thanks to my father.

I left Express Scripts in search of a new set of challenges, seeking a leadership role with a growth-oriented healthcare company that focused relentlessly on a mission to make a difference. When I left Express Scripts, I had no idea what my next position would be, but I had the confidence that I would find it, and I did. Today, I am the CEO of Envolve Health, a wholly owned subsidiary of Centene Corporation in St. Louis, and a Fortune 66 company.

I now have responsibility for more than 4,500 employees who provide flexible and affordable healthcare solutions, including access to a comprehensive suite of supplemental health benefits (pharmacy, behavioral health, disease management, dental, and vision, to name a few), wellness, and back-office support solutions for partners nationwide. I am proud to work for a company that encourages its employees to give back in the form of our time, resources, and talents to our communities, striving to make a difference in the lives of those who are less fortunate.

I've learned a lot along my journey. The following are the guiding principles I embrace every day:

- Take every opportunity you are provided (and push for others you want) to keep learning and growing your entire life. Never settle for the status quo and always set the bar exceptionally high; be your toughest critic.

- Don't let anyone tell you that you "can't" do something. Those were always fighting words to me and inspiration to prove the critics wrong, which I always did. Fear, uncertainty, and doubt are derailers; take care of yourself and stay strong, in body and mind, every day.

- True living is all about connecting with others. Your professional network, if you nurture it, will bring you endless opportunities. Never underestimate the power of relationships. I submit that they are everything we have.

- We all go through adversity; face each challenge with an accountable, ownership-first attitude, and don't play the victim. Anyone who blames others is not a leader. Focus on finding the lessons learned that enable positive change.

- Dare greatly in your life. You've got one shot at this. Develop the whole you and live as one person. Be authentic and live in the moment. Pay attention to the signs in your life. Take care of you and always have an attitude of gratitude.

CHAPTER 25

BECOME THE PRESIDENT OF A STATE BOARD OF PHARMACY
*While Leading a Major Integrated Health Network as
Chief Pharmacy Officer*

Amy Gutierrez

President, California State Board of Pharmacy
Vice President and Chief Pharmacy Officer, Kaiser Permanente
National Pharmacy Programs and Services

I am grateful for the circuitous and serendipitous routes my professional career has taken because these routes have provided a variety of opportunities to hone my leadership skills. In a way, I was destined to be a pharmacist. I was born in Cuba and arrived in the United States with my immigrant parents, who left everything behind after Fidel Castro came into power. My mother obtained her pharmacist license in the states, and my first pharmacy experiences involved typing prescription labels in the inner-city community pharmacies where she worked, using my Spanish language skills. I learned firsthand of the struggles that patients experience with medication affordability. These early experiences solidified my desire to make a difference in my future profession, as well as to be part of a team that focused on access to quality health care.

I attended the University of Southern California and earned my PharmD degree among a professional class that produced multiple pharmacist leaders that I still greatly admire. As a newly minted pharmacist, I was determined to utilize my newly acquired clinical skills. I accepted a position as a pediatric clinical pharmacist with the Los Angeles County Department of Health Services, starting what would be a thirty-two-year career in a government healthcare system that provides care for the underserved. Our county health-care system provides care to all, regardless of insurance status, and did so years before the Affordable Care Act became law.

Over the years, I assumed positions with increasing leadership responsibility and specifically sought opportunities that would provide growth. One of these roles would turn out to be quite challenging because it was located at an inner-city hospital that was in the midst of political and regulatory strife, and, therefore, it was under intense media focus. I didn't know it at the time, but this experience would serve to provide a strong leadership foundation and regulatory skills that were key in future roles.

During my last eleven years with this county healthcare system, I served as the chief pharmacy officer, developing a corporate pharmacy leadership team that initiated a multitude of medication management, care, and patient access improvements in hospital, ambulatory, emergency services, and correctional health settings.

Along the way, I was appointed to the State Board of Pharmacy by the governor of California, and I have served in this role for more than five years. I have been honored to serve in a leadership role on the Board of Pharmacy, as vice president for a year, and as president for the last three years. I have had the opportunity to provide leadership during the development of multiple state regulations that have impacted our profession, including expanded pharmacist scope of practice changes and safety-focused sterile compounding regulations. The most rewarding part of this responsibility was the ability to be a true patient advocate.

Earlier this year, I accepted a new leadership role as the vice president and chief pharmacy officer for Kaiser Permanente, one of the largest integrated healthcare networks in the nation and an organization that is at the leading edge of clinical pharmacy care. I am honored to be helping shape our professional pharmacy vision and leading pharmacy efforts that continually improve quality and access for the millions of patients we serve across the United States.

Reflecting on my professional path, I have the following recommendations for those embarking on a pharmacist career:

- Embrace new challenges as opportunities for growth; keep challenging yourself and seek opportunities to hone your clinical and leadership skills.

- Do not be afraid of tackling a crisis head-on. You may learn far more when things go wrong than when they go right.

- Clinicians have the responsibility to utilize their clinical skills in a leadership role. Despite my role as a pharmacy leader, I always consider myself to be a clinical pharmacist first. However, as a leader, I have the additional ability to establish policies and vision that will impact patient outcomes for more than one patient at a time.

- Find out what it is about our great profession you love, and focus your passion and efforts in this area. Take your time and explore all that pharmacy has to offer, and consider nontraditional pharmacist roles as you find the best professional fit.

- Keep the patients at the center; they are the ultimate reason why we do what we do.

- Develop and cultivate professional networks; they are extremely valuable. Find a good mentor who will challenge you along the way. Then, be an inspirational mentor and learn to identify and nurture future potential leaders.

CHAPTER 26

BECOME THE LEADER OF 340B PRICING IN THE U.S. MARKET
Supporting our Nation's Safety Net Providers
Through the 340B Drug Pricing Program

Christopher Hatwig

President, Apexus

Pharmacy wasn't always a part of my career plan. After earning a bachelor's degree in biology at the University of Arkansas, my goal was to pursue a PhD in biochemistry. However, a wise professor sensed that I wasn't a good fit for a career conducting repetitive tests on lab rats. Fortunately, my lab experience exposed me to the pharmacy school. I applied, was accepted, and earned my bachelor's degree in pharmacy.

During my pharmacy studies, another mentor encouraged me to pursue an advanced degree and residency training at one of the top pharmacy administration training programs in the country. He recommended the University of Wisconsin, Ohio State, and the University of Kansas. I had the good fortune of matching with the University of Wisconsin residency program and was exposed to an endless number of mentors and peers for the next two years and beyond.

After graduating and completing the residency, I took a position with Parkland Health & Hospital System, the major safety-net provider for the North Texas region. During my tenure there, we received funding to expand clinical pharmacy services to ambulatory clinics, build out central fill and mail facilities, and open twelve clinics with dedicated pharmacies in medically underserved areas of the community. We were far ahead of our time and became a model for other systems across the country.

The ambulatory pharmacy program grew to 130 ambulatory pharmacists providing direct patient services. The system was filling more than 10,000 outpatient prescriptions a day — accounting for 86 percent of Parkland's total drug expenditures.

The U.S. government introduced the 340B Drug Pricing Program in 1992. Parkland's senior leaders were instrumental in getting the legislation passed, and I had the unique chance to learn about and lead the program from the ground up.

Many of you work at 340B hospitals today and are aware that the program provides key safety-net hospitals and clinics with access to deep discounts on outpatient drugs. During my thirteen years at Parkland, I experienced firsthand the shortcomings of the program's first prime vendor — a pharmaceutical distributor — selected by the Health Resources and Services Administration to manage contracting, distribution, and support.

I accepted a position with Healthcare Purchasing Partners International (HPPI), a national group purchasing organization that won the next proposal cycle for the prime vendor role in 2004.

Apexus spun off from HPPI, and the Health Resources & Services Administration (HRSA) renewed and expanded our prime vendor role two additional proposal cycles, in 2009 and 2014. We anticipate we will participate in the next proposal cycle in 2019.

Our success has come from building an effective team that understands, anticipates, and meets customer needs. We're now a staff of more than seventy serving more than 30,000 participating providers. We've saved participants $4.4 billion since 2004 — including $1.07 billion in 2016 alone. I'm proud of the education and technical assistance offerings we've created that support operational compliance in the marketplace for all stakeholders.

What prepared me most for my career are the professional relationships and experiences I've had. These concepts have shaped my approach and guided my accomplishments:

- **Have passion for your work.** Use your passion to drive your work, because it can be contagious. When you do, work really doesn't seem like work at all. Remember that passion comes with emotion, and unregulated emotion can weaken your effectiveness. Passion combined with emotional control gives you a calm confidence that can move mountains.

- **Build professional networks and relationships.** Develop relationships with mentors, business partners, and peers. You'll learn more than you ever could from management articles and books, and you'll have allies as you work to meet your goals and influence outcomes.

- **Build effective teams.** Develop teams whose loyalty and competence you can trust. Trust leads to empowerment and even greater accomplishment. Remember that each team member brings unique skills. Choose team members whose strengths and weaknesses balance one another.

- **Drive hard and maintain high standards**. Take accountability seriously and set goals that make you stretch. But don't let "perfect" get in the way of "better." We're only here for a short time.

- **Be adaptable.** Learn to adapt, or run the risk of being swallowed up in the past. Welcome new situations and challenges, make adjustments, and find new ways of approaching people and problems.

You can apply these concepts to your business and personal life. Find something to be passionate about, stay connected, and invite smart, committed people to share your journey. Stay flexible and be ready for wherever the future leads you. Good luck in your career journey.

CHAPTER 27

BECOME A REGULATORY PHARMACIST AT THE NATIONAL INSTITUTE FOR ALLERGY AND INFECTIOUS DISEASES (NIAID)

Binh Hoang

Pharmacist
Office of Regulatory Affairs,
Division of Microbiology and Infectious Diseases
NIAID/NIH

Being raised by a single mother along with my nine other siblings in Vietnam, I did not have much choice but to work hard and to find my way around. My mom barely finished third grade because my grandmother passed away during war time when my mother was nine years old, but she always reminded us to make our education a top priority. She made it possible for us to continue with our education. Thanks to "The Land of Opportunity," I arrived in America during my high school years knowing no English. I worked as a cashier at a fast-food restaurant and later as a pharmacy technician, and I made up my mind to attend pharmacy school.

After graduating from pharmacy school, I worked in retail, an outpatient clinic, clinical research, and a product-management program. Prior to joining the National Institutes of Health (NIH), I was at Thermo Fisher Scientific and spent thirteen years supporting HIV clinical trials for the NIH, the National Institute of Allergy and Infectious Diseases (NIAID), and the Division of AIDS (DAIDS).

During my tenure at Thermo Fisher Scientific, I managed clinical supplies that were being shipped globally to more than 100 clinical sites in twenty-eight countries. I collaborated with the NIH on the development of the protocols and determined the total amount of drug, vaccine, and ancillary supplies needed for each protocol. I also served as the primary liaison to hundreds of clinical pharmacists around the world regarding all aspects of the clinical trial process. I worked very closely with the manufacturers to plan for receipt of supplies during the lifespan of the studies.

With more than thirteen years of experience in clinical trials, I have accumulated a wealth of knowledge in export and import pharmaceutical product regulations and requirements, knowledge of design and implementation of clinical trials, and knowledge of good clinical practice. I also have extensive experience managing and dealing with customs brokers and freight forwarders. In addition, I was fortunate enough to be involved in reviewing, analyzing, writing, and editing materials for government contract proposals for two winning contract cycles.

While working at Thermo Fisher, I managed to complete my MBA in health informatics at New England College. I also finished the Pharmacy Leadership Academy program from the American Society of Health-System Pharmacists (ASHP).

I now serve as the pharmacist for Division of Microbiology and Infectious Diseases (DMID) -supported clinical trials in enteric and hepatic diseases, respiratory diseases, and sexually transmitted infections. In that capacity, I am responsible for coordinating, collaborating, and providing pharmaceutical expertise during protocol development and implementation; providing accurate and efficient advice about the dispensing of study product at clinical sites; and maintaining overall responsibility for pharmacy-related inquiries and issues. I also oversee the functions of the product support team.

My tips for grads are as follows:

- Integrity: Learn from successes and mistakes, be accountable, be a team player, make and meet commitments, and cultivate a strong work ethic.

- Develop yourself: Be willing to take on new challenges, seek ideas and feedback from others, and be a mentor.

- Drive continuous learning: Desire to advance and build up career-oriented skills, focus on the output, constructively confront and solve problems, and take pride in your work.

- Don't forget the power of networking.

CHAPTER 28

BUILD A REGIONAL CHAIN OF DRUGSTORES

T.J. Johnsrud

Founder and President
NuCara Management Group

I am the son of a cheesemaker from northeast Iowa. I grew up in a small town called Schley, which was a bump in the road with our cheese factory on one side and a tavern on the other. I went to a one-room schoolhouse with one teacher for all seven grades then on to the big city of 400 in Protivin, Iowa. Neither of my parents attended high school, much less college, but advanced education was a primary goal for my three siblings and me. After high school, I studied liberal arts at Creighton University in Omaha, Nebraska, before transferring to the University of Iowa College of Pharmacy. The transition from a one-room schoolhouse, followed by a small high school, to a Jesuit university was huge. I was woefully ill-prepared to take on the load of freshman classes that Creighton demanded. I didn't flunk out my freshman year as I'd feared, and, ultimately, my time at Creighton made a profound mark on my life. I always say that the Jesuits taught me how to live, and the University of Iowa taught me how to make a living.

After graduating from the University of Iowa, I worked for seven years at Paramount Pharmacy in Cedar Rapids, Iowa. During that time, I already had the bug to own my own store and despite a lucrative offer to stay with Paramount when the opportunity arose, with a deep breath I struck out on my own. Did I have any thought of one day being called an entrepreneur? No. But with the support of the only physician clinic in the small town of Conrad, Iowa, I took the $100 in my pocket and my family of four and took a chance. I secured a bank loan for $24,000 (with the help of the physicians) and I risked opening my first pharmacy. The rest can only be called a "crooked goat path up the side of a mountain."

From this single pharmacy, the NuCara network began to grow. Did I wake up one morning and say, "Now I'm going to be an entrepreneur"? Once again, no! So, what is an entrepreneur? I believe an essential characteristic is to have confidence in your ability, to recognize opportunities when they come along, and to have the courage and willingness to accept the risk that comes with your convictions. It's OK to be scared, and if you aren't, then you don't understand risk. Entrepreneurs not only see what is, they see what can be, and they are willing to accept all the risks and challenges that come with effecting change.

After more than forty years as a pharmacist, I've made as many mistakes as I've had victories, but that first pharmacy has now grown through strategic partnerships to more than thirty locations in six states, with ancillary businesses in home medical equipment, sterile and non-sterile compounding, an internet veterinary medicine company, and real estate.

It's been hard but gratifying work, and that work has been recognized with many accolades from my peers. Perhaps the most meaningful to me was the "Osterhaus Medal for Lifetime Achievement" named for my friend, Bob, which was awarded by the University of Iowa. My career has not only been spent building the NuCara brand, but just as important, providing opportunities to serve people and for others to grow.

I now have a young management team in place, and my time can be devoted to further business development. NuCara plans to continue expanding its network, including its most recent acquisitions in Wisconsin, Iowa, and Texas. And, for me, it's all still fun!

My tips for grads are as follows:

- Set out with the goal to make change, not just make money.
- It's important to understand business and management, but having said that, many business decisions are intuitive. Pharmacy today is more than dispensing medication.
- Find a mentor who will challenge your ideas and still foster your vision.

CHAPTER 29

BECOME AN INNOVATION LEADER
From pharmacist to innovation junkie

Saul Kaplan

Founder and Chief Catalyst
Business Innovation Factory (BIF)

My thought process coming out of high school was no more com-plicated than, "I love science, and it would be nice if a college di-ploma resulted in a job!" Pharmacy fit the bill. I wasn't signing up for a career, just looking for a start. I wanted something I could build on without a clue where it might lead me. A degree from the University of Rhode Island (URI) School of Pharmacy in the 1970s was the perfect prescription. I knew by my second year that I wouldn't spend my career filling prescriptions, but I valued the foundation I received at URI. I couldn't tell you how I planned to leverage a pharmacy degree, but I had confidence that it would set me up for a successful career. I have been grateful for my pharmacy education every day since then.

Saul Kaplan

I went on to launch a career with many twists and turns as an innovation junkie and strategist. I believe there is always a better way. I have dedicated my career and life to enabling those around me to make what's next easier and safer to manage. My career has followed the simple principle of always staying on a steep learning curve. I have always done my best work when I stretch myself to learn and do something new. I never cared about job titles, how many people reported to me, or how much money I made. I knew those things would come if I kept myself on a steep learning curve, always willing to tackle new challenges.

After pharmacy school, I wanted to learn how business and large organizations work and how emerging technologies change markets. I combined my analytical foundation from pharmacy school with an MBA from Rensselaer Polytechnic Institute (RPI) in the strategic management of technology. From there, I leveraged both degrees to work in the pharmaceutical industry for Eli Lilly & Company, first in sales and then in the home office as a marketing manager. I had the incredible opportunity to work on the U.S. introduction of Prozac. It was a young marketing manager's dream job. I learned the difference between market-making and share-taking. Most people and organizations are share-takers, competing for market share in a defined industry with known competitors. I became interested in market-makers, the people and organizations that redefine markets. My career has been defined by enabling market-makers.

From Lilly, I became a road warrior consultant, first with Arthur D. Little and then as a senior partner at what became Accenture. I'm still absorbing what I learned during those halcyon days traveling around the world working with pharmaceutical and medical products companies, and enabling and leading consulting practices and teams that were focused on innovation.

I became interested in the difference between the innovation rheto-ric coming out of the C-suite and the real work being done at mid-levels in most of the companies with which I consulted. The rhetoric was about transformation, but the reality was more focused on in-cremental improvements to the way companies worked at the time. There was nothing wrong with tweaks, but it seemed to me that a different approach to innovation was needed if transformation was the goal. Again, organizations were much better at share-taking than market-making.

I was fortunate to be able to retire at an early age from Accenture a few years after its IPO, but my wife wasn't in the market for a strategist at home to advise on household operations. I made the mistake of raising my hand in front of the newly elected governor in my home state of Rhode Island, and the next thing I knew I was working as the No. 2 at the state's economic development agency. Soon after I joined the agency, its director went back to Wall Street, and I found myself leading the agency.

I had become an accidental bureaucrat, and it completely changed my worldview and approach to innovation. Instead of seeing in-novation through the lens of large institutions, I learned to see it through the lens of the citizens, students, and patients they served. In working on the state's economic development strategy, I began to see the state as a real-world sandbox to develop transformational models in government, education, and healthcare.

I created the Business Innovation Factory (BIF) at first as a local program in Rhode Island, and when I left state government, I ex-panded it to serve government, healthcare, and education leaders across the country to explore and test practices and new business models to help make transformation safer and easier to manage.

We live in a time that screams for transformation, and the best we seem to be capable of is tweaking what works today. BIF is trying to change that.

I am proud of my pharmacy background and how I have been able to combine and recombine what I have learned along the way to take on and create new roles that didn't exist or I couldn't have imagined when I started. The truth is that none of us can predict what we'll be doing in the future. All we can do is learn how to confidently reinvent ourselves. Reinvention is the most important life skill in a rapidly changing world. A pharmacy education is a wonderful foundation that can open up many new career and life paths, if we let it.

CHAPTER 30

**BECOME THE MARKET LEADER AND EXPERT
IN PROVIDING TRAINING FOR BOTH STERILE COMPOUNDING
PRACTITIONERS AND REGULATORS**

Eric S. Kastango

Founder of Clinical IQ and Critical Point

My journey into pharmacy started by happenstance when I was in seventh grade. During a career day, I visited with an architect and a pharmacist. I was really interested in being an architect, but after attending a summer architecture program at Carnegie Mellon University in the summer between my junior and senior year of high school, I found out architecture was not going to be my chosen path. I loved math and science and applied to Ohio State University for chemical engineering and the Massachusetts College of Pharmacy for pharmacy school. I was accepted into both schools but chose pharmacy because it was closer to home. This was the first of many forks in the road that led me to where I am today.

My galvanized passion for pharmacy and patient safety began when I started working as a pharmacy technician at Brigham and

Women's Hospital (BWH) in Boston, Massachusetts. I was still in college at the time. During my first three years at Massachusetts College of Pharmacy and Allied Health Services, I struggled academically. I did not understand how what I was studying would apply in the real world. It wasn't until I started working at BWH that I understood "the why behind the what," and with that understanding, I improved my academic performance. I graduated in March 1983, became a New Jersey Registered Pharmacist in May, and set out to make a difference in the world.

As a pharmacist, I worked diligently to hone my knowledge and clinical and business acumen. I practiced pharmacy in a number of settings, including hospitals, community, and home care, in a number of different roles, including as the corporate vice president of pharmacy services for Coram Healthcare Corporation. I also managed an FDA-registered cGMP manufacturing operation for Baxter Healthcare Corporation.

In 1997, seeking to use this knowledge to advise others, I teamed with a colleague to start my first consulting company, Cognitive Design Associates. Our mission was to facilitate robust sterile compounding standards of practice. To do so, we developed one of the first computer-based training programs, called Good Compounding Practices, and detailed standard operation procedures. After two years, our company was acquired by Coram Healthcare, and I launched my second consulting firm, Clinical IQ, LLC.

One of my mentors encouraged me to reflect on a mission statement for my new business. I thought carefully about what I wanted to accomplish. I wanted to fundamentally change the practice of sterile compounding in the United States. It was an audacious goal.

Since the inception of Clinical IQ, my team and I have worked to improve the compounding practices and facilities of hundreds of pharmacies and consulted on hospital building projects, training of personnel, and remediation of non-compliant compounding operations. I have worked closely with the National Association of State Boards of Pharmacy and many individual state boards of pharmacy and departments of public health to assist them in responding to sterile compounding practice issues, as well as to educate their staff.

Most recently, I completed a significant project at National Institutes of Health (NIH), where my team and I assisted the organization in remediating their FDA 483 observations and helped redesign their new sterile compounding area. The NIH pharmacy department moved into their new sterile compounding area in May 2017. This year, I was able to grow the business from two to seven consultants.

Through the launch of a second company called CriticalPoint, LLC, I turned to scalable education and training to improve staff competency and patient safety. My team and I have created a comprehensive curriculum of in-person and web-based training for both sterile compounding practitioners and regulators. In its twelve years, we have reached more than 1,000 pharmacy professionals working in hospitals, community pharmacies, nuclear medicine and radiopharmaceutical sites, and home infusion settings worldwide.

Throughout my career, I have challenged myself to continue to learn and to give back. I completed an MBA from University of Phoenix while starting my first two businesses. I have written and published in both traditional peer-reviewed journals and web-based publications. I was a volunteer expert as a member of the Sterile Compounding Expert Committee of the United States

Pharmacopeial Convention, Inc. (USP) from 2005 to 2013. In this capacity, I assisted in writing USP's public quality standards for sterile compounding, USP General Chapter 797. I was also a member of the Compounding with Hazardous Drugs Expert Panel from 2010 to the present day. I also worked with The Pew Charitable Trusts as a sterile compounding adviser to their Drug Safety Project.

I have been honored to receive three significant professional and public health awards: The American Society of Health-System Pharmacists selected me as a Fellow (FASHP) in March 2001. This designation recognizes pharmacists who have excelled in pharmacy practice and distinguished themselves through service and contributions to the pharmacy profession. In May 2014, I was co-recipient of the Henry Cade Memorial Award, presented by the National Association of Boards of Pharmacy in recognition of assistance provided to the national and state boards of pharmacy to protect the public health. Most recently, in December 2016, I received a Cheers Award from the Institute for Safe Medication Practices for my ongoing work related to sterile compounding safety.

My advice to any pharmacist is that your future is not limited, and, quite frankly, unlimited opportunities lie in front of you if you have a passion, but, more importantly, have the energy and discipline to become the best you can be in your chosen area of passion.

CHAPTER 31

BUILD AND RUN THE MARKET-LEADING COMPANY IN OUT-SOURCED STERILE PRODUCT COMPOUNDING

Rich J. Kruzynski

Immediate Past President, PharMEDiumHealthcare Corporation Current: RJK Pharmacy Innovations

In the fifth grade, I would walk the mile home from basketball practice in the steel town of Latrobe, Pennsylvania., and I passed two independently-owned retail pharmacies along the way — there were no chains at the time. One of the pharmacies had a soda fountain where I would sit each time on the circular stool and down a cherry Coke before going home to dinner. I couldn't help but notice the professional aura of the pharmacist as he filled prescriptions and counseled patients (he was eventually given national recognition for inventing the banana split at that very fountain!) I would tell my parents all about it over the evening meal. They listened intently.

Little did I know that the other pharmacist in town, a member of our church, was also influencing my parents' guidance of their young son. At the time, parents could only mentally connect with tangible professions like a nurse, lawyer, doctor, and druggist. All were guiding me toward a job with which they could identify, that they thought would pay well, and that matched up with my strong suits of math and science. So, given my cherry Coke experience, I applied to the University of Pittsburgh and ultimately entered the pharmacy school.

I had many pharmacy and non-pharmacy experiences during those educational years. Looking back, I realized that diving into each one, getting the most out of each endeavor no matter how seemingly insignificant, reaped an intellectual, educational, and financial payday years later. I earned the "normal" hours for the Pennsylvania-issued license through the two independent pharmacies mentioned above.

I earned the "traditional" hours for licensure working as a pharmacy intern at the local hospital. But during the summer before my last school year, I really had my eyes opened with a non-traditional experience, a National Pharmaceutical Council internship at Abbott Laboratories, which is a big pharmaceutical company in Chicago. It was so non-traditional that I had to fight with the Pennsylvania State Board of Pharmacy to count those industry hours toward licensure.

I was not pursuing the traditional pharmacist career route. I was captivated by the few RPh/MBAs there were at Abbott that summer, and I saw the professional, fulfilling careers they developed. Filled with variety and a bent toward creativity/innovation, their marketing positions used pharmacy, science, math, and business skills to create leadership, true value, and marked impact. Indeed, there was a whole other world out there for pharmacists, and it was very non-traditional! After graduating with my bachelor's in pharmacy, I first decided to work for a retail chain that's now CVS, but I soon applied for the MBA program at the University of Chicago, concentrating in finance and marketing.

We all like it when a plan comes together. The RPh/MBA was a very unique combination at the time, and it was particularly attractive to big, Midwestern healthcare manufacturers. Not surprisingly, I had many job offers. I joined Baxter Healthcare Corporation in Deerfield, Illinois, upon completion of my MBA, and I spent the next twenty-three years in rising positions of authority.

I hope I brought value to many aspects of the established pharmacy-related businesses (mostly intravenous therapy areas), and I was not afraid of pioneering new things. Management took note. I soon found myself mired in the clouds of startup concepts and businesses, things never before tried at all, let alone by a big company. Sterile product compounding as a service to hospitals was one of these, and it became known as "outsourcing" business. It's hard to fathom, but this very franchise started in the cafeteria on a napkin that was handed to me by a senior executive; I was the first employee in this entrepreneurial initiative.

Over two decades at Baxter and for the dozen years as president of this business, which Baxter sold to private investors (creating PharMEDium Healthcare Corporation), I helped shape not just the company but the entire U.S. sterile product outsourced compounding industry, servicing more than 3,000 hospitals.

PharMEDium was the sterile compounding leader, and many times I was the main spokesperson to the "stakeholders." That included the hospital pharmacy community at large, professional organizations, state boards of pharmacy, the FDA and other federal regulators, and to members of Congress and their staff. I can't tell you how many times I came to appreciate and value the formal education from the universities, the learnings from informal experiences with which I challenged myself, the big company training programs, and a honing of some essential skills to present clear, concise, and compelling ideas persuasively.

This was a thirty-year program design loaded with bends, turns, setbacks, and reloads. My proudest achievements are creating a company that was known for innovation in a traditionally unimaginative pharmacy sector—innovations that created 1,200 jobs—assistance on Capitol Hill that created important federal safety legislation for patients (the Drug Quality and Security Act signed in 2013 by President Obama), thirty-seven U.S. patents for safety labeling of sterile compounds, and, of course, the creation of more than $2 billion worth of value for our investors with the sale of the business in 2015.

While challenged to work with many personality types over the years, I was privileged to be a part of many teams, both as leader and member. So much was accomplished on our entrepreneurial mission by the imaginative and passionate work of those many individuals.

Today, I am retired but involved with nonprofit advisory boards and councils for three pharmacy schools. I also teach a class on leadership to the Masters of Science in Pharmacy Business Administration (MSPBA) students at the University of Pittsburgh. I'm also involved with for-profits, principally as an investor and a board member of etectRx, specifically in pharmacy areas. I also do some informal mentoring of twenty-somethings and thirty-somethings.

My tips for grads:

- Get to know yourself and what you are good at, what you like. With any luck, those will be one and the same and will be a great source of satisfaction to you.

- Live with passion. Surround yourself with others whose careers rival yours.

- Initiate and embrace innovation. I am convinced that even the best ideas can be enhanced.

- You will have many teammates, mentors, and bosses during your career. Cling to the good ones. Consider yourself very fortunate to not spend a lot of time around the occasional bad one.

- Read, read, read. Learn as much as you can from every experience. Example: Learning from the seemingly insignificant responsibility of managing the hospital narcotics vault as a pharmacy intern may have contributed to some of the greatest value in the programs we developed.

- Build exceptional presentation and public-speaking skills.

- Never, ever give up!

CHAPTER 32

ESTABLISH A VETERINARY PHARMACY

Jeff Langer

Owner, The Pet Apothecary

When you discover an unfulfilled need and you are able to fill it, go for it.

My father, Jack Langer, owned a retail pharmacy for more than thirty years, and his father owned it before him. When I graduated from pharmacy school in 1976, I continued on to graduate school but quickly realized that wasn't my calling. I eventually went to work for my father at Jack Langer Pharmacy & Gifts for fifteen years. Being an independent retail pharmacy surrounded by large chains, we were always looking to do things a little differently than other pharmacies to set ourselves apart. I became a certified diabetic educator, which was very helpful for our pharmacy. One other thing we found was compounding medications. We encouraged physicians to send us their prescriptions that needed to be compounded and even taught them about compounding options.

Over the years, I realized that every couple of weeks, a veterinarian would call either with a prescription that needed to be compounded or with a wide range of questions about what we could compound. I could see there was a need for compounded prescriptions for animals. In 1995, my father and I sold our drugstore to Osco Pharmacy, a retail pharmacy chain that was new to Milwaukee. I continued to work for Osco after the sale of our store, but I knew I didn't want to work there for the rest of my career. My wife, Patti, also a pharmacist, suggested starting a compounding pharmacy just for pets. In 1999, we started The Pet Apothecary in our basement on a shoestring budget as I continued to work for Osco. Eventually I was able to make our pet pharmacy my full-time job. Today it is a thriving, lucrative business that employs thirteen people.

My advice is simple: Don't be afraid to fail! We opened and closed four other pharmacies, and we manufactured a liquid soap for sensitive skin that we couldn't afford to market.

CHAPTER 33

BECOME A QUALITY ASSURANCE/REGULATORY AND DEVELOPMENT EXECUTIVE

Suzanne Levesque

President
Pharmacists without Borders — Canada

I knew I wanted to be in the healthcare field, and I chose pharmacy as a career. I wanted a profession that offered many options: retail, hospital, industry, and government. The thought of owning my own pharmacy to create a business was a driver in my choice.

During the four-year pharmacy program, I worked in retail pharmacy and soon learned that the practice of community pharmacy was not for me. With a pharmacy degree in hand from the University of Montreal, my options were industry and government. As many people would tell me, a pharmacist starts in industry through sales, but, unfortunately, that was not my strength nor my interest.

Luckily, through contacts I heard about this small over-the-counter (OTC) generic company called Sabex that was recruiting a pharmacist for their quality control position. It was 1984, jobs were scarce, and I needed to pay back my student loans. I was always interested in the manufacture of drugs and pharmacopoeias, and so this job fit perfectly with my interests.

Newly hired and highly motivated, more responsibilities soon fell upon me, including drug information, narcotic and controlled substances management, and regulatory affairs. Over the course of twenty years, I grew the quality and regulatory departments to more than seventy-five employees, professionals, and managers. I worked for two great pharmacists who mentored me daily; and, with other colleagues, we became a great and successful team.

To maintain my competencies and develop my skills, continuous learning was the key to my career growth. To keep abreast of the continuous regulatory changes to Good Manufacturing Practices (GMPs) and because we were a sterile manufacturing company, I got involved with the Parenteral Drug Association (PDA) based in the United States.

I attended many PDA conferences, eager to learn everything needed to help the company be the best in its field. PDA was such a great association that I soon got involved in their Canadian chapter, organized conferences in Canada, and eventually became chapter president. My involvement with PDA allowed me to be on program and regulatory committees either as a member or chair. After obtaining an MBA 1998 from the University of Sherbrooke, I was asked to submit my candidacy to the board of directors of PDA in the United States and was elected for two terms (1999-2004).

My regulatory affairs responsibilities allowed me to learn about the regulatory environment for registering drugs for sale in Canada and the United States. Because regulatory affairs is very close to development, I was very much involved in defining development requirements for generic submissions. Negotiating and defining research protocols with Clinical Research Organization (CRO) was also under my responsibility for development projects that required bioequivalence studies.

This small OTC/generic privately owned company of thirty-five people in 1984 later sold to Novartis in 2004 and grew to become a more than 1,000-employee company at Sandoz, Canada. At Sandoz, Canada, I became development site head for the Canadian development center, reporting to the global development head in Germany. I was responsible for the development of injectable and ophthalmic generic drugs for the United States and Canada, and also for Europe and emerging markets. I managed a team of more than fifty scientists, and I had the opportunity to visit many development sites around the world and network with many people of different cultures. I am proud of having been part of this great journey from Sabex to Sandoz and feel that my vision and drive for building a great company was achieved.

I retired from my career in industry in 2010 and returned to university to update my knowledge of pharmacy. I wanted to return to my community of pharmacists. One of the courses I took was "The Humanitarian Pharmacist." I then became involved with Pharmacists Without Borders Canada and was appointed president of the organization in 2016.

The pharmaceutical world has been part of my entire life encompassing different roles. I could not have planned such a career, and, in retrospect, I feel that my desire to learn, create, and build organizations from the ground up has been a key personal trait of mine.

Life is full of surprises, and you must be open to take on new opportunities and challenges. The profession of pharmacist can be just that!

CHAPTER 34

BECOME THE PRESIDENT OF A GLOBAL RESEARCH-BASED PHARMA COMPANY

Joe Mahady

Former President, Wyeth Pharmaceuticals

I don't remember a time in my life when pharmacy wasn't a central theme. I grew up with an older sister who had been born with devastating cardiac defects. I recall the fear, sadness, and challenges that confronted my parents. In those early years, I developed an appreciation for just how precious and fragile human life can be. I also learned just how awe-inspiring and great health care could be when setting out to save a life. My sister, Kathy's, life was initially saved by pioneering physicians and surgeons at the Johns Hopkins Hospital. There were also the pharmacists around the corner at Cavallo's Pharmacy in Garfield, New Jersey, who were the most visible and constant partners in helping my parents care for Kathy.

I was too young to understand the medicines, but I could not miss seeing how much my parents depended on who and what was behind that pharmacy counter. So, when sixth grade brought the offer of being an after-school stock boy in that pharmacy, I signed on for that 50-cents-per-hour pharmacy job, and, in many respects, I never really left.

I became licensed and practiced in that very same pharmacy and could have easily followed that course save for one development in my life. In the year prior to my graduation, I was selected for an internship program offered by the Student American Pharmaceutical Association and the National Pharmaceutical Council. That internship was with a pharmaceutical division of Warner Lambert. During that internship, I had the opportunity to rotate through many different functional areas of a pharmaceutical company. It wasn't any one of those rotations that interested me; indeed, it was the collection of all those functions that excited me and had me committed to joining the industry.

I applied for many roles, most of which had requirements that were way beyond my qualifications, and I was rightly rejected or ignored. But then a company called Ayerst Laboratories was looking for a pharmacist to join its Regulatory Affairs department. I moved out of R&D, earned an MBA, joined the commercial operations, and progressed through many business roles leading to my last operating role as president of Wyeth Pharmaceuticals. My management team had responsibility for a 45,000-person workforce, more than $20 billion in annual sales, nearly $4 billion in R&D spending, and leading products in small molecules, biotechnology, vaccines, and infant nutritional.

A pharmacy degree was required for my first position, but my pharmacy education and experience was an everyday asset to me in every position I held. I retired from my active operating role after thirty years and feel so fortunate to be able to say that I loved what

Joe Mahady

I was privileged to do for all those years. The industry has collected many critics over the years, and on occasions those criticisms have been deserved, but I left work each day knowing that millions of people were leading better and often longer lives because of Wyeth products.

Was it the pharmacology and pathology courses that helped me in my industry roles? Yes, and did learning pharmacokinetics and clinical chemistry help? Absolutely, but it was the time I spent behind the counter with direct patient contact that helped convert my academic education into a better understanding of what our medicines and information mean to patients and their families, and how challenged all of that is by the complex system we call health care.

My tips for grads are as follows:

- Never forgo the opportunity to learn/practice in direct contact with patients. Regardless of the career path you choose, this firsthand experience will always be an asset.
- Find out what is out there, and don't expect that your curriculum or school will do that for you. Most pharmacy school programs focus on their core curriculum with experiential programs concentrated in clinical or retail environments. But there can be so much more out there for you. Give yourself the opportunity to see what options there are, and go after them.
- Understand that healthcare has many business functions and elements that are common to most businesses, but health care is not like any other business, and we must operate each day with that understanding.

    a. Our medicines can alter human physiology.

b. Our medicines improve, extend, and save lives, and such power can also cause harm.

c. Our medicines can cost hundreds to hundreds of thousands of dollars per year.

d. Who gets which medicines and why isn't always clear to the patient.

For all of the reasons above and so many more, you must execute your healthcare roles with a fiduciary-like approach. It is not just "what we do" in healthcare, but "how we do it" that is so important.

- Just because it is not illegal doesn't make it right.

- Give yourself every chance to love what you do.

CHAPTER 35

BECOME THE LEADER OF A CHAIN STORE GIANT
Helping People on Their Paths to Better Health Through Pharmacy

Larry J. Merlo

President and CEO, CVS Health

When I was a teenager growing up in Charleroi, Pennsylvania, I was lucky to have a high-school chemistry teacher who recognized my passion for science and urged me to pursue a career in pharmacy.

I knew it was a good fit for me because I wanted to make a difference in people's lives. But it wasn't until I entered pharmacy school at the University of Pittsburgh that I realized the significance of the path I had chosen and how pharmacy could make the world a better place.

After graduation, I became a pharmacist in Washington, D.C., with Peoples Drug. Over the years, I took on new challenges and positions of greater responsibility as a field leader within CVS Pharmacy, which had acquired Peoples. I didn't set out to be a CEO; I was just determined to be the very best pharmacist I could be.

Through hard work, good coaching, and a little luck, I was able to advance step-by-step in my career until I was fortunate enough to be named president and CEO in 2011. Many other pharmacists have moved into executive roles at CVS Health, just as I did, and it is a deep understanding of the pharmacist-patient relationship that guides our decision-making.

Purpose is very important to us at CVS Health. If you walk into the lobbies of many corporations across the country, you will see their mission statement on the wall. Some call it their vision. At CVS Health, we have a purpose: "Helping people on their path to better health." We use those eight simple words as a guidepost in making business decisions, continually innovating to stay ahead of the transformative changes taking place in health care today.

According to a Gallup Poll, Americans cite nurses and pharmacists as the nation's two highest-ranking professions in terms of honesty and ethics. At CVS Health, we employ both. It's a high calling, and I can't think of a more exciting time for graduates to be starting out in health care. Now, more than forty years after entering pharmacy school, I am still inspired by my chosen profession and very proud to be a pharmacist.

Throughout my career, I've relied on five basic principles to guide my path:

- **Take advantage of opportunities that come along without being afraid of failure.** Stay committed to winning and don't be deterred by obstacles. They make you stronger and more creative.

Larry J. Merlo

- **Work hard and never give up.** Be persistent and do what it takes to win—the right way.

- **Act with integrity.** When you do the right thing for the right reasons, you gain credibility and build trust, all of which contribute to success.

- **Communicate—broadly and continuously.** In the absence of good communication, people fill in the blanks themselves. Clear, direct communication is essential to understanding and alignment. The integrity of leaders is measured through the connection of their words and actions, so your walk should be consistent with your talk. In addition, I have always made two-way communication a priority. I embrace the importance of talking with CVS Health colleagues at all levels of the organization to hear about their experiences, successes, challenges, thoughts, and ideas. From my early days in the company until today as CEO, I have learned a lot by talking with and listening to colleagues across the organization.

- **Lead with purpose.** People want to be inspired by a larger mission; they will rise to the challenge of high expectations. At CVS Health, every decision we make is viewed through the lens of our purpose: Helping people on their path to better health. By using our purpose as a guide for our actions, we ensure that what we say and what we do are aligned with our values. Our customers and clients expect this from us, and I'm proud to say that we are delivering on that promise across our organization.

CHAPTER 36

COMBINING PHARMACY AND LAW

Ned Milenkovich

Principal, Much Shelist, P.C.

I am a strong believer that a rewarding career is an essential element in a balanced life. Knowing that each person has a unique blend of interests, motivations, and personalities, I recognize that what "balanced" means to me may not work for someone else, and vice versa. I stress the importance of balance, but I understand that I can only dictate its form for myself. My career offers a perfect counterpoint to my other life interests. Even better, the work itself is balanced, blending four key interests: health care, law, journalism, and government/public service.

As an undergraduate at The Ohio State University, I attended a "Biological Sciences Day" and immediately recognized the opportunities available to me in the sciences. Ultimately, I recognized that one of my passions centered around health care. As a result, I embarked on pharmacy studies to obtain my pharmacy degree. Thereafter, I continued my scholastic development by pursuing a doctor of pharmacy degree, which was not only a natural out-growth of those health care interests, but it also provided me with additional career options. I knew that after graduation, I could work as a pharmacist in any number of settings, pursue additional training in medical school, or give in to the law bug.

I come from a lineage of lawyers that includes my father and grand-father. Moreover, I knew that I wanted to marry my interests in the law with health care. So, after earning my law degree from The John Marshall Law School in Chicago, I began working at various law firms, where I established a broad legal practice in health care. As co-chair of the healthcare practice at my current firm, I have the opportunity to advise healthcare, drug, and pharmacy clients on a range of business and regulatory issues. I am also an active member of the National Association of Boards of Pharmacy, the American Society of Pharmacy Law, and the Illinois Association of Health Care Attorneys.

Separately, my work in journalism began in high school, where I was an editor for my high-school newspaper. After law school, I began to create a social media presence, writing on legal topics in health care and pharmacy. This led to nearly ten years of publish-ing regular columns in *Drug Topics* and serving on the publication's editorial board, after which I moved to *Pharmacy Times*. At *Pharmacy Times*, I serve on the editorial board, write regular columns, and am a guest host for the publication's weekly web newscasts, which ex-plore a range of topics facing the industry.

Finally, public/government service has always been my passion. I have been named to the Illinois State Board of Pharmacy by two governors and am currently the vice chair of this state governmen-tal administrative body, and I also serve on the Dean's Corporate

Council of The Ohio State University College of Pharmacy. I am also a member of the Illinois Pharmacists Association, and various other healthcare groups.

Pharmacy has been a fantastic springboard for pursuing a number of professional interests. During a recent presentation to members of the Phi Lambda Sigma Honor Society (of which I am a member) at The Ohio State University, I offered the following career suggestions to future pharmacists:

- Enjoy what you do: Life is too short to not have passion for the things that occupy your day.

- Find the gravitational force that pulls you, then align your training and work experience so you can pursue your passions more effectively.

- Life is fluid: Internal changes and external circumstances will affect your opportunities and your decisions. That's OK: Make choices. Be open to surprises. Test ideas. Evolve.

- Find the right balance for you, at work, at home, and in the world.

CHAPTER 37

WORK FOR THE DEA

*A Career in Law Enforcement and Regulatory Control—
Using a Pharmacy Degree to Protect the Public Health and Safety*

Joseph T. Rannazzisi

**Drug Enforcement Administration (DEA), retired
Founder of Due Diligence Compliance, LLC**

I was raised in Freeport, New York, in the 1960s and 1970s with my mother, father, and sister. My father became a schoolteacher after a combat tour in Korea with the U.S. Army. My mom was a homemaker and worked in a retail jewelry store. I lived in a blue-collar neighborhood that was home to many military veterans, police officers, firefighters, and other public servants. It was the kind of neighborhood where everyone knew each other, and there was always a game of baseball, football, or street hockey to join. This is where I learned the value of public service.

I always knew I wanted to be a police officer, but I also wanted to have a degree that was different from other applicants who were pursuing a career in law enforcement. I worked in two independent pharmacies during high school and was impressed with how patients relied on pharmacists to provide medical advice and guidance concerning drug therapy. That experience convinced me to pursue a pharmacy degree, and I decided that Butler University was the ideal place to learn the profession. I didn't realize how well my pharmacy degree would serve me.

I graduated and became a pharmacist at the Indianapolis Veterans Administration Hospital. I served as a staff pharmacist before beginning my career with the Drug Enforcement Administration (DEA) as an investigator and special agent. My application to DEA was rejected twice before I was accepted to the special agent academy. During my career, I served in different capacities and positions of increasing responsibility as a special agent, including clandestine laboratory coordinator, homicide task force supervisor, section chief, assistant special agent in charge, and deputy chief (Office of Enforcement Operations-Headquarters). During these assignments, I either personally investigated or supervised investigations concerning violations of the Federal Controlled Substances Act. I experienced and participated in all aspects of drug law enforcement, and my pharmacy degree gave me a distinct advantage over many of my colleagues.

In January 2006, I was appointed to the position of deputy assistant administrator in the Office of Diversion Control, where I supervised and coordinated all criminal and regulatory investigations concerning the diversion of pharmaceutical controlled substances and listed chemicals from legitimate distribution channels.

Throughout my career as a pharmacist and then law enforcement officer, my job was to serve and protect the public. This is especially important today as thousands of people are victims of overdose from diverted pharmaceuticals every year, and this trend continues unabated. I retired after thirty-two years of federal service from a profession that I considered a passion rather than a job.

Public service will not make you wealthy, but it will provide you with a personal enrichment that money will never provide. It also is one of the few professions where you can retire at a fairly young age and pursue new employment opportunities. I am currently a consultant for law firms and also speak about issues concerning drug diversion, opioid abuse, and synthetic drugs.

My tips for grads are as follows:

- Select a career that you are passionate about. It will make your employment a profession, and the years will fly by quickly.

- If you want the job of your dreams, you might have to make multiple attempts before success. Don't get angry if you are initially rejected; learn from this failure and try again. Employers like people who are persistent.

- Always treat every project and job task as an interview for a new position. People like a finished product that is polished and on time. Believe it or not, people are watching what you do.

- Volunteer and ask questions. You may not need to understand a particular program or initiative now, but job duties and program responsibilities always change, and you want to be as versatile as possible.

- Use your formal education to your advantage. Answer questions and provide support to your coworkers who don't have your educational background. Become the office expert in a specific area that interests you. My area of expertise was clandestine laboratory investigations. I became one of the "go-to" special agents concerning all aspects of the clan lab program, and that exposure helped me advance in my career.

- Always pursue more education and training—you can never have enough.

BECOME THE HEAD OF OPERATIONS AT A GLOBAL PHARMACEUTICAL COMPANY

From scientific research and technology, to manufacturing and quality, to running a business, assuring supply of medicines to 30 million patients around the world

Azita Saleki-Gerhardt

**Senior Vice President, Operations
AbbVie**

Growing up, I received conflicting words of encouragement from my parents: you can do anything you set your mind to, but nothing you did was ever perfect. These competing philosophies formed the foundation of a diverse career starting with a bachelor's, master's and doctorate in pharmaceutics, culminating in leading operations for a global pharmaceutical company, with many stops along the way.

I've always had a passion for helping people, and I knew early on that a degree in pharmacy would let me do that. But I was also interested in understanding all the steps it took for a medicine to get developed and eventually reach the hands of patients who needed it. That's what steered me to pharmaceutical research at Abbott Labs after graduation, where I spent several years as a scientist developing and revising drug formulas to make them better for our patients.

For example, one of my first projects was reformulating an antibiotic for pediatric use to make it taste less bitter. We wanted to ease the burden of taking the medicine, both for parents and kids. That reformulation led to my first patent.

I then grew curious about how the drugs we were developing in the labs were manufactured consistently, how we made sure they met the varying needs of our patients, and how we could improve them. That's when I started working on the challenges associated with scale-up and manufacturing for large patient populations, the critical steps necessary to ensure our products are always of the highest quality, and what it takes to make them consistently available.

Over many years in a variety of roles, I oversaw the technical work necessary to transfer diverse medicines, from small molecules to biologics, active drug substance to drug product, oral products to injectables, and from the design lab to the manufacturing floor. I led the team responsible for overseeing the complex quality requirements of our internal and external network that would meet global regulatory agencies' rigorous standards.

All of these experiences and roles have led me to where I am today, leading global operations at AbbVie. I lead a team of more than 6,400 people around the world, encompassing scientific, engineering, business, quality, supply chain, security, purchasing, and manufacturing professionals responsible for the supply and distribution of all AbbVie products, as well as a number of enterprise-wide services.

My education in pharmacy has helped me in every step of my career. Its fundamental principles taught me to ask the right questions and advocate for what is important for the patient, no matter which role I was in. I learned that it is critical to know the impact we can make, whether it is on one patient suffering from a disease, or on 1 million patients around the world. An education in pharmacy allows us to make that connection and deliver better outcomes.

Today, my team works to make a remarkable impact on more than 30 million patients every year who are suffering from a variety of unmet medical needs. Knowing that makes it easy to get out of bed every morning and go to work!

During my career journey, I've learned valuable lessons through my own experiences and from leaders and mentors:

- No matter your position or level, there are always opportunities to learn and grow. Many times when I was making a decision to switch roles, my only real criterion was whether it would challenge me to either learn something new or improve on a skill or capability I already had.

- It's smart to seek out mentors and guides for advice and direction, but you can only rely on one person: yourself. Have confidence in your capabilities and ability to learn and grow, and be persistent and determined to succeed.

- Never be afraid to explore the unknown, but be sure to do it wisely. Embrace smart risks, and get out of your comfort zone. Don't fear failure because you've tried something new. When you fail (everyone does), learn from your mistakes. That you didn't get it right the first time isn't as important as what you learned and how you responded.

CHAPTER 39

BECOME A SENIOR POLICY ADVISER AT FDA
And an Intrapreneur in Your Organization

Juliette Toure

Senior Policy Adviser
CAPT, United States Public Health Service
Division of Psychiatric Products
Food and Drug Administration

I first learned of the term "intrapreneur" while working on my MBA. Gifford and Elizabeth Pinchot first coined the term, defining intrapreneurs as "dreamers who do. Those who take hands-on responsibility for creating innovation of any kind within a business." I immediately identified with it and realized it was a common theme in all of my positions, whether in consulting, managed care, or regulatory environments. Looking back, I realize it has been a critical part of my professional journey and led me to where I am today.

You may be thinking, "Intrapreneurship in government—how can that be?" I will be the first to admit that government hierarchy, bureaucracy, and processes are unique and can be frustrating. However, I believe every organization, private or public, has its own rules that can hamper innovation or progress if you let them. I also believe government is the perfect place for innovation, shaping and driving large-scale change, and spurring "profitable" ideas for not only the public (public health in my line of work) but also for businesses.

In all of my government jobs, there has always been this sense of "building the plane as it's flying," because many initiatives are given nearly impossible time frames and limited resources. Regardless of my varying roles, they have all been rich opportunities to "think outside the box," fix things that plague us as healthcare providers, learn from failures, and improve processes — everything that entrepreneurs do.

I've been an officer in the public health service on deployment in response to a public health disaster. I've served as a subject matter expert and principal designer for the Part D Plan Finder at the Centers for Medicare and Medicaid Services (CMS). I've been a senior policy adviser at the FDA who looks for opportunities to streamline internal processes and I've worked with experts to develop policies that raise the bar in regulatory science to advance global drug development in psychiatry.

So, take some time to be a dreamer. As you think of your next career moves, here are some things to think about:

- **Be responsible.** I relearned the definition of "responsible" from Sadhguru's Inner Engineering program. Many people view being responsible as a burden; it's usually associated with carrying the burden of others. However, if you break the term down into its subparts, **"respond"** + **"able,"** it simply means having the ability to respond. When you see a problem, you should think, am I responsible? Am I able to respond? If you can't, then don't complain about the outcome. If you can, then try to be part of the solution.

- **Look for and fill the need.** You don't need to wait for your boss to tell you about a problem to bring it to the surface. As many before have said, unless you take risks, you will not know what's possible. I am not advising you to fly solo—you should run your ideas by others, particularly your boss and other stakeholders. Be open to listening to their concerns because they can help mold your ideas for success.

- **Be a catalyst for change.** Often, you cannot single-handedly bring about the change that's needed. Look for who you need on your "team" inside and outside your organization, realize your own limitations, and empower others to bring the change that's needed.

HEAD UP GLOBAL MEDICAL AFFAIRS IN A
MAJOR PHARMACEUTICAL COMPANY

Liia Vainchtein

**Vice President, Global Medical Affairs,
Takeda Pharmaceuticals, Inc.**

The train announced the last stop in a language that I didn't understand. My father and mother stood up with my brother, a toddler, in one arm and luggage in every other. I was a 14-year-old hating every moment of this journey. What I didn't know then was that this was the first of many journeys that would make me the woman I am now. I only spoke Russian and was now forced to live as a stranger in a strange land because we were not welcome in the one I was born into. It was 1992 when I arrived in the beautiful and remote canal city of Groningen in the Netherlands from another, very industrial city that I used to call home in Kazan, Russia, in the former Soviet Union. The fall of the USSR happened months before and led to the migration of many families like ours in search of a new home.

Courage comes from many places. Mine came from stories that my grandmother, Gita, told me. During the train ride to Groningen, I remembered what Gita recalled of her mother, Faina, rushing Gita and her sister to the train station in Mariupol, Ukraine as the Nazis overran the country looking to intern the Jews, Gypsies, and other "undesirables" who still lived there. It was 1941, and nothing was certain for them. My great-grandmother put her two daughters on a train to Russia so they would be out reach of the Nazis. Even though Faina didn't know whether her daughters would make it across the border to Russia, she knew what would happen if they stayed in Ukraine. This was not a choice; it was a desperate act.

Faina decided to stay in Ukraine as long as possible. She was a head pharmacist at the local hospital and believed she had to care for the patients there. Being a pharmacist, she was led to believe that she would be considered "essential staff" and would not be taken by the Nazis. Things got worse over the next few months because no one was essential in the Nazis' "Final Solution." After seeing other members of the family taken to concentration camps, she decided to flee and look for her daughters who were now more than 1,600 km away in Kazan in the Republic of Tatarstan. She arrived three months after her daughters made it to safety, but the loss of family and the journey took its toll on her. Life would never be the same for our families; we were always visitors in our new home.

Two things in Faina and Gita's story made me resolved to win no matter what: One was that I needed to make them proud that their struggles in life gave me the courage to seek success no matter what the circumstance, and the other was that I wanted to dedicate myself to helping others, whether they be patients or people who needed the strength to find the path to success.

Liia Vainchtein

I learned fluent Dutch within months of arriving in Groningen, but I never lost my heritage or mother tongue. I, too, wanted to become a pharmacist like Faina, but to do so, I had to excel in my high-school academics above many of the other students. With my parents' moral support and a belief in myself, I achieved a master's of science in pharmacy, followed by a doctorate of pharmacy (PharmD) and finally pursued and obtained a doctorate of philosophy (PhD) in analytical chemistry, studying anti-cancer drugs.

Yet, these academic accomplishments did not fulfill me. I knew I could help more people by working on promising new drugs. So, I joined the pharmaceutical industry and performed many different roles, from research and development to medical affairs to compliance. Along the way, I was blessed to meet many great mentors and friends who taught me and guided me. It is to them that I am so grateful. Now, when given the opportunity, I guide and groom many promising people to pay it forward.

As a woman, I know it's not always easy to make the mark the way a man can make it; I don't allow that as an excuse but rather a way to push forward through obstacles. Being a wife to a caring and supportive husband/mentor and a mother to three wonderful children gives me the strength to look for solutions no matter what the circumstance. At work, I know that what I do makes the difference in every life that our medicines touch, from heart disease to cancer to pregnancy. What I do is part of the solution to helping others lead better lives.

How I behave as a female executive influences others to also strive for success. Mentoring women unlocks the potential of both the mentor and mentee: I learn their life stories and what they feel gets in their way. Most of the time, it is their own perception of what others feel are the limitations of being a woman. This struggle for women to feel empowered about who they are and not by how others define them is one that still continues. It is the glass ceiling for us that is being broken.

Life has taken me from the Soviet Union to the Netherlands to the United Kingdom and now to the United States, a long way from where Faina, Gita, and the others came from, but I know that all of us have been following Our North Star down the path to success, not just for ourselves but for our families and children, as well as the lives we touch along this journey of life.

CHAPTER 41

BECOME THE CEO OF A GROUP PURCHASING ORGANIZATION

Curtis J. Woods

President and CEO of Pace Alliance

I grew up on a small farm in western Kansas. Working on the farm set my social values and work ethic for life. I had to be responsible for the care of farm animals and make independent decisions at a young age.

I had no plans to become a pharmacist. I liked science; therefore, I pursued a chemistry degree in college. However, the thought of working in a science laboratory for the rest of my life seemed horrible. As I was nearing the final semester in chemistry, I decided to apply to pharmacy school. Pharmacy offered me the opportunity to apply chemistry and work independently.

After graduation, I worked in both hospital and retail settings. I enjoyed the interaction with the physicians, nurses, and patients. One of my strengths was the ability to communicate with people from all walks of life and in different professions. As a pharmacist,

I could assist other healthcare providers and help patients use their medications appropriately.

During my clinical practice, I became knowledgeable about the purchase of pharmaceuticals in both hospital and retail settings. Hospitals had already organized to form buying groups to purchase medications at favorable prices. Independent pharmacies had not yet done so. When the opportunity came up to help start a buying group for independent pharmacies, I signed on. I left clinical practice to help create one of the original and most successful buying groups for independent pharmacy.

There were many challenges to starting and operating a buying group for independent pharmacies. The first challenge was to get a significant number of independent pharmacies to join together in a buying group. The second challenge was to convince drug companies to negotiate with the buying group for preferential pricing. My clinical knowledge as a pharmacist and the values I learned growing up assisted me in becoming the CEO of the buying group, Pace Alliance.

I offer the following tips and advice:

- Be honest. Patients, business colleagues, and friends deserve your honesty.
- Show up. Be on time and come prepared.
- Be a good listener. This will help you be a better communicator.
- Show compassion. Be empathetic. This applies to both the clinical practice of pharmacy and the business world.
- You will be most successful when you achieve a balance between your work and family. Your jobs and careers may

change, but always value the people who are most important to you.

- Continuing education is a lifelong endeavor. Never think you know it all. Be willing to learn more.

CHAPTER 42

BECOME THE CEO OF A PHARMACEUTICAL COMPANY FOCUSED ON ANTIBIOTIC DEVELOPMENT

David S. Zaccardelli

Acting CEO
Cempra Pharmaceuticals, Inc.

I was raised on the East Side of Detroit with my two brothers and sister by loving parents who created the foundation for our education and work ethic. My mother, an Olympian and all-around superwoman provided for all our needs and made sure we were always supported. My father, who was employed for more than thirty years at the same company, instilled the clarity of hard work and ensured we were educated. To this day, I am not sure how they provided financial support to all of us to complete our education with no debt. It's an amazing gesture and one I carry on with my children.

I always enjoyed science, biology, and learning how things work. However, I also wanted to experience how a business is created, built, and run. In college, it is very difficult to do both science and business; however, I was fortunate to receive my PharmD from the University of Michigan. I learned during the pharmacy program that I preferred to not treat patients as a clinical hospital pharmacist or in the community setting. Being involved in drug development in the pharmaceutical industry was for me, and I completed a fellowship in drug development and clinical research at the University of North Carolina.

After eight years of roles with increasing responsibility in clinical research, I formed my own company with two partners, and we created a contract services company focused on formulation development and manufacturing. Within seven years, we grew a successful company and sold it. I received my MBA the old-fashioned way, from direct experience. I didn't realize it then, but this experience set the foundation for the next fifteen years.

As a clinical researcher, drug developer, and someone who was experienced in chemistry, manufacturing, controls (CMC), and good manufacturing practice (GMP), I was able to differentiate myself and ultimately become COO of a mid-size pharmaceutical company. Along the way, we built excellent teams, obtained multiple life-saving drug approvals, and built a strong company. I learned that being around talented people and developing mutual trust is the fuel for success and professional enjoyment.

With success comes the challenge of determining what's next, and I enjoy drug development, building teams, and growing businesses by being on the board of directors for several companies. All of these interactions led to countless opportunities. If you are aware and keep pushing in a suitable direction, you will extract your true talent and contribute to the success of others and yourself.

Interestingly, my daughter just graduated with a PharmD from the University of North Carolina — another generation of pharmacists to carry our legacy forward.

Key messages and learnings:

- Follow your gut and passions. You may not get to a goal on the path you envision, but that is actually the best part.

- Differentiate yourself. Learn something others do not know. Develop skills that serve a wide range of areas. Take risks and always look for opportunities — they are important in ways you do not immediately know.

- Practice having a strong work ethic — it is not taught. True success and achievement can't be obtained without it.

- Change is constant; if you embrace change, you will be successful in whatever you do.

- Live in the moment — the past and future do not actually exist. You need to take full advantage of the present, and then you will arrive at where you are meant to be.

CHAPTER 43

WORK WITH PRIVATE EQUITY INVESTORS TO ACQUIRE COMPANIES, BUILD THEM UP, AND SELL THEM

George S. Zorich

CEO, ZEDPharma Advisors, Inc.

I grew up in Milwaukee. Neither of my parents attended college, yet my sister and I seemed to be told daily that we were going to college for a better life. No one among my relatives was a pharmacist, but I always had an interest in chemistry. I was the middle-school kid who went to the corner drugstore and purchased sulfur, potassium nitrate, and charcoal to make gunpowder for fireworks or to launch a rocket. The gunpowder cones and fireworks always worked; the rocket launch always failed. My chemistry and science interest eventually got me going in the direction of pharmacy school, and although I was on a waiting list, I got in thirty days before my PH-1 year. I'm thankful that someone gave up his or her slot, which allowed me to enter pharmacy school.

After graduation from pharmacy school, I worked in health care for more than thirty years, starting in sales at Eli Lilly and Company. My career included executive positions in Big Pharma, biotech, generics, distribution companies, and startups. During the final fifteen years of my career, I focused on building up and selling companies as president or CEO. I worked with private equity to acquire companies and develop the best growth and exit strategy for each company. I could not have accomplished the second half of my career without all the hard work and experiences gained in the first half.

When speaking to pharmacy students today about career opportunities, some will ask how they can get on a career path where you run a pharmaceutical company and then sell it for hundreds of millions of dollars. The simple answer is you never can plan for that with certainty. You obtain your first job, work hard, doing the best job possible while waiting for or creating opportunities. I never knew what my final career moves would be in pharmacy school, or even shortly thereafter. I simply worked hard, pursued areas where I had strengths, capitalized on many, and found that success would breed more success. I fell on my face more than a few times, but every career move was an effective building block to the next step, more experience, and greater opportunities.

Although I'm retired from day-to-day operations, I'm currently a board member for several privately held companies involved in pharmaceutical development. I also serve on the University of Wisconsin School of Pharmacy Board of Visitors and enjoy working with the dean, faculty, and students in the Industry Pharmacists Organization (IPhO).

Currently, a quarter of my time is invested with nonprofits on a volunteer basis, including Brothers United and ReNew North Chicago—both are mentoring and jobs-training programs for young men in North Chicago.

I'm passionate about what I call "maximizing the pharmacy degree" for the benefit of society, including how pharmacists should form a bigger part of the answer for reducing total drug costs nationwide, not just dispensers of drugs. I'm also an advocate for more entrepreneurship, leadership, and selling skills being taught to our college students. Finally, I believe everyone should pay it forward by mentoring young people.

My tips for grads are as follows:

- Wherever your first job is, work hard and strive for excellence in every aspect of the job.

- Do all the small things well, including items that take zero skill (e.g., being on time, following up in a timely manner, having a willingness to learn, going the extra mile, and, finally, always being prepared for meetings). People—including your next potential employer—notice these traits.

- Become an expert in something essential—be the "go-to" person for that part of the business.

- Network relentlessly: It will assist in building a career, but I always found it fun, too.

A NOTE ON THE WRITING

In the *LEADERS* section, participants were asked to use creativity to tell their stories and provide their tips or advice for young pharmacists. My only contribution was to write the header for each entry. I found that the *LEADERS* were so humble that they undervalued their career accomplishments, so I wrote their headlines to reflect the breadth of their experience. Clearly, humility is required of all leaders, and this group exemplified it.

Two priorities in my life are family and mentoring/giving back.

My family--including nine grandchildren.

Mentoring a small group of future leaders from the
University of Wisconsin School of Pharmacy.

Our fourth year of mentoring some great young men with unlimited potential from the NCCHS class of 2018.

CPSIA information can be obtained
at www.ICGtesting.com
Printed in the USA
FFOW03n0415121017
41021FF